From prosperity to austerity

MANCHESTER
1824

Manchester University Press

From prosperity to austerity

A socio-cultural critique of the Celtic Tiger and its aftermath

Edited by Eamon Maher and Eugene O'Brien

Manchester University Press

Manchester and New York

*distributed in the United States exclusively
by Palgrave Macmillan*

While copyright in the volume as a whole is vested in Manchester University Press, copyright in individual chapters belongs to their respective authors, and no chapter may be reproduced wholly or in part without the express permission in writing of both author and publisher.

Published by Manchester University Press
Oxford Road, Manchester M13 9NR, UK
and Room 400, 175 Fifth Avenue, New York, NY 10010, USA
www.manchesteruniversitypress.co.uk

Distributed in the United States exclusively by
Palgrave Macmillan, 175 Fifth Avenue, New York,
NY 10010, USA

Distributed in Canada exclusively by
UBC Press, University of British Columbia, 2029 West Mall,
Vancouver, BC, Canada V6T 1Z2

British Library Cataloguing-in-Publication Data
A catalogue record for this book is available from the British Library

Library of Congress Cataloging-in-Publication Data applied for

ISBN 978 07190 9167 4 hardback

ISBN 978 07190 9168 1 paperback

First published 2014

The publisher has no responsibility for the persistence or accuracy of URLs for any external or third-party internet websites referred to in this book, and does not guarantee that any content on such websites is, or will remain, accurate or appropriate.

Typeset in Sabon and Gill Sans by
Servis Filmsetting Ltd, Stockport
Printed in Great Britain by
Bell & Bain Ltd, Glasgow

To our wives and families:

Liz, Liam, Marcella and Kevin;
Áine, Eoin, Dara and Sinéad

For their unstinting support and for putting up with us

Contents

List of figures

Notes on contributors

Ruth Barton is Head of the Department of Film Studies at Trinity College Dublin. Her publications include: *Jim Sheridan, Framing the Nation* (2002), *Irish National Cinema* (2004), *Acting Irish in Hollywood* (2006), *Screening Irish-America* (editor, 2009) and *Hedy Lamarr, The Most Beautiful Woman in Film* (2011). She has written numerous articles on Irish film and is involved in a number of research projects on Irish cinema and on women's film history. Her current research is on the Irish émigré director Rex Ingram.

Justin Carville is Lecturer in Historical and Theoretical Studies in Photography and Visual Culture Studies in the School of Creative Arts at the Institute of Art, Design & Technology, Dun Laoghaire. A former Government of Ireland Senior Research Scholar in the Humanities and Social Sciences (2003–2004), he has guest-edited a special Ireland-themed issue of *The Journal of Popular Visual Culture* and an issue of *Photographies* on the photographic image and globalization. His first book, *Photography and Ireland*, was published in 2011. He is currently researching the connections between photography, ethnography and the visualization of Irish identity, for which he was awarded an IRCHSS Research Fellowship.

Bryan Fanning is a professor in the School of Applied Social Studies at University College Dublin and is a leading expert on immigration and its impact on Irish society. His books include *New Guests of the Irish Nation* (2009), *Immigration and Social Cohesion in the Republic of Ireland* (2011) and *Racism and Social Change in the Republic of Ireland* (1st edition 2002, 2nd edition 2012).

Eóin Flannery is Senior Lecturer in Contemporary Literature in the Department of English and Modern Languages at Oxford Brookes University, UK. He is the author of three books: *Colum McCann and* *the Aesthetics of Redemption* (2011), *Ireland and Postcolonial Studies: Theory, Discourse, Utopia* (2009) and *Versions of Ireland: Empire, Modernity and Resistance in Irish Culture* (2006). He is also the editor of three volumes: *This Side of Brightness: Essays on the Fiction of Colum McCann* (2012), *Ireland in Focus: Film, Photography and Popular Culture* (2009) and *Enemies of Empire: New Perspectives on Imperialism, Literature and Historiography* (2007). He is currently writing a book entitled: '*Listening Deeply*': *Ecology, Postcolonialism and Social Justice in Irish Cultural History*, completing a study of the work of the novelist, dramatist and short story writer, Eugene McCabe and editing a special number of *The Journal of Ecocriticism* on 'Ireland and Ecocriticism'.

Brendan Geary FMS, PhD, is a Marist Brother and counselling psychologist. He is currently the Provincial of the Marist Province of Europe Centre-West, which includes Ireland. While studying and working in the United States, he specialized in work with victims and perpetrators of sexual abuse. He has published papers on sex offenders, counselling and spirituality. He co-edited *The Christian Handbook of Abuse, Addiction and Difficult Behaviour* (2008). He has also co-edited the following two books with Joanne Marie Greer: *Sexual issues: Understanding and Advising in a Christian Context* (2010) and *The Dark Night of the Catholic Church: Examining the Child Sexual Abuse Scandal* (2011). He was invited to work as a facilitator and presenter at the Symposium on child sexual abuse held at the Gregorian University in February 2012 entitled 'Towards healing and renewal'.

Kieran Keohane is Senior Lecturer in Sociology, at the School of Sociology and Philosophy, University College Cork, and **Carmen Kuhling** is Senior Lecturer in Sociology and Women's Studies at the University of Limerick. Both hold PhDs from York (Canada). They are cultural analysts working in the interpretative tradition, informed by social theory, Continental philosophy, political anthropology and psychoanalysis. They are co-authors of *Collision Culture: Transformations in Everyday Life in Ireland* (2005) and *Cosmopolitan Ireland: Globalization and Quality of Life* (2007), as well as of numerous essays and articles published in the *Irish Journal of Sociology*, *Irish Review*, *Irish Sociological Chronicles* and other journals.

Eamon Maher is Director of the National Centre for Franco-Irish Studies in IT Tallaght and editor of the Reimagining Ireland book series with the Peter Lang Oxford branch. His most recent monograph is '*The Church* *and Its Spire': John McGahern and the Catholic Question* (2011) and he is currently writing a study of the Catholic novel in the twentieth century. He is co-editor (with Catherine Maignant) of *Peregrinations and Ruminations: Franco-Irish Connections in Space and Time* (2012) and is currently working on a collection of essays with Máirtin Mac Con Iomaire entitled *'Tickling the Palate': Gastronomy in Irish Literature, Culture and the Public Imagination.*

Catherine Maignant is Professor of Irish Studies at the University of Lille and President of the French Association for Irish Studies. After writing a PhD on early medieval Irish Christianity, she now specializes in contemporary Irish religious history. Her research interests include the New Religious Movements, the response of the Catholic Church to secularization, interreligious dialogue, Celtic Christianity and the religious aspects of globalization. She co-edited, with Eamon Maher, *Peregrinations and Ruminations: Franco-Irish Connections in Space and Time* (2012).

Victor Merriman is Professor of Performing Arts at Edge Hill University in Liverpool. He is the author of articles and book chapters on postcolonialism and late twentieth-century Irish theatre. He was Guest Editor for a Special Issue of the online journal *Kritika Kultura* on Radical Theatre and Ireland (2010). He was a member of An Chomhairle Ealaion/The Arts Council (1993–98), and chaired the Council's Review of Theatre in Ireland (1995–96). His monograph *Because We Are Poor: Irish Theatre in the 1990s,* was published in 2011.

Sylvie Mikowski is Professor at the University of Reims Champagne-Ardenne, where she lectures in Irish Studies and English Literature. She has published *Le Roman irlandais contemporain* (2004) and edited *Aspects of the Irish Book from the 17th Century to Today* (*Revue LISA*, 2005), *Histoire et mémoire en France et en Irlande History and Memory in France and Ireland* (2011). She also co-edited *Ireland: Zones and Margins* (2004), *The Book in Ireland* (2007) and *Ecrivaines irlandaises/ Irish Women Writers* (to be published in 2014). She has also contributed articles and book chapters on various contemporary Irish writers, including John McGahern, Deirdre Madden, Joseph O'Connor, Colum McCann and Sebastian Barry. She currently edits the literary section of *Etudes Irlandaises,* the French journal of Irish Studies.

Brian Murphy is a lecturer in hospitality, tourism and gastronomy at the Institute of Technology, Tallaght. Prior to becoming involved in education, he spent a number of years working in management positions in the hospitality sector in Ireland and abroad. He recently completed a PhD on the role of 'place and story' in modern perceptions of French wine culture. He has also published a number of book chapters detailing his research findings in this area.

Neil Murphy received his PhD from University College Dublin. He is currently Associate Professor of contemporary literature at NTU, Singapore, and has previously taught at the University of Ulster and the American University of Beirut. He is the author of *Irish Fiction and Postmodern Doubt* (2004), and has co-edited three collections of essays, the most recent of which is *Aidan Higgins: The Fragility of Form* (2009). He is also the editor of the revised edition of Higgins's *Balcony of Europe* (2009) and has co-edited (with Keith Hopper) a special issue of the *Review of Contemporary Fiction* to coincide with Flann O'Brien's centenary (2011). In addition, he has published numerous articles and book chapters on contemporary Irish fiction, postmodernism and theories of reading, and is currently writing a book on aesthetics and contemporary fiction.

Eugene O'Brien is Senior Lecturer and Head of the Department of English Language and Literature in Mary Immaculate College, Limerick. His publications include: *Seamus Heaney – Creating Irelands of the Mind* (2002), *Seamus Heaney and the Place of Writing* (2003), *Seamus Heaney: Searches for Answers* (2006) and *'Kicking Bishop Brennan up the Arse': Negotiating Texts and Contexts in Contemporary Irish Studies* (2009). He co-edited: *Reinventing Ireland through a French Prism* (2007), *Modernity and Postmodernity in a Franco-Irish Context* (2008) and *Breaking the Mould: Literary Representations of Irish Catholicism* (2010). He is currently working on a monograph on Seamus Heaney as a European intellectual, and editing a collection on the later poetry of Seamus Heaney.

Mary Pierse teaches Irish feminisms and related feminist theory on the MA programme in Women's Studies at University College Cork. She has previously taught courses on Victorian and fin-de-siècle literature, and on colonial literature, at the School of English, UCC, where she was IRCHSS Post-Doctoral Research Fellow (2004–6) and later a Research Fellow. She is editor of the five-volume set *Irish Feminisms 1810–1930* (2010) and of *George Moore: Artistic Visions and Literary Worlds* (2006). She has published on the writings of Moore, Kate Chopin, Arthur Conan Doyle and Antonio Fogazzaro, as well as on the poets

Dennis O'Driscoll and Cathal Ó Searcaigh. An ongoing research interest is the investigation of synaesthetics at the fin-de-siècle. She is a board member at the National Centre for Franco-Irish Studies and serves on editorial boards and scientific committees for publications in Ireland, France and Spain.

Gerry Smyth is a musician and academic working in Liverpool, UK. He is the author of a number of works on the subject of Irish popular music, including *Noisy Island* (2005) and *Music in Irish Cultural History* (2009).

Acknowledgements

The editors would like to acknowledge the help and support of the Institute of Technology in Tallaght, and Mary Immaculate College, University of Limerick, for their encouragement of this and other similar initiatives. We would also like to acknowledge the enthusiasm and dedication of the contributors to this volume. It has been a real privilege working with such a professional outfit, and through this work, gaining a fuller appreciation of the socio-cultural consequences of the Celtic Tiger and a clearer sense of where we are as a country.

Introduction

Eamon Maher and Eugene O'Brien

In August 1994, the UK economist Kevin Gardiner, an employee of the US investment bank Morgan Stanley, coined the term 'Celtic Tiger', to liken Ireland's unexpected economic take-off to the successes of the Asian tiger economies (Gardiner 1994). As so often happens with attractive terms, it quickly became part of the lexicon, mainly because it was a flattering metaphor for the prosperity that seemed to flood into the Irish economy in the 1990s and the early years of the second millennium. Looking back with the benefit of hindsight, however, it is still seen as a time of prosperity and growth, but also of greed and of grand desires, a far cry from Robert Emmet's dream of an Ireland that had finally taken its place among the nations of the earth, at least in terms of material wealth. There were confident assertions that Ireland had confounded all existing economic theory and that, in the fashionable jargon of the period, growth would be exponential, 'going forward'. Gene Kerrigan makes the point that, in the mythology of the time, the culture of the entrepreneur was seen as all-pervasive:

> Some time during the Celtic Tiger era, being in business became old-fashioned. There arose the concept of the entrepreneur – people with risk running in their veins, with minds hewn from solid blocks of ambition. You became an entrepreneur in the same way as you might have once become a poet – by declaring yourself to be one. (Kerrigan 2012, p. 36)

This was an example of the new confidence that was to be found in Ireland, a confidence that stemmed from the belief that a new economic paradigm had been born. Even in 2008, when glimmers of doubt were being cast as to the ongoing viability of the Celtic Tiger, the Economic and Social Research Institute, an independent research agency, gave the following prediction in its *Medium-Term Review* from 2008 to 2015:

> While our understanding of the key factors driving the economy has evolved over recent years, our view of its likely medium-term growth rate has not. The forecast for the growth in GNP over the period 2007–2015

is identical to what it was when we published the last *Review* in December 2005, an average of around 3¾% a year. (Fitzgerald et al. 2008, p.vii)

With such positive economic figures being announced on an almost weekly basis, perhaps there was a feeling that there would be plenty of time in which to discuss the macro-strategy of how best to spend the wealth. In the meantime, conspicuous consumption and production were the norm, and property prices increased annually as overly generous tax-breaks were given to developers who, in turn, erected more and more buildings, shopping malls, apartment complexes and hotels. This process was seen as pro-cyclical in that tax-breaks were given to developers, who in turn borrowed more money to develop more properties, and the banks, in their turn, borrowed from European banks in order to have sufficient liquidity to maintain this cycle of lending for property development. The tax paid on the resultant property transactions meant the exchequer was awash with money.

Contextually, it is important to remember that in the 1980s, Ireland had been in a deep recession, with savage cuts made to public services, hospital wards being closed down and infrastructural work at a standstill. Emigration served as an economic tool which helped to keep the country afloat, but there was little sense of economic buoyancy. Allied to a very conservative political system, with the two main parties Fianna Fáil and Fine Gael very much ideology-free zones, social liberalism in Ireland was not allowed to flourish; consequently the *Zeitgeist* of the late 1960s had never permeated the Irish mindset. The Catholic Church steered the moral conscience of Irish society through its hugely influential role in the realms of health and education. It controlled the vast majority of schools in the country, while maintaining a strong presence on the governing boards of most of the universities as well. Socially and culturally, therefore, 1980s Ireland was quite a stagnant place.

However, in the broader global frame, change was afoot. Ireland had joined the EEC in 1973 and, from that point onwards, Ireland would benefit from the European structural funds to the tune of €17 billion. This money was mainly targeted at infrastructural development, the impact of which was to become most apparent during the 1990s. The influx of significant investment in the building and construction sector, with the aim of providing a more sophisticated road and rail network, was the stimulus that kick-started a more consumer-driven culture. Another major turning point was the English pound leaving the European Exchange Rate mechanism in 1992. This placed severe pressure on the Irish punt, which forced the Irish government, on 27 January 1993, to devalue the punt by 10 per cent. This caused consternation in Irish financial circles at the time, but it had two long-term consequences. Firstly, a number of institutions and individuals who had seen the devaluation coming made a killing on trading of the currency in the financial markets, and this introduced the notion of speculation as a viable possibility for Irish financial institutions. Until then, it is fair to say that the Irish financial sector was quite insular, being governed by a sense of probity and conservatism in terms of global investment. Having long been in the giant shadow of the City of London financial services industry, it would take time for the Irish sector to come out into the light: devaluation was a significant initial factor in that process.

Secondly, the reduced currency made Irish exports significantly more competitive and this resulted in something of an export boom. So from the early 1990s, there was a lot more liquidity in the Irish economy, and construction and building had become very important aspects of Irish economic activity. In macro-economic terms, the trend was to espouse a neo-liberal economic model, which favoured light touch regulation and which saw the market as the key to regulating economic activity. In Irish politics, a new party, the Progressive Democrats, espoused this paradigm and began, with the aid of Fianna Fáil, to introduce a low tax, high-spend economic model with significant privatization of public utilities. This meant more money in people's pockets and, with a huge increase in demand for houses and apartments, fuelled by the traditional Irish desire for home-ownership, the construction industry increased exponentially, and the Celtic Tiger was born.

Higher salaries meant that new apartment blocks, shopping centres, luxury gated developments began to dot the towns and cities of the country, while the gentrification of inner cities proceeded apace. Flexible financial and planning regulations, a low corporation tax, and a blind eye turned to white-collar crime and corruption between developers and planning agencies, provided huge opportunities for growth: 'the politicians kept the regulation light, they re-zoned like mad, they created tax-breaks' (Kerrigan 2012, p. 63). Irish property speculators, spurred on by the success they were enjoying at home, began to spread their wings abroad. Prestigious London properties were bought by newly wealthy Irish, which resulted in the term 'CRISPY' (Cash Rich Irish Seeking Property) being coined. While their grandparents and parents might have slaved as navvies or construction workers to build the imposing buildings of London, the Celtic Tiger generation of Irish investors were now buying these buildings. At the height of the Celtic Tiger, the Irish gross domestic product was the second highest in Europe, and this led to a transformation in the self-perception of the Irish, who realized to their satisfaction that they were no longer the poor relation of Europe or the colonized property of the UK.

To illustrate this paradigm shift, here is a (possibly apocryphal) story of one Irish property developer who walks into the marbled foyer of an opulent Mayfair apartment block:

'Who owns this place?' he asks the doorman in the top hat.

'Don't know, Paddy,' is the reply.

'Well, you do now,' says the Irishman and turns on his heel and walks jauntily away from his investment.

The almost non-existent regulation, generous tax incentives and the ongoing boom in the property market, facilitated by an aggressive banking system led by Anglo-Irish Bank, meant that in a sense Ireland had skipped the slow process of modernity, which involved the painstaking build-up of a manufacturing base, and instead had moved to the postmodern model of financial services, investment and a seemingly never-ending property bubble.

However, this affluence proved illusory, and the sudden dramatic bursting of the property and building bubble meant that prosperity has been followed by austerity and the erstwhile Tiger is now a very bedraggled and scraggy metaphorical animal. This seismic shift has an exact date, 29 September 2008, when the chief executives of the Bank of Ireland and Allied Irish Banks sought, and received, a financial guarantee from the Irish government, one that would also apply to Anglo-Irish Bank, which at that point was perilously close to collapse. The results are well known to anyone with even a passing interest in Irish affairs: there was a major run on the Irish banks, which were seen to have a liquidity problem, and bank debt was quickly turned into sovereign debt. The Troika of the European Union, the International Monetary Fund and the European Central Bank arrived in Dublin and the bail-out – which three senior Ministers claimed they knew nothing about only days previously – was put in place. Ireland slipped into a sharp depression from which it has yet to emerge. Unemployment soared, along with tax increases, and empty semi-developed housing and commercial building sites became the concrete manifestation of an economy that was not experiencing the promised 'soft landing', but rather a startling crash-landing into recession. The mourning period had its own associated terminology, with terms like 'senior debt', 'bondholders' and 'haircuts', which in their turn became part of colloquial vocabulary.

Given the suddenness of this shift from prosperity to austerity, it is hardly surprising that there have been a number of books attempting to explain and understand this phenomenon in Irish life. Some of the earlier ones like *The Making of the Celtic Tiger: The Inside Story of Ireland's Boom Economy* (MacSharry and White 2000); *The Celtic Tiger: Ireland's Continuing Economic Miracle* (Sweeney 1999) and *Inside the Celtic Tiger: The Irish Economy and the Asian Model* (O'Hearn 1998), attempted to explain the reasons for the dawning of prosperity. Their common approach was to examine the economic factors which coalesced to bring about extremely vigorous growth in the Irish economy at this time, and the shared inherent assumption in all of these studies was that Ireland had hit on the right formula to stimulate rapid expansion: a young, educated work force, a low corporate tax regime and an English-speaking population in a country with easy access to the European market. Ireland really appeared to have all the trump cards necessary for economic success. So, as budget surpluses continued unabated for a decade and a half, any initial incredulity gave way to a naive belief that an economic miracle had taken place in Ireland, that emigration would be a thing of the past, and that dole queues would be replaced by longer lines at ATMs as salaries soared and consumer spending grew apace. From a socio-cultural perspective, David McWilliams's *The Pope's Children: The Irish Economic Triumph and the Rise of Ireland's New Elite* (McWilliams 2005), attempted to categorize the new generation of successful Irish people, coming up with particularly memorable classifications such as 'DIY Declan', 'Low GI Jane', 'Breakfast Roll Man', 'Yummy Mummy', 'Decklanders' and the 'HiCos'. All of these sobriquets were economically derived. It was as if economics had now become the master discipline and Ireland was, in Fukuyama's terms, in the realm of a specific end of history (Fukuyama 1992), as we had traversed beyond the traditional cycles of economics and had moved into a new paradigm.

There were of course books that argued that all was not well with Celtic Tiger Ireland, that it was built on faulty foundations and tended to benefit the rich more than the poor. Kirby, Gibbons and Cronin produced a compelling critique of what they viewed as the dominant neo-liberal approach to economics that encouraged people to believe that Ireland had never had it so good, that the country had a rosy future and that full employment and increased wealth would continue. *Reinventing Ireland: Culture, Society and the Global Economy* (2002) remains one of the best interrogations of the comfortable consensus that developed between government, the media and business interests. This consensus held that anyone who opposed the current ideology was against progress, was rooted in the past, or was incapable of seeing the benefits to all of our exceptional prosperity. It is not without significance that the one power block that might have been capable of putting forward a different vision, the Catholic Church, was itself in turmoil at this point in the wake of the on-going revelations about clerical abuse of children, and hence found it difficult to highlight social inequality and the dangers associated with unbridled desire for material goods. But then again, it was extremely difficult to fight against what were strongly ingrained myths. Kirby argued that the concentration of power in the hands of economic and political elites meant that there was a widespread positive reading of Ireland's miraculous 'reinvention' that was based on a fundamental misunderstanding, namely 'that the interests of the whole of Irish society are equated with the interests of those elites who are benefiting from this newly invented Ireland'. He continued:

> But this reading has also taken on a power in its own right, promoting economic growth as an end in itself and equating social success with the enrichment and conspicuous consumption of wealthy elites. (Kirby et al. 2002, pp. 32–33)

It is clear now that Kirby's reading was accurate, but it was not one that found widespread support at the time. According to economists, Ireland underwent a major cultural transformation during the Celtic Tiger years, one that eagerly embraced globalization and the ideals of Western capitalism. *Reinventing Ireland* viewed the close identification between culture and economic forces as a dangerous development, as it largely deprived dissenting voices of any real forum.

In *From Prosperity to Austerity*, we probe a little further and ask why it was that our writers and artists, along with politicians, economists, academics and the media in general, failed to alert the public in an adequate manner to the dangers associated with the Celtic Tiger. Why was there no major novel, for example, that exposed what was really happening in Ireland at that time? Could it possibly have had something to do with the increased funding of the arts during this period, a support that made it more difficult to avoid being part of the consensus that held sway? It could be said that novelists like John McGahern and William Trevor had other interests and concerns than those of the Celtic Tiger era, but many of the younger generation eschewed engaging with what was a fascinating project: the artistic representation of a society in flux. Dermot Bolger deserves mention for his angry depiction of the 1980s, *The Journey Home* (1990), which laid bare the sordid relationship between politics and business and the havoc it wreaked on hapless citizens. For some reason, there is no equivalent fictional representation of the 1990s and beyond, apart from some references in the genres of crime fiction and chick lit.

The End of Irish History? Critical Reflections on the Celtic Tiger (2003) developed a similar narrative to that of *Reinventing Ireland*. In the Introduction, Colin Coulter outlined just how difficult it was to get a public airing for a negative interpretation of what was really happening to Irish society during the Celtic Tiger years:

> In striving to advance a systematically distorted vision of the era of the Celtic Tiger, mainstream commentators have conspired to conceal and defend the interests of that small body of individuals who have been the principal beneficiaries of the boom years. The orthodox reading of the turn that the Irish Republic has taken over the last generation should be regarded, therefore, as not merely intellectually feeble but politically reactionary as well. (Coulter and Coleman 2003, p. 18)

Perhaps the advent of austerity and the general disillusionment with the Celtic Tiger makes it easier for us to outline its main fault lines in this book. However, our aim is not merely to point out the obvious negative spiral precipitated by the years of inflated house prices and impressive government surpluses, but rather to show what impact these huge transformations have exerted on the Irish psyche. Why was it that the lonely voices that warned the economy was over-heating, that the concentration on construction was posing a danger to our fiscal stability, that there was no question of our having a 'soft landing', were not listened to? It undoubtedly was due to the cosy consensus that was being peddled by politicians and business leaders, aided and abetted by media outlets who saw their advertising revenue soar during these years, and a public that did not want to face up to the reality that the economic miracle was no more than a chimera. By tracing the path from prosperity to austerity, we will be endeavouring to illustrate in a detached and systematic fashion the myriad factors that contributed to what has been a major socio-cultural, as well as an economic, upheaval.

The sudden downturn naturally also gave rise to a number of books, seeking to analyse the depressing transition from boom to bust that was predicted in some of the studies already mentioned above. In 2009, there were some notable accounts of the economic and political catastrophe: in *The Bankers: How the Banks Brought Ireland to Its Knees* (Ross 2009), Shane Ross detailed the actions of the people in charge of Allied Irish Banks, Bank of Ireland and Anglo-Irish Bank; Fintan O'Toole's *Ship of Fools* (O'Toole 2009) examined the nexus between developers, bankers and politicians and looked at the hubris that brought about the collapse; *Ireland's Economic Crash: A Radical Agenda for Change* (Allen 2009), saw the crisis as a tipping point and set out an agenda for economic change, including a scheme of public works. Matt Cooper's

Who Really Runs Ireland? (Cooper 2009) looked at the elite corridors of power and at a crony capitalism that, in a light-touch regulatory environment, encouraged relationships between politics and business. That latter point was further and more closely examined in Martina Devlin's and David Murphy's *Banksters: How a Corrupt Elite Destroyed Ireland's Wealth* (Devlin and Murphy 2009). These books sold very well, underlining the obvious fascination in Ireland with unveiling the real reasons for our economic collapse.

As the structural economic flaws that permeated Irish society came under the critical microscope, 2010 brought the publication of other books which attempted to analyse the reasons for the financial meltdown. In *Wasters* (Ross and Webb 2010), Shane Ross and Nick Webb outlined the phenomenal waste of public money by the State and semi-State sector over the period of the Celtic Tiger. Fintan O'Toole offered a prescriptive account of an alternative route, building from the corpse of the Tiger in *Enough Is Enough: How to Build a New Republic* (O'Toole 2010), wherein he set out an agenda for political, fiscal and administrative change in Ireland. Peadar Kirby examined the economic and political flaws in the system that led directly to the downfall in *Celtic Tiger in Collapse: Explaining the Weaknesses of the Irish Model* (Kirby 2010). David J. Lynch's title, *When the Luck of the Irish Ran Out: The World's Most Resilient Country and Its Struggle to Rise Again* (Lynch 2010), explains the broad outline of his thesis, even though this book also takes some account of cultural products such as U2 and Riverdance, which he sees as indicative of the enduring success of certain Irish cultural phenomena. In 2011, in *How Ireland Really Went Bust*, Matt Cooper produced a more in-depth account of the events leading up to the actual bank collapse and the entry of the Troika into Irish politics (Cooper 2011), while in 2012 Fintan O'Toole provided a critique of the republicanism of Ireland in *Up the Republic! Towards a New Ireland*, and Gene Kerrigan assessed the rise and fall of the Celtic Tiger in *The Big Lie – Who Profits from Ireland's Austerity?*

So it is clear that there has been serious analysis of the Celtic Tiger in all of its phases, and hence it is necessary for a book such as this to state clearly why there is a need for it, and to explain what new perspectives it can bring to bear in order to achieve some understanding of what happened in Ireland during this period, and how we should learn from it. Our thesis is that all facets of the crisis have to do with aspects of language, structure and ideology, and it is these particular lenses which may shed light on hitherto unacknowledged effects of this pivotal period of Irish history. There are a number of issues involved here. Firstly, we see the Celtic Tiger period as broadly spanning the mid-1990s to the present, and we see it as involving both the prosperity and the resultant austerity. It is important to remember that no economy exists independently of the country which it serves; in fact, one could argue that the constant focus on the economy, and the way in which cures and suggestions are posited for the economy, is actually an error. One should also realize that 'economy' is a noun used to summarize and encapsulate the buying and selling that are done in a country. In technical terms, this figure of speech is called a catachresis (a misuse or misapplication of a word to explain a term which has no name) or a metalepsis (where one thing is referred to by something else that is only remotely associated with it), where there is an incorrect name given to a phenomenon. While this may seem far removed from the issues of sovereign debt and bank bail-out, nevertheless we would maintain that correct terminology would allow for a more accurate assessment and critique of what is going on. The Celtic Tiger, for good or ill, affected people, society, culture, lived lives; this has gone largely unnoticed in the current crisis, with its predominant focus on matters economic.

At the beginning of June 2012, the IMF and ECB provided €4.5 billion to Greece as part of what has been loosely termed the Greek bail-out. The use of language here would suggest that this money is bailing out a leaking ship, providing funds to pay Greek workers, in order to maintain societal norms and living conditions. However, this is an incorrect reading of the term, as nearly €4 billion went straight back to the European Central Bank – the difference being that the money was now a payment of sovereign debt. The same happened in Ireland where, out of its bail-out, some €60 billion went to reinforce the banks, which is code for paying their debts and *de facto* making those debts Irish sovereign responsibility. The purpose of this transaction is in fact to transfer private debt, from private speculators and bondholders and bankers, into sovereign debt, which means, in effect, that this bail-out worked to socialize private debt and serve as a guarantor for these to whom the money is owed. This money is no longer owed by private citizens or limited companies which can become bankrupt; instead, it is now owed by a country, a sovereign State, which makes the debt a lot less unsure. To understand the language here is to have a greater understanding of how the etymology of economics, arcane and specialized as it is, affects the language of a culture and a society.

Cultural analysis can also bring to light behaviours which would seem to run contrary to the dictates of common sense. Thus, when we see how Ireland, despite warnings in 2008 and 2009, repeated the tax exemptions given to builders and developers which were initially awarded to stimulate a dormant construction and property sector; or when the current government, despite protestations long and loud in the election of 2010 that they would not be bound by the Bank Guarantee of the bail-out by the Troika, has nevertheless repeated the exact policies of austerity against which it railed while in opposition. This would appear to go against political wisdom and economic sense, which is where once more a cultural analysis can be useful. Sigmund Freud postulated that, as well as the pleasure principle, the desire to achieve some form of pleasure as a core motivation of human behaviour, there existed 'in the mind a compulsion to repeat which overrides the pleasure principle' (Freud 1961, p.16). Cultural analysis of the First World War further developed this thesis:

> Victims of shell shock were regularly reported to suffer recurring nightmares in which they re-lived, with similar feelings of terror, the same traumatic incidents that had triggered the shell shock. This was in direct contradiction to Freud's ideas about one of the purposes of dreams. As well as being the vehicles of wish-fulfilment, dreams were there to rework emotionally distressing material so that it did not disturb sleep. Yet these traumatised soldiers were repeating a deeply distressing experience time and again. How could this repetition-compulsion fit in with the pleasure principle? After thinking long and hard about repetition-compulsion, Freud was forced to the conclusion that it was a manifestation of an instinct in direct contradiction to the life instinct or the pleasure principle. This was Thanatos (from the Greek word for 'death'), the death instinct or those impulses aimed at destruction or an escape from all stimulation into a state of inorganic inertia. (Rennison 2001, p.85)

There are aspects of current political behaviour in Europe that would accord with this death instinct, and we would contend that analysis such as that provided in this book can be very valuable in attempting to understand the Celtic Tiger and its aftermath. Cultural critiques help also to focus on the trite tautologies which have passed for analysis over the last number of years. It is time to emphasize the redundant nature of the almost phatic phrase: 'we are where we are', or the escapist mantra of 'we all partied'. First of all, these phrases are patently not true and secondly they are typical of the vacuous language that dominated public discourse in Ireland during the past two decades. While it may seem that such a critique has limited relevance for serious economic issues, this book argues that it is through language that such issues are either confronted or evaded. The two aforementioned phrases underscore a line of thought which espouses helplessness in the face of forces beyond our power, which in turn means that there is no onus to make any changes in society or culture.

A more overt focus on language and nomenclature might also have alerted us to the transitory nature of the prosperity in Ireland. As already noted, the term Celtic Tiger came into being in 1994, but, rather than being invented, it was appropriated from a number of Asian economies such as Indonesia, Singapore, Malaysia, Thailand, South Korea and China. Owing to large amounts of investment, these economies grew with great rapidity between the 1980s and the 1990s, but then were rocked by the financial crises of 1997 and 1998, which were largely due to difficulties with debt-servicing and banking. Interestingly, the Celtic Tiger repeated the trajectory of its Asian relatives, and experienced something like the same consequences. One of the problems in Tiger economies was that wealth was concentrated in the hands of an elite, and the same can be said of Ireland, where those at the top of the social pyramid have not really felt the full impact of the recession, and this is especially true of the bankers, speculators, regulators and the political classes who have been seen as culpable in not exercising due vigilance of the Irish finances.

The effect of exceptional wealth, followed by massive indebtedness, on the collective unconscious of the Irish people has never really been addressed; neither has there been scrutiny of the attendant sense of religious disenchantment that has characterized Irish society, albeit over a more extended time-line. A high point of Catholic hegemony in Ireland was perceived to be during Pope John Paul II's visit to Ireland in 1979, with Church appeal and sway particularly apparent when Father Michael Cleary and Bishop Eamonn Casey 'warmed up' the crowd of over 280,000 young people in Galway on 30 September. One could also trace the beginning of the end of that hegemony from 1992, when the same Bishop Eamonn Casey admitted that he had had an affair with Annie Murphy, and that he was father to her son. In his turn, Michael Cleary was discovered to have had a sexual relationship with his housekeeper Phyllis Hamilton for a number of years. Their son, Ross, lived with the couple without ever being acknowledged as Fr Cleary's offspring. Cleary was a skilled communicator with a special appeal for young people, which made him a popular figure with his superiors, who were also impressed with his conservative pronouncements on the issues of pre-marital sex, contraception and abortion. The scandals surrounding these two high-profile clerics caused a level of spiritual shock in Ireland that one could see as paralleling the economic shocks of recent years, and the subsequent revelations of misconduct by other priests and religious meant that many people were left bereft of any sense of spiritual security.

Again, while there have been, as already noted, numerous reports on the facts of the abuse of children and of Church complicity in not reporting these abuses, there has been little or no analysis of the effect on the mind-set or on the sense of identity of people who defined themselves as Catholic but were now rocked to the core by the clerical abuse scandals and the culture of secrecy and cover-up that followed. The Church showed itself to be just another human institution whose culture of 'group think' allowed it to justify everything in the interests of preserving its power and prestige, irrespective of the suffering their actions or inaction caused for other people. In Ireland, the socio-cultural elite, numbering amongst them the Church, the banks, republicanism, the Fianna Fáil party, the wealthy, were central to the sense of 'ourselves' as a society. The other studies of the period that we have already mentioned, many of which provided key insights into certain aspects of the phenomenon, were not in a position to assess the full range of socio-cultural effects of the Celtic Tiger and its aftermath on the Irish psyche.

This book of essays is a first step towards filling this lacuna. It could be said that the net effect of the Celtic Tiger on the Irish socio-cultural sphere was to accelerate development from a premodern culture to a postmodern one, without ever passing through the slow developmental process of modernism and modernization that has been the pattern in most other Western economies and societies. The slow *embourgeoisement* of these European cultures has left a strong legacy of literature, music and, more recently, film, through which the gradual changes in society were expressed and commented upon. However, such was the speed of the Irish economy's growth that these concomitant socio-cultural paradigms had not evolved. Literature and culture are means by which language can be used to signify the traumatic real of an event. All of the economic jeremiads have not brought a genuine understanding of the profound effect of the Celtic Tiger on the Irish people's communal sense of self. It is the unconscious aspects of this period, the repressed and suppressed narratives, which may provide some important measure of comprehension. To understand the nature of this inanimate beast, a forensic examination of its insides is necessary.

While acknowledging the contribution of Ging, Cronin and Kirby, who examined the legacies of the Celtic Tiger in *Transforming Ireland* (2009), we believe that more time had to elapse in order to assess the full impact of the transition from prosperity to austerity. Kirby, in particular, has been consistent in his exposition of the dangers associated with the unquestioning embrace of neo-liberal discourse. We read the following lines in the Introduction to *Transforming Ireland*: 'in the explicit rhetoric of neoliberalism, the significance of culture as an aesthetic or political endeavour is almost wholly consumed by the discourse of corporate profit' (Ging, Cronin and Kirby 2009, p. 9). Our desire in this book is not so much to view the political and economic consequences of the Celtic Tiger but rather to consider how exactly the move from boom to bust affected our social and cultural outlook, our eating and drinking habits, our religious behaviour, our literature and visual culture. In brief, we propose to assess how a new sense of 'Irishness' has had serious socio-cultural ramifications, in addition to the politico-economic fallout that has been well traced in other studies of the period.

In his *The Political Unconscious*, Fredric Jameson makes the point that there are underground master-narratives always present in our cultural matrix, and that they are ideologically operative in much of our thinking. The task of the intellectual, then, is to unearth aspects of this political unconscious through 'the dynamics of the act of interpretation' (Jameson 1981, p. 3). Jameson sees this unconscious as an absent cause, and as something that is available only in textual form; he further suggests that access to 'the Real itself necessarily passes through its prior textualisation, its narrativisation in the political unconscious' (Jameson 1981, p. 26). The 'Real' refers to the world beyond language, to that which cannot be symbolised in language, it is 'what resists symbolisation absolutely' (Lacan 1991, p. 66); it is therefore that which is 'without fissure' (Lacan 1988, p. 97), it hints at what lies beneath the symbolic order, things that have an effect, but that cannot be said. The aim of this book is to bring the 'Real' of the socio-cultural consequences of the Celtic Tiger out of the darkness and to begin a debate that is, in some respects, equally important as the numerous economic analyses of recent times. The realms of language, fiction, drama, film and public culture provide a supplement to the economic aspects of society, as they both contribute to, and are largely constituted by, the economic paradigm. This book will analyse how culture and society are mutually informing discourses and how this synthesis may help us to understand more fully what happened in this period, and, more importantly, why it happened.

The opening chapters of the book examine one of the great signifiers of Irishness – the Catholic Church. In the opening chapter, Eamon Maher argues that Catholicism's grip on Irish society was on the wane long before the advent of the Celtic Tiger. Both before and during the years of unprecedented economic prosperity, there was continued questioning of Church authority, particularly in the area of sexuality. Maher concludes that the perceived religious 'crisis' that one associates with the Celtic Tiger years might well be an opportunity for renewal for the Church. Catherine Maignant develops this theme by suggesting that, while many assume that the Celtic Tiger has devoured religion, examination of various data does not support this analysis. She suggests that the Irish religious market has evolved from being monopolistic to becoming more pluralist, and she goes on to explore the nature of today's religious market in Ireland from the perspective of the Celtic Tiger values as echoed by religious market theories and by the post-secularization theory. Finally, Brendan Geary looks at how assumptions about the Catholic Church have been shattered by the reports of child sexual abuse and their subsequent cover-ups, and he examines how the institutional Church has reacted to these events. He notes that, as in Spain, the Netherlands and Poland, the bishops in Ireland are adopting a defensive rather than an open, engaging stance. He suggests that new forms of leadership will be needed to form new and progressive responses to this crisis.

Popular culture is one of the few cultural areas to address the Celtic Tiger directly. In Chapter 4, Eugene O'Brien argues that cultural unconscious of the Celtic Tiger is to be found in the humorous narratives of Paul Howard and his fictional Celtic Tiger cub, Ross O'Carroll-Kelly. Freud has noted that 'the realm of jokes has no boundaries' and it is in humour that the repressed 'Real' of the Celtic Tiger can be made to return. Like dreams, jokes use the same techniques of condensation, indirect representation and displacement, and this chapter examines what they reveal. When Bono sang 'Uncertainty can be a guiding light' on the title track from U2's album *Zooropa* (1993), many people felt him to be perfectly attuned to an emerging sense of Irish identity. It was, moreover, a message that was taken up in various ways in subsequent popular musical engagements with modern Irish identity. In Chapter 5, Gerry Smyth examines the music of U2, The Script and Jedward as signifiers of aspects of the rise and fall of the Celtic Tiger.

In Chapter 6, Sylvie Mikowski asks why is it that women writers should have turned to the depiction of rich, globalized Ireland far more readily than their male counterparts. She shows how Deirdre Madden, Éilís Ní Dhuibhne and Anne Enright have each found a way to express in their fiction the ineradicable permanence of sexual difference in a world where economic and sexual liberalism combine to erase that disparity. In Chapter 7, Justin Carville explores the significance of the photograph's capacity to present a moment that is simultaneously disappearing and becoming. Drawing on recent debates on the accelerated distribution and circulation of media imagery and the gaze of contemporary photography, Carville opines that the aesthetics of topographical photography provided a visual critique of the cultural politics of the Celtic Tiger. Bryan Fanning, in the following chapter, argues that the large-scale immigration into Ireland during the Celtic Tiger period had its roots in a post-1950s nation-building project of economic development which superseded an economically and culturally isolationist Irish-Ireland period. The lack of political debate about this post-1990s immigration is an eloquent silence and Fanning attempts to fill the void by offering an insightful discussion of immigration in the Celtic Tiger period.

Images of subjectivity have certainly changed during and after the Celtic Tiger. In Chapter 9, Kieran Keohane and Carmen Kuhling analyse the transformation that the Irish subject has undergone, and is still undergoing, in connection with the period popularly dubbed the Celtic Tiger. Looking at the history and literature of the monstrous, the chapter posits connections between Celtic Tiger and nineteenth-century vampires, twentieth-century native gombeen men, to the twenty-first-century zombie slaves that we have become, in thrall to foreign paymasters and senior bondholders. Mary Pierse, in Chapter 10, looks at the role of women writers who furnish important images of societal change and paint portraits that are vital for social history. Perceived constraints, relationship difficulties, negotiation of economic, religious, educational and social environment, attitudes to family and children all feature in fiction written in this millennium by Anne Enright, Éilís Ní Dhuibhne, Edna O'Brien, Belinda McKeon, Cláir Ní Aonghusa and others.

During the Celtic Tiger years, Ireland's gastronomic culture and the story of Irish hospitality changed dramatically. In Chapter 11, Brian Murphy argues that Ireland has been revolutionized in terms of dining and drinking practices during the Celtic Tiger years, and has, in fact, developed its own version of a gastronomic cultural field. Examining gastronomy as an index of how Irish people started to see themselves in a different light, he traces the notion of food and wine as socio-cultural signifiers.

Literature and film have also, in their different ways, attempted to represent the Celtic Tiger. It is sometimes said that high-culture writers said comparatively little about the Celtic Tiger. Neil Murphy, comparing contemporary writers with Joyce, Beckett and Flann O'Brien, notes the complex and nuanced relationship between these texts and their cultural contexts. Against this literary background, Murphy's chapter reflects on some of the ways that novelists John Banville and Dermot Healy deal with issues of representation and artistic response during the years since the mid-1990s.

In Chapter 13, Vic Merriman reviews selected examples of Irish theatre's critical engagement with the building industry, and the nexus of crony relationships between developers, legislators, banking and media which underpinned the hegemonic tone of Celtic Tiger Ireland. He considers the interventionist works of the 'theatre of the nation' during the 1990s while also examining the role of critical mediation in reception and analysis of the work of artists.

Chapter 14 sees Eóin Flannery providing a summary critical survey of different poetic responses to the Celtic Tiger period, to its imprints on, and legacies for, contemporary Irish society. Considering this era in recent Irish history in terms of modernization, urbanization, ecological thought and activism, Flannery addresses the works of the following poets: Derek Mahon, Rita Ann Higgins, Paul Durcan, Dennis O'Driscoll, Alice Lyons and Dave Lordan. Finally, Ruth Barton looks at Irish cinema and considers the role of the Irish Film Board, the growth of digital filmmaking, and the influence of funding on the way films were made. She probes the shift from films that celebrate the new spaces of globalized Dublin such as *About Adam* (2001) and *Goldfish Memory* (2003) to those that that focus on Ireland as a dangerous space inhabited by a disenfranchised underclass – *Intermission* (2003) and *Garage* (2007).

In socio-cultural terms, therefore, it is clear that the critical period covered in this book brought about significant changes in the perception of Irish identity. Ireland's sense of itself became more confident, more assured and more globally oriented, as many of the chapters in this book demonstrate. The dominance of the Catholic Church gradually diminished, and a more secular, European sense of Irishness came into being along with the financial prosperity that accompanied the Celtic Tiger. Now that we have entered the period of austerity, we are even more confused than we were before the mid-1990s, as the self-image has now become less assured and more uncertain. Fintan O'Toole is of the opinion that Ireland failed to grasp to glorious opportunity presented by the Celtic Tiger and instead succumbed to contradictory energies:

> on the one hand the great buzz of consumerism and a surging, apparent endless property bonanza and on the other the terrible, heart-stopping thud of revelations that everything you believed in – the holiness of clerics, the decency of nationalism, the idea of public service – was a lie. It was much easier to drown out the insistent whisper of the second of those realities with the triumphant roar of the first than to take on the hard task of making a republic. (O'Toole 2012, p. 44)

It is hard to say with any degree of certainty whether establishing a true republic is the answer to Ireland's current problems, but at least it is a worthwhile suggestion as to how to emerge from the impasse in which Ireland finds itself. The chapters that follow do not attempt to come up with solutions to what is an existential as much as an economic crisis; rather, they seek to show how looking at the rise and demise of the Celtic Tiger through a socio-cultural lens can bring fresh insights and offer some succour to a society in flux.

Works cited

Allen, Kieran (2009) *Ireland's Economic Crash: A Radical Agenda for Change*, Dublin: The Liffey Press.

The Cloyne Report (2009) *Report of Investigation into Catholic Diocese of Cloyne*, available: www.justice.ie/en/JELR/Pages/Cloyne_Rpt [accessed 2 August 2012].

Cooper, Matt (2009) *Who Really Runs Ireland?* Dublin: Penguin.

Cooper, Matt (2011) *How Ireland Really Went Bust*, Dublin: Penguin.

Conlter, Colin and Coleman Steve (2003) *The End of Irish History? Critical Reflections on the Celtic Tiger*, Manchester: Manchester University Press.

Devlin, Martina and Murphy, David (2009) *Banksters: How a Corrupt Elite Destroyed Ireland's Wealth*, Dublin: Hachette Books.

The Ferns Report (2005) Report of Investigation into Catholic Diocese of Ferns, www.bishop-accountability.org/ferns/ [accessed 21 August 2012].

FitzGerald, John, Bergin, Adele, Conefrey, Thomas, Diffney, Sean, Duffy, David, Kearney, Ide, Lyons, Seán, Malaguzzi Valeri, Laura, Mayor, Karen, Tol, Richard SJ, (2008) (Economic and Social Research Institute) *Medium Term Review 2008–2015*, ESRI Forecasting Series, No. 11, Dublin: ESRI, www.esri.ie/UserFiles/publications/20080515155545/MTR11_ES.pdf [accessed 23 August 2012].

Freud, Sigmund (1961) *Beyond the Pleasure Principle*, translated and newly edited by James Strachey. London: Hogarth Press.

Fukuyama, Francis (1992) *The End of History and the Last Man*, London: Penguin.

Gardiner, Kevin (1994) 'The Irish Economy: A Celtic Tiger', *Morgan Stanley Euroletter*, 31 August.

Ging, Debbie, Cronin, Michael and Kirby, Peadar (2009) *Transforming Ireland: Challenges, Critiques, Resources*, Manchester: Manchester University Press.

Jameson, Fredric (1981) *The Political Unconscious: Narrative as a Socially Symbolic Act*, Ithaca: Cornell University Press.

Kerrigan, Gene (2012) *The Big Lie – Who Profits from Ireland's Austerity?* Dublin: Transworld Ireland.

Kirby, Peadar (2010) *Celtic Tiger in Collapse: Explaining the Weaknesses of the Irish Model*, London: Palgrave Macmillan.

Kirby, Peadar, Gibbons, Luke and Cronin, Michael (2002) *Reinventing Ireland: Culture, Society and the Global Economy*, London: Pluto.

Lacan, Jacques (1988) *The Ego in Freud's Theory and in the Technique of Psychoanalysis 1954–1955*, *The Seminar of Jacques Lacan Book II*, edited by Jacques-Alain Miller, translated by Sylvana Tomaselli, Cambridge: Cambridge University Press.

Lacan, Jacques (1991) *Freud's Papers on Technique 1953–1954*, *The Seminar of Jacques Lacan Book 1*, translated by John Forrester, New York: W. W. Norton.

Lynch, David J. (2010) *When the Luck of the Irish Ran Out: The World's Most Resilient Country and Its Struggle to Rise Again*, London: Palgrave.

MacSharry, Ray and White, Padraic (eds) (2000) *The Making of the Celtic Tiger: The Inside Story of Ireland's Boom Economy*, Cork: Mercier Press.

McWilliams, David (2005) *The Pope's Children: The Irish Economic Triumph and the Rise of Ireland's New Elite*, Dublin: Gill and Macmillan.

The Murphy Report (2009) *Commission of Investigation Report into Catholic Archdiocese of Dublin*, www.justice.ie/en/JELR/Pages/PB09000504 [accessed 21 February 2012].

O'Hearn, Denis (1998) *Inside the Celtic Tiger: The Irish Economy and the Asian Model*, London: Pluto Press.

O'Toole, Fintan (2009) *Ship of Fools: How Stupidity and Corruption Sank the Celtic Tiger*, London: Faber.

O'Toole, Fintan (2010) *Enough Is Enough: How to Build a New Republic*, London: Faber.

O'Toole, Fintan (2012) *Up the Republic! Towards a New Ireland*, London: Faber.

Rennison, Nick (2001) *Freud & Psychoanalysis*, Harpenden: Pocket Essentials.

Ross, Shane (2009) *The Bankers: How the Banks brought Ireland to Its Knees*, Dublin: Penguin Ireland.

Ross, Shane and Webb, Nick (2010) *Wasters*, Dublin: Penguin Ireland.

The Ryan Report (2009) *Report of the Commission to Inquire into Child Abuse*, www.childabusecommission.ie/rpt/ [accessed 2 August 2012].

Sweeney, Paul (1999) *The Celtic Tiger: Ireland's Continuing Economic Miracle*, Dublin: Oak Tree Press.

1

Crisis, what crisis? The Catholic Church during the Celtic Tiger years

Eamon Maher

Any book purporting to offer a socio-cultural critique of the Celtic Tiger cannot fail to deal with the thorny issue of Irish Catholicism. There is a commonly held belief that the Celtic Tiger hastened a wave of aggressive secularism that proved fatal to the hallowed status of organized religion in Ireland, and particularly to the majority faith, Roman Catholicism. However, such a perspective fails to recognize the steady decline in vocations to the priesthood from the beginning of the 1970s, a situation that could well have been the motivation for Pope John Paul's visit to the island in 1979. As more challenges to the Church's position on moral issues such as contraception, divorce and abortion came to the fore, and as the erstwhile deference to the Church and its priests dissipated, neo-liberal values began to take root. A more educated population was no longer willing to accept being dictated to on issues that they considered matters of individual conscience, and so there began a slow process of secularism. Charles Taylor's take on such a development is interesting from an Irish perspective:

> One understanding of secularity then is in terms of public spaces. These have been allegedly emptied of God, or any reference to ultimate reality. Or, taken from another side, as we function within various spheres of activity – economic, political, cultural, educational, professional, recreational – the norms and principles we follow, the deliberations we engage in, generally don't refer us to God or to any religious beliefs; the considerations we act on are internal to the 'rationality' of each sphere – maximum gain within the economy, the greatest benefit to greatest number in the political area, and so on. This is in striking contrast to earlier periods, when Christian faith laid down authoritative prescriptions, often through the mouths of the clergy, which could not be easily ignored in any of these domains, such as the ban on usury, or the obligation to enforce orthodoxy. (Taylor 2007, p. 2)

During the Celtic Tiger years, the majority of Irish people were unde-niably in favour of 'maximum gain within the economy', believing, mis-takenly, that 'a rising tide lifts all boats', a maxim that fails to specify that it tends to lift the boats of a few to an inordinate degree while leaving the others firmly attached to their moorings. When it came to politics, there was a distinct tendency to espouse the ideal of 'the greatest benefit to the greatest number', a philosophy that led to planning corruption, but also to the silencing of dissenting voices, especially those who expressed reservations in relation to the direction the country was headed. It was viewed as heresy to question the dominant view of the political class that the good times would roll on for ever, that Ireland had finally assumed its place at the top table of wealthy nations and would continue to stay there. The celebrated author and then priest John O'Donohue predicted such a trend in an article that appeared in *The Furrow* in 1993:

> Now that religion is in demise, industrial society has taken over its role and in a very subtle way colonizes and controls the territory of the sacred. Human longing is very effectively taken over and steered into glamorous and exciting *culs de sac*, where its energy is numbed and vulgarized in false patterns of gratification. (O'Donohue 1993, p. 617)

From being a model of orthodoxy, a society where the various institutions of the State were strongly influenced by Catholicism, where loyalty to Rome or deference to the dictates of bishops informed the behaviour of people in their public and private lives, Irish society reached the stage where religion was relegated to a private, personal concern. In addition, because of the clerical abuse scandals and the mismanagement of same by the Catholic hierarchy in the 1990s, the Church lost its moral standing, with the result that a strong advocate for the poor and marginalized was no longer capable of making its voice heard to the extent that it might have done in the past.

In order to assess the degree to which Catholicism declined as a reference point for Irish people, I think it is worthwhile to consider the theories propounded by the French philosopher Pierre Bourdieu, who is quoted in a number of the chapters in this book. Bourdieu highlighted the concept of 'habitus', which he defined as:

> the product of the work of inculcation and appropriation necessary in order for those products of collective history, the objective structures (e.g. of language, economy, etc.) to succeed in reproducing themselves more or less completely, in the form of durable dispositions, in the organisms (which one can, if one wishes, call individuals) lastingly subjected to the same conditionings, and hence placed in the same material conditions of existence. (Bourdieu 1997, p. 85)

In both primitive and sophisticated cultures, a set of commonly accepted values bestow symbolic capital on certain individuals who are viewed as encapsulating what is considered desirable or acceptable within that culture. In Ireland, it was the case for many years that being regarded as a 'good' Catholic was an obvious advantage if one wanted to work in primary or secondary education, succeed in politics or business, climb to high positions in the civil service, and generally enjoy the esteem which is often showered on the righteous. The elites in a society have a vested interest in inculcating a certain '*doxa*' – that which is beyond question – as it allows them to preserve their privileged status without the threat of social unrest.

The 'habitus', however, does not remain constant, and in the Ireland of the second half of the twentieth century, and during the era of the Celtic Tiger in particular, the focus shifted from God to Mammon in a spectacular fashion. The spiritual was replaced by the material as the desired cultural capital and one's position in society was gauged more by what car one was driving than by the number of times one was seen in church. Bourdieu explains how:

> symbolic interests (often described as 'spiritual' or 'cultural') come to be set up in opposition to strictly economic interests as defined in the field of economic transactions by the fundamental tautology 'business is business'; strictly 'cultural' or 'aesthetic' interest, disinterested interest, is the paradoxical product of the ideological labour in which writers and artists, those most directly interested, have played an important part and in the course of which symbolic interests become autonomous by being opposed to material interests, i.e. by being symbolically nullified as interests. (Bourdieu 1997, p. 177)

This, in my view, accurately captures the paradigm shift that occurred within Irish society: there was a change of emphasis from the symbolic capital to a search for real 'capital', as encapsulated by disposable income, car(s), property portfolios, holidays, eating out and so on. According to Fintan O'Toole, social conservatives are incorrect in offering the loss of religious faith as an adequate explanation for the amorality that characterized the Celtic Tiger years. For one thing, the Church had revealed its own desire to protect the institution at all costs by placing its reputation above the safety of children. Also, in the Taoiseach of the time, Bertie Ahern, the Church had one of its staunchest allies, a person who railed against the 'aggressive secularism' of those who dared to question the Church's control of education for example. The real problem with the decline in the Church's authority was that there was no real 'civic morality' to take its place:

> The Irish had been taught for generations to identify morality with religion, and a very narrow religion at that. Morality was about what happened in

bedrooms, not in boardrooms. It was about the body, not the body politic. Masturbation was a much more serious sin than tax evasion. In a mindset where homosexuality was a much worse sin than cooking the books, it was okay to be bent as long as you were straight. (O'Toole 2009, p. 183)

As Irish culture became fixated on the pursuit of material wealth at all costs, there was a move away from the religious 'habitus' that had held sway for a number of centuries. In the words of the sociologist Tom Inglis, Ireland went from a culture of self-denial to one of self-indulgence (Inglis 2006, pp. 34–43). Whereas in the past self-indulgence was considered a mortal sin, at the zenith of the Celtic Tiger it became a type of rite of passage, something that underlined one's freedom to do things that no longer had the stigma of sin attached to them. The danger, as Inglis saw it, was that when the fear associated with self-indulgence was removed, people failed to grasp the potential harm unbridled hedonism can have:

> In the attempt to express and realise oneself through consumption, through discovering new goods, tastes and pleasure, people run the risk not just of becoming self-consumed but of eliminating themselves through their addictions. (Inglis 2006, p. 42)

When evaluating the legacy of the Celtic Tiger, it is crucial to point out that it instilled a desire for instant gratification that ended up having a deleterious impact on many people. Catholic guilt did fulfil some worthwhile purposes: it often served as a brake on extreme behaviour like excessive drinking or violence; it preached honesty, respect for others, moderation, fidelity within marriage. That is in no way to downplay the many negatives fundamental Catholicism also brought with it, such as an unhealthy attitude to sex and to everything associated with the body. The Irish are not good at half-measures, however. They tend to adopt an all or nothing approach, especially when it comes to religion. In this regard, Inglis offers a convincing assessment of what emerged during the Celtic Tiger years:

> The Irish ... have become the same as their Western counterparts in their immersion in the material world, their pursuit of pleasure, quest for excitement, fulfilment of desire, obsession with consuming and obsession with self. They have moved from being quiet, poor Catholic church mice embodying a discourse and practice of piety and humility, to becoming busy, productive, self-indulgent rats searching for the next stimulation. (Inglis 2007, pp. 189–190)

So how did we get to this point? A brief look backwards is necessary to understand the factors that brought about such a dramatic change. In the Introduction, we discussed the impact the revelations surrounding Bishop Eamonn Casey and Fr Michael Cleary had in the early 1990s. Much worse was to come in the exposure of clerical abuse scandals contained in the Ferns (2005), Ryan and Murphy (both in 2009), and Cloyne (2011) reports, which revealed an institutional mindset that bears all the hallmarks of 'groupthink'.

In his 2007 study of abuses by the American military in the Abu Ghraib prison in Baghdad, Philip Zimbardo found himself frustrated by the unwillingness of anyone in authority to accept blame for what went on. The power of the 'System' rendered soldiers and officers incapable of viewing the actions of the military in a critical, objective manner. Zimbardo uses the term 'groupthink', a concept devised by his former teacher, the Yale psychologist Irving Janis, to explain the bad decisions made in groups composed of largely intelligent, well-meaning people: 'Such groups suppress dissent in the interest of group harmony, when they are an amiable, cohesive group that does not include dissenting viewpoints and has a directive leader' (Zimbardo 2007, p. 354). He cites the disastrous Bay of Pigs invasion of Cuba in 1961 and the mistaken conclusion of the Bush cabinet that Iraq possessed weapons of mass destruction that started the allied invasion of that country in 2003, as two glaring examples of groupthink. In Ireland, the Church hierarchy's poor management of the clerical abuse crisis was caused, not so much by malevolence on the part of the bishops, as by a spectacular incapacity to view the problem for what it was, a cancer that could not be cured by moving offending priests to different parishes or sending them away for treatment.

It is clear that the Catholic Church is not the only institution that is prone to groupthink. Recently the national broadcaster RTÉ was found guilty of the same fault in 2012 when it allowed a *Prime Time Investigates* programme, *Mission to Prey*, to be aired alleging that a priest, Fr Kevin Reynolds, had raped a woman and fathered a child by her while working as a missionary in Kenya. The priest had offered to undergo a paternity test to refute the allegations, but the programme producers, convinced they had their facts right, declined the offer and went ahead with the broadcast. RTÉ subsequently issued a full apology and had to pay damages for this serious error of judgement. The raft of revelations of abuse of various kinds by priests in recent years could well have led to an expectation of guilt in the case of Fr Reynolds. What saved many clerical child offenders in the past was precisely the opposite view: very few could conceive of any priest or religious being responsible for heinous crimes against children. So the system can work in different ways, but the end result is always severe myopia when it comes to the faults within a group where orthodoxy and lack of critical capacity hold sway.

The spectacular fall from grace of the Catholic Church in Ireland in the past few decades can be gauged by the fact that the majority of people no longer see the Church as a moral arbiter, and refuse to allow its teachings to impact on their daily lives, especially when it comes to controlling their sexual behaviour. A survey of Irish Catholics carried out by Amárach Research on behalf of the Association of Catholic Priests in Ireland found that Church teachings on sexuality had 'no relevance' for 75 per cent of respondents or their families. In addition, 87 per cent of respondents believed that priests should be allowed to marry and 77 per cent were in favour of women priests (Amárach 2012). Weekly Mass attendance is now at 35 per cent and the congregations are predominantly middle-aged and older. There is a marked disconnect between official Church teachings and the way in which Catholicism is lived and practised on the ground. In addition, the age-profile and conservative nature of the Irish hierarchy are an obstacle to communicating in a meaningful manner with the Irish people, and with the young in particular. A commonly voiced criticism levelled at the Church is the degree to which this man-made institution fails to reflect the teachings and example of its founder, Jesus Christ, a man who identified with the poor, befriended a prostitute and spoke kindly to a tax collector. He was slow to judge or to issue reproaches. He spoke of freedom and rebirth, of love of self and love of neighbour. He was kind and tolerant. Such was the inspiration of the witness he provided that this followers were prepared to run the risk of death to spread the good news of which he was the living incarnation. The prescriptive messages coming from the Vatican in recent times could be viewed as starkly out of tune with Christ's message.

In spite of this rather pessimistic picture, is it accurate to use the term 'crisis' to describe what is happening in the Irish Church at present? What is so bad about a once-powerful institution being humbled, if that results in its rediscovering what should have been its primary mission in the first place, namely looking after the poor and the marginalized? It is quite noticeable how many people, even some of the harshest critics of the Church, speak admiringly of the work done by the Jesuit priest Peter McVerry or Sister Stanislaus Kennedy. Why is this? It is quite simple really: these are two examples of religious people who live out the Gospel message of unconditional love for the have-nots of society, for those who are the victims of homelessness, drug addiction, depression, unemployment, the inevitable results of the two-tier society that is Ireland at present. Fr McVerry regularly called the government to task

during the prosperous Celtic Tiger period for missing a golden opportunity to tackle poverty in a meaningful manner. Seán Healy, Director
of CORI (Conference of Religious of Ireland), has similarly been to the
fore in highlighting the plight of poor people, whom his organization
seeks to protect from the most swingeing budget cuts. The politicians
didn't listen, mainly because vested interests find it difficult to commit
themselves to a programme that will disturb the status quo. The Church
in general should never have become another arm of the State, a role it
assumed in Ireland during the decades after independence. The French
priest-writer Jean Sulivan (1913–1980), writing in 1976, recognized the
opportunity presented by the diminished status of the Church:

> When the Church's prestige diminishes, when freedom shatters various
> forms of hypocrisy, when priests who for centuries have been under pres-
> sures that forced a large number to choose between a dishonest vocation
> and social disgrace are able to make their own decisions a little more freely,
> when churches begin to recognize that they can no longer use their politi-
> cal weight to influence moral decisions, there are clear signs of a Christian
> renaissance which, obviously, has nothing to do with social structures.
> Where did we get the idea that faith existed in order to prop up the social
> order of this world? (Sulivan 1988, p. 149)

These are insightful lines, especially when one considers that they were
written almost forty years ago. Sulivan was a prophetic voice in a country
where distrust of the political leanings of the Church was evident from
before the time of the Revolution, where fall-off in religious practice was
noticeable as early as the 1930s. Georges Bernanos's *Diary of a Country
Priest* (1936) evokes the massive dechristianization of the French rural
parish of Ambricourt, which its disconsolate pastor describes in the
following terms: 'I wonder if man has ever before experienced this con-
tagion, this leprosy of boredom: an aborted despair, a shameful form
of despair in some way like the fermentation of Christianity in decay'
(Bernanos 1999, p. 3).

In spite of such apathy, this saintly priest, who is viewed by himself and
his superiors as an abject failure in his administrative duties, manages to
bring healing to the local countess, who is in rebellion against God for
the unjust death of her son at an early age. He also provides the type of
spiritual presence that causes people to marvel at the mysterious inner
force that drives him to persevere against all the odds. He seems to literally assume the cancer at the heart of his parish, which eventually kills
him. His last words, 'All is grace', show an acceptance of his fate and
an awareness that the Christian path, if it is to be lived in an authentic
manner, inescapably involves pain and suffering.

In the past, there were plenty of energetic, powerful parish priests in Ireland who ruled with an iron fist and accepted no challenge to their authority. It is more common now to see an older, overworked and disillusioned clerical caste who carry out their ministry in parishes that occasionally remind one of Ambricourt. Feeling betrayed by their leaders and exposed to the sometimes unjustified rancour of the public, they continue to perform their duties in parishes the length and breadth of the country. People no longer go to church out of a sense of obligation, and that is a good thing. There is no longer the same fear of eternal damnation, no longer the same level of guilt about perceived wrongdoings. In fact, the whole awareness of sin is very hazy in a society that has shed the shackles of sexual repression and is intent on pursuing pleasure at every opportunity. The Celtic Tiger is not solely responsible for this change in attitude, but it certainly contributed to the development of a groupthink that equated financial enrichment with happiness. Now that austerity has replaced prosperity, there is uncertainty about where to turn for comfort and reassurance. Maybe it is time to return to the original notion of Christian community advocated by Jean Sulivan:

> Brothers and sisters who meet together in truth – that's the Church. The rest is only a big, necessary apparatus which fulfils its function when it permits them to live in communion. The empire doesn't interest me. I accept the remains of empire provided that something is stirring inside it, the creative liberty of men and women wounded by the Gospel. (Sulivan 1988, p.6)

Such sentiments would be unlikely to meet with approval in the Vatican, where conformity to the Church's authority and teaching is paramount. It appears to have forgotten that faith needs to be freely chosen and to contain a set of values that, when lived truly, lead to a fulfilled inner life. By concentrating on dogma, by insisting that its adherents accept the magisterium's pronouncements on all issues pertaining to Catholic doctrine, the Church risks alienating a large number of its potential allies. The New Testament contains very little by way of laws and obligations, and yet Rome continues to issue admonishments to those Catholics who remarry outside the Church, to men and women in homosexual relationships, to priests who dare to stray from the party line on key issues like contraception, women priests, abortion, the Immaculate Conception and so on. When one considers that these pronouncements come from the same Church that sought to indemnify itself against the liability linked to the sexual abuse it knew some of its priests had been engaged in for many years and that it had done little to eradicate, it is difficult not be sceptical. In the view of the historian Louise Fuller, such an attitude leaves the Church open to the accusation of hypocrisy: 'The implications for the Church go far beyond the abuse issue with which these reports deal to the question of Catholic culture as such, so flaunted, admired and even envied in the past' (Fuller 2011, p. 484).

A key event took place in July 2011, when the Taoiseach of the day, Enda Kenny, made a blistering attack on the Catholic Church in the wake of the Cloyne report. The fact that the comments came from the leading politician of the State, and a practising Catholic, made the impact all the more significant. In a country where in the past it would have been an act of political suicide to criticize the hierarchy, where deference and obsequiousness to Rome were the norm, suddenly we were exposed to comments such as the following:

> for the first time in Ireland, a report into child sexual abuse exposes an attempt by the Holy See to frustrate an enquiry in a sovereign, democratic republic.
>
> ... the Cloyne report excavates the dysfunction, disconnection, elitism – the narcissism – that dominate the culture of the Vatican to this day. The rape and torture of children were downplayed or 'managed' to uphold, instead, the primacy of the institution, its power, standing and 'reputation'.
>
> [Ireland no longer a country] where the swish of a soutane smothered conscience and humanity and the swing of a thurible ruled the Irish-Catholic world.
>
> This is the *Republic* of Ireland 2011. A republic of laws, of rights and responsibilities; of proper civic order; where the delinquency and arrogance of a particular version, of a particular kind of 'morality', will no longer be tolerated or ignored. (Dáil Report 2011)

Kenny's speech marks a watershed in Church–State relations. There was no attempt by the Taoiseach to couch his sentiments in the language of diplomacy. Hard-hitting, uncompromising, emotional, Kenny's words gave vent to the frustrations felt by Catholics and non-Catholics alike in relation to how young people had been allowed to endure the most horrible crimes, sometimes perpetrated by priests about whom serious allegations had already been made, but who were allowed to continue their ministry and to have access to more hapless victims. The Taoiseach echoed the *Zeitgeist* of the nation. This is evident in the almost universal praise that was heaped on his speech afterwards. He may well have gone too far in inferring that the Vatican had obstructed the investigation into clerical child abuse, but that is not of any great significance. What matters is the way in which he articulated the feelings of anger that have convulsed Irish people since the initial revelations of clerical child abuse came into the public domain.

There is another important aspect to this speech and that is that it was delivered at a time when anger at the banks, the developers, the politicians and all those associated with the collapse of the Celtic Tiger was at its zenith. The policy of austerity was biting and scapegoats were being sought. The various tribunals had already revealed that politics and big business were aligned to an unhealthy degree. But the view persisted with many that the Church was above such corruption. When it was shown to be just another institution marked by the same desire to protect itself come what may against the accusations that were hurled at it, when it was shown to have overseen a deliberate attempt to hide the extent of clerical sex abuse, this was a massive deception for those who had been devoted followers or silent admirers all of their lives. Convicted paedophile priests Donal Collins, Seán Fortune, Ivan Payne, Brendan Smyth joined the list of corrupt politicians on the Irish hate list. They all had betrayed the trust placed in them by the people, and the exposure of their crimes meant that Ireland would never be quite the same again.

Don O'Leary's recent study of Irish Catholicism's relationship with science cites the Jesuit academic Michael Paul Gallagher's dialogue with students in University College Dublin that led him to take a particular interest in religious unbelief, which, he argued, was far less imputable to ideologies than to culture. O'Leary concludes:

> By the 1990s it seems that there had been a shift from a conscious and deliberate denial of God amongst unbelievers to a vague disengagement from faith. Unbelief was based more on scepticism about big ideas rather than on a deliberate rejection of God. (O'Leary 2012, pp. 235–236)

This sea change had coincided to a large degree with the clerical abuse scandals and the first stirrings of the Celtic Tiger. Instead of being imputable to any real rejection of God, the move to a more sceptical outlook on life was a cultural phenomenon, one that impacted negatively on religion in the same way as it did on other aspects of Irish life such as politics and republicanism. Lionel Pilkington argued that the 'consumerist utopia of Celtic Tiger Ireland considers the idea of justice and equality as increasingly irrelevant to Celtic Tiger success' (Pilkington 2002, p. 138). While this assertion contains more than a grain of truth, it does not fully explain the disillusionment experienced by so many in the post-Celtic Tiger era. Long before there was any economic transformation, people were increasingly looking to new forms of spiritual experience that were more attractive than the rather drab rituals they encountered in most Catholic churches. A renewal of its liturgy, a reappraisal of its approach, a re-engagement with the spirit of the times, that is what the Catholic

Church will have to undergo if it is to have any hope of remaining a relevant force for those thirsting for satisfying spiritual experience. Don O'Leary is correct in seeing the importance of culture in any successful initiative to win back people to Catholicism: 'In the long term, the dominance of Roman Catholicism in the religious marketplace in Ireland will be determined by its ability to reform itself, so that it can adapt to a rapidly changing cultural milieu' (O'Leary 2012, p. 239).

The late John McGahern, a writer who suffered more than most at the hands of a repressive, puritanical Church that was responsible for his losing his job as a primary school teacher after his second novel, *The Dark*, was banned in 1965, was always careful to distinguish between the institution and its rituals. The former, in the rural north-west midlands in which McGahern grew up, was primarily concerned with control and power. But this did not take from the beauty of its sacraments that lifted people's eyes from the avaricious earth and revealed the possibility of another, more wholesome, universe. In his essay 'The Church and its Spire', we read:

> I have nothing but gratitude for the spiritual remnants of that [Catholic] upbringing, the sense of our origins beyond the bounds of sense, an awareness of mystery and wonderment, grace and sacrament, and the absolute equality of all women and men underneath the sun of heaven. That is all that now remains. Belief as such has long gone. (McGahern 2009, p. 133)

McGahern outlines the experience of a number of Irish men and women who find themselves attached to the sacramental side of Catholicism and yet no longer capable of believing many of the Church's pronouncements. Such a situation is far from constituting a crisis in my view. The Eucharistic Congress returned to Dublin after eighty years in June 2012. While the numbers attending the various talks and Masses that were organized around the event were way down on the heady days of 1932, there was still quite an amount of interest among the public for what was happening. The *Irish Times* editorial of 9 June, entitled 'Church at Crossroads', observed that Ireland had moved on from the time when the last Congress was hosted in Dublin: 'That world is dead', it stated. 'Ireland will never again be a monolithic culture in which a single hierarchal institution can enjoy such prestige.' In order for the Church to maintain a role for itself in the new Ireland, the editorial argued, it would have to find a way of reconciling those who favour a return to the discipline and certainties of the past and the 'cultural Catholics' who, while attached to their Catholic identity, refuse to be dictated to in matters of faith. The editorial concludes:

What's so terrible about 'cultural Catholicism' – the idea that the broad church is deeply intertwined with the way Irish people think and feel and, however occasionally, pray? There is a deep well of respect and affection for Catholic tradition even among those who do not wish to obey an all-male celibate elite and who make up their own minds about spiritual and moral questions. If the church pushes such people away, it will make itself a sad and bitter thing and, in the process, impoverish Irish culture as a whole. (*Irish Times* 9 June 2012, p. 17)

The Celtic Tiger and its aftermath undoubtedly transformed Irish society and rocked the people's faith in corporate institutions. But when it comes to analysing its impact on the Catholic Church, it has to be acknowledged that, far from creating a 'crisis', it instead posed the same type of questions of the Church as it did of other institutions. As a result of this, it may well fulfil the prophecy of Jean Sulivan and find inspiration from its lowly status: 'Like the storm-clouds of the exodus, the Church's face is more luminous today than when it seemed to rule. It has found glory in its humiliation' (Sulivan 1988, p.149). Only time will tell.

Works cited

Amárach Survey (2012) *A Survey carried out for the Association of Catholic Priests of Ireland*, available: www.associationofcatholicpriests.ie/wpcon tent/uploads/2012/04/Contemporary-Catholic-Perspectives.pdf [accessed 3 November 2012].

Bernanos, Georges (1999) [1936] *The Diary of a Country Priest*, translated by Pamela Morris, New York: Carroll & Graf Publishers.

Bourdieu, Pierre (1997) *Outline of a Theory of Practice*, translated by Richard Nice, Cambridge: Cambridge University Press.

Dáil Report (2001) available: www.youtube.com/watch?v=m05MXrqbDeA.

Fuller, Louise (2011) 'Critical Voices of Irish Catholicism: Reading the Signs of the Times', *Studies An Irish Quarterly Review*, 100: 400 (Winter), pp. 477–488.

Inglis, Tom (2006) 'From Self-Denial to Self-Indulgence: The Clash of Cultures in Contemporary Ireland', *The Irish Review*, 34 (Spring), pp. 34–43.

Inglis, Tom (2008) *Global Ireland: Same Difference*, New York and London: Routledge.

McGahern, John (2009) *Love of the World: Essays*, London: Faber.

O'Donohue, John (1993) 'The Horizon Is in the Well: A Reflection on Secularization and Marginalization', *The Furrow*, 44: 11 (November), pp. 615–621.

O'Leary, Don (2012) *Irish Catholicism and Science: From 'Godless Colleges' to the 'Celtic Tiger'*, Cambridge: Cambridge University Press.

O'Toole, Fintan (2009) *Ship of Fools: How Stupidity and Corruption Sank the Celtic Tiger*, London: Faber.

Pilkington, Lionel (2002) 'Religion in the Celtic Tiger: The Cultural Legacies of Anti-Catholicism in Ireland', in Peadar Kirby, Luke Gibbons and Michael Cronin (eds), *Reinventing Ireland: Culture, Society and the Global Economy*, London: Pluto, pp. 124–139.

Sulivan, Jean (1988) *Morning Light: The Spiritual Journal of Jean Sulivan*, translated by Joseph Cunneen and Patrick Gormally, New York: Paulist Press.

Taylor, Charles (2007) *A Secular Age*, Cambridge, MA: The Belknap Press of Harvard University Press.

Zimbardo, Philip (2007) *The Lucifer Effect: How Good People Turn Evil*, London: Rider.

2

The Celtic Tiger and the new Irish religious market

Catherine Maignant

Many assume that the Celtic Tiger has devoured religion. However, a careful examination of data does not fully support this analysis. In the view of recent developments, it may even be argued that religiosity remained part of life for most Irish people throughout the Celtic Tiger years. John Waters once commented that in spite of Ireland's disaffection with the Catholic Church 'there [was] no such thing as an ex-Catholic' in Ireland (Waters 1997, p.63). Yet the country changed beyond recognition from the 1990s onwards. On the one hand, it seems that the Irish religious market evolved from being monopolistic to becoming more pluralistic. On the other hand, Catholicism itself, and people's understanding of what it means to be a Catholic in contemporary Ireland, evolved from a strict adherence to Roman precepts to more individualized perceptions. In the words of Tom Inglis, the major transformation may have been that 'the dominant Catholic habitus of self-denial' was gradually 'transformed into a culture of self-realization and indulgence through a decline of the Catholic Church and the religious field, and their replacement by the media and the market' (Inglis 2008, p.79). Nevertheless, if the 'Celtic Tiger factor' no doubt accounts for some aspects of religious changes, its nature and impact need to be carefully investigated, for there is no easy explanation to the phenomena that this chapter will seek to identify.

Carmen Kuhling argues that 'Ireland simultaneously inhabits pre-secular, secular and post-secular modernities', that it is 'simultaneously enchanted and disenchanted' (Cosgrove et al. 2011, p.207). Contradictions and paradoxes abound and the time-frame itself is not fully coherent with explanations focusing to an inordinate degree on the Celtic Tiger factor. As a result of the economic take-off, Ireland has arguably been brought into closer conformity with other Western European societies, even though it has retained many specific characteristics. It may be useful as a consequence to examine Irish contemporary complexities in the light of recent theses put forward to

explain religious evolutions around the world. The traditional secularization hypothesis is clearly outdated, but its updated forms may
prove relevant to the Irish case, if only because they clarify the correlation between religion and economic development. Religious market
theories for their part defend the controversial notion that liberal
and neo-liberal economic theories have their religious counterparts.
They suggest that religious choice in a pluralist society is regulated by
rational decisions based on supply and demand, competition and consumer needs. As concerns Celtic Tiger Ireland, this suggests raising the
issue of whether or not Irish people have succumbed to consumerism
in that area of their life.

The purpose of this chapter is to analyse the nature of the Celtic Tiger
and post-Celtic Tiger religious market in Ireland from the perspective
of Celtic Tiger values as encapsulated by religious market theses as well
as by secularization and post-secularization theories. It will argue that
the Celtic Tiger is only one of many causes of recent changes, but that it
may be understood as a catalyst in the chemistry of religious evolution.

In order to assess the impact of the Celtic Tiger on religiosity in
Ireland, the first sources to be examined are international, European
and national survey results as well as census returns. The critical examination of this data charts decisive changes in religious commitment
in the past decades, but the direct correlation with the Celtic Tiger is
problematic. Census reports show that the decline in identification with
Catholicism started in the 1960s, and that it was slow and regular. No
specific acceleration was registered during the Celtic Tiger years. At the
turn of the twenty-first century, levels of affiliation were comparable to
those of 1861 (91.6 per cent in 1991 and 88.4 per cent in 2001 against
89.4 per cent in 1861). Besides, EVS surveys suggest that belief in God
remained remarkably stable over the period (95 per cent in 1981, 96
per cent in 1990, 96 per cent in 1999, and still 90 per cent in 2008).
Nevertheless a clear decline was reported in Catholic practice (church
attendance and confession), in vocations and in the level of confidence
in the Church (51 per cent had a great deal of confidence in the institution in 1981, 40 per cent in 1990, 22 per cent in 1999 (Cassidy 2002,
p. 58), and 18.6 per cent in 2008 (EVS 2008, Irish Catholic Bishops'
Conference 2010, p. 17). Yet disaffection with the Church was no doubt
provoked by revelations of scandals and abuse from 1992 onwards, and
it seems only marginally connected with the level of religious vitality,
which, however difficult to assess, cannot be restricted to weekly Mass
attendance.

Kieran Keohane and Carmen Kuhling interestingly suggest that the
deliberate choice of the term 'Celtic' in preference to 'Irish' to define the

Celtic Tiger corresponds to the collective desire to reject the Catholic and nationalist past, as well as 'to repudiate their failures and their ethical practices of repressive self-sacrifices and asceticism' (Keohane and Kuhling 2004, p. 147). If this is so, the drop in Catholic practice cannot be ascribed to the economic take-off of Ireland. In the same way, rejecting the model initiated by the De Valera era does not mean ceasing to be religious or even Catholic. In 1999, when Ireland still had one of the highest rates of formal religious practice, 76 per cent of Irish people thought of themselves as religious. If there was a sharp decline in later years (67 per cent in 2005 and a striking 47 per cent in 2012 according to the WIN-Gallup international poll), the connection with the economic situation is again unclear. Indeed, the spectacular 22 per cent drop between 2005 and 2012 (to be set against the 9 per cent international average) must be understood in the context of the post-Celtic Tiger period, following the devastating publication of the reports exposing child abuse by religious (*Global Index of Religion and Atheism* 2012, p. 5). It can be argued that such revelations were made possible by the decline in deference to religion and by the simultaneous increase in self-confidence which characterized the Celtic Tiger years. Conversely, this should not make us overlook the fact that, when this period came to a close, Ireland's attachment to Catholicism was still strikingly strong. In 2008, the very year the current crisis started, Tom Inglis noted: 'Although Catholics may have become detached from the teachings and regulations of the Church as a guide as to how to live a moral life, being Catholic is still an endemic part of most people's lives' (Inglis 2008, p. 148).

In the same way, atheism emerged in 1961 and increased very slowly. Assessing the level of unbelief is extremely difficult, however, as survey findings appear contradictory. In 1999, Eoin Cassidy commented on Ireland's exceedingly low proportion of atheists according to the EVS survey (1 per cent) by saying: 'however indifferent people may be to religion, atheism is not a concept they identify with' (Cassidy 2002, p. 60). More recent international results tend to indicate that Irish respondents to international surveys may no longer be as shy, since 4 per cent of atheists were recorded in 2005 (*Eurobarometer* 2005, p. 9), 4.7 per cent in 2008 (EVS 2008, Irish Catholic Bishops' Conference 2010, p. 14) and 13 per cent in 2012 (WIN-Gallup international poll 2012), which makes Ireland one of the top ten least religious countries in the world (*Global Index of Religion and Atheism* 2012, p.4). In Ireland itself results are strikingly different. The 2011 census mentions only 0.9 per cent of self-professed atheists and 5.88 per cent of people stating no religion. It may be more difficult to be honest about unbelief when answering an Irish survey. That said, censuses since 1961 point to a regular increase in the number of people with no religion (3905 atheists in 2011, as opposed to 320 in 1991, for instance). The sharpest increase, it is true, came between 1991 (1.9 per cent of the total population) and 2002 (3.5 per cent), but the proportion remained low. More recent data highlights a comparable post-Celtic Tiger increase between 2006 and 2011. Nevertheless, owing to contradictory survey results and the existence of other factors justifying the growth of atheism and agnosticism, the correlation between the Celtic Tiger and the increase in the number of people with no religious affiliation remains impossible to determine in any systematic way. What can be said at best is that if the 1960s ushered in a new era, changes accelerated in the 1990s and early 2000s.

The analysis of the 'other religion' tables proves clearly more rewarding. They concern the people who identify neither with the Catholic, Church of Ireland, Presbyterian, Methodist or Jewish faiths. Whereas the 'no religion' proportion decreased after 1926 to reach an all-time low of 0.2 per cent in 1961 (the same proportion as in 1861), their numbers sharply increased in the 1980s to reach 1.1 per cent in 1991, 2.3 per cent in 2002 and 3.3 per cent in 2006. In 2011, they reached nearly 5.5 per cent (Census 2011) of the whole Irish population, a new sign of continuity between Celtic Tiger and post-Celtic Tiger years. Pluralism therefore appears to be a characteristic of Celtic Tiger dynamics. This confirms that religion continued to make sense for Irish society as a whole throughout the boom, albeit in a new multicultural context favoured by economic developments. For the first time in history, Ireland became a country of immigration, and migrant religions developed, notably Islam, introduced by newcomers from Asia, Africa or Eastern Europe, which has become the fastest growing religion in the Republic. Muslims represented 1.1 per cent of the population in 2011 (Census 2011). The important immigration from Eastern Europe for its part accounts for the significant proportion of Orthodox believers, 1 per cent of the population according to the latest census. Other migrant religions include Hinduism, African Pentecostalism, Taoism, Baha'i and Buddhism.

Buddhism, however, did not just develop as a result of immigration and is not connected to the Celtic Tiger in the same way as other migrant religions. Laurence Cox and Maria Griffin borrow Nattier's typology, and distinguish between '"import Buddhism" brought by people living in Ireland, "export Buddhism" driven by teachers from abroad, and "baggage Buddhism" arriving as part of migrants' cultures' (Cosgrove et al. 2011, p. 65). Only the third type is the product of the Irish economic boom. The first type developed among Irish adepts of the American counter-culture in the 1960s and 1970s and its history, therefore, results from Ireland's initial phase of internationalization. The second type is chronologically associated with the Celtic Tiger but has only oblique connections with its values. It was brought into Ireland by second-generation European Buddhists, who came to Ireland as missionaries and have contributed to the development of the Irish counter-culture, notably the 'New Age ethic' (Kuhling 2004), which is yet another addition to the Irish religious landscape in recent years.

Syncretistic New Religious Movements almost systematically refer to Buddhism as a source of inspiration, and hybridization or creolization is one of their key features. Celtic Buddhism originating in Scotland was thus imported into Ireland, but it is only one of many attempts to combine and intertwine widely diverging creeds. Radical forms of Celtic Christianity, which actually also draw some of their inspiration from Buddhism, belong to the same category. Different forms of New Age religiosities have developed in recent years: neo-paganism, including various forms of neo-druidry and Celtic spirituality, wicca and other types of witchcraft and neo-shamanism to mention but a few. The cult of the Great Goddess in different shapes has also grown, and Ireland has become the base for an international religion of the goddess: the Fellowship of Isis. These movements appear under the unsatisfactory label of 'pantheist' in recent censuses, which seem to underestimate their numbers. These movements emerged in the 1970s and 1980s, but they became more and more visible from the 1990s, even in official records: 202 'pantheists' were identified in 1991, 1106 in 2002, 1691 in 2006 and 1940 in 2011 (Census 2011), nearly a tenfold increase in twenty years.

New Religious Movements are particularly interesting to investigate, since they epitomize the contradictions of the time with regard to consumerism and the market economy. As a matter of fact, New Agers generally reject the values of capitalism and condemn consumerism. Many of them are foreigners, mostly Europeans, who settled in the Republic because of their skewed image of Ireland, ultimately based on the nationalist ideological construct of the first half of the twentieth century. They saw Ireland as a premodern, pastoral country, a romantic land of magic where ancient supernatural spirits had survived the maelstrom of liberal and neo-liberal values, which had destroyed them elsewhere. They expected that a country so full of liminal places would offer a more authentic experience of a life close to nature and respectful of the earth. The English-born neo-pagan and witch Bev Richardson, the founder of Castle Pook Centre in 1995, is a good example of this type of approach.

Adepts of New Age and New Religious Movements also condemn any form of institutional religion, particularly Christian churches which, in the words of Dara Molloy – a former Catholic priest who now defines himself as a druid and Celtic monk – created 'the monotheistic myth' which initiated 'the journey towards globalization'. In his view, 'the first global products and services were created by corporate Christianity' (Molloy 2009, p. 4), which must be denounced and replaced by a spirituality likely 'to give a framework, a context and a depth of meaning to a lifestyle' specific to each bioregion. 'For this to work', he continues, 'the spirit has to be put back into the material world. That spirit must be recognized and respected in animals, in plants, in the natural landscape and seascape and in the cosmos' (Molloy 2009, p. 314). If we are to believe that Celtic Tiger Ireland moved 'from Catholic capitalism to consumer capitalism' (Inglis 2008, p. 256), New Age and New Religious Movements provided certain responses for people who refused to surrender to both dynamics and were in need of healing, reconciliation and rebirth in a dehumanized world.

Motivations are difficult to pin down, however, and New Agers often contribute to, rather than dissociate themselves from, the capitalist ethos. In his analysis of postmodern spirituality, Jeremy Carrette notes that 'the spiritual community is transformed by the values of individualism, as tradition and space become fragmented into commodities to be purchased in the spiritual supermarket' (cited in Partridge 2004, p. 364). The related markets of astrology, alternative therapies, spiritual healing and health foods illustrate the capitalist spirit that is part of the New Age philosophy. The target of selling goods and making people buy them is central to New Age beliefs, as is illustrated by a pagan and metaphysical shop in Dublin, which likes to advertise on the internet. It describes itself as 'extremely pagan friendly with several witches and pagans working on staff' and is proud to offer 'a wide range of goods and services' including tarot cards, angel cards, incense blends, music for relaxation, but also 'a whole range of therapists and readers providing physical, emotional and neuro-therapy as well as serving the divinational and psychic needs of the community' … 'and so much more!' (Children of Artemis 2008) – no doubt an extremely profitable business.

In the same way self-professed holism is often another name for extreme individualism. The self and the body are at the core of New Age preoccupations. Wellbeing is the target to be reached. Partridge suggests that the development of alternative spiritualties corresponds to 'a move away from a religion that focuses on things that are considered external to the self (God, The Bible, the Church) to "spirituality", which focuses on the self and is personal and interior'. He explains the connection with deep ecology by saying that spirituality is 'a quest for full humanity' and 'a path that, while focusing on the self, seeks to extend to all life' (Partridge 2004, p. 17). All things are interconnected and eventually commune in a reinvented form of *anima mundi* beyond worldly realities.

The desire for self-realization explains the link with the capitalist ethos, and the sacralization both of the self (Heelas 1996) and of the body justify consumer behaviour. People in need of healing may choose what they think best for them in the spiritual supermarket, they can express preferences, pick and mix, and buy a spiritual identity specifically suited to them. This approach naturally stands in sharp contrast to what characterizes traditional religions, in which religious identity is necessarily inherited in package form. The elaboration of new identities of the type described above is arguably a symptom of the authority-crisis which characterizes late modern societies. Today, communication and information make for innovation rather than transmission. In the context of distrust in institutional churches, better education, increased affluence, regular foreign holidays, the media and the internet bring exotic or archaic creeds to the attention of people in need of answers to their existential questions and who have put the past behind them.

The Celtic Tiger turned Ireland into one of the most globalized economies in the world. It also opened the country to international influences precisely at the time when old models were being abandoned. As already stated, a long transition period had started in the 1960s, but late modern preoccupations began flooding in from the 1990s. In the religious field, this means that the tendencies identified above were not restricted to the tiny community susceptible to New Age discourses. The similarity between New Age values and values professed by an increasing proportion of Christians from that period onwards is striking.

For Catholicism, the majority religion in Ireland, this particularly impacted on obedience, as is evidenced by the contrast between the proportion of people who identify as Catholics and those who trust the Church and respect its moral dictates. The pick and choose or *à la carte* attitude has become the norm, particularly in the area of tolerance and sexual morality. The sacralization of the body, and the 'feel-good' ideal, have replaced the shame and guilt which were the trademark of Irish Catholicism since the nineteenth century. Self-denial has been replaced by self-realization and relativism has gained ground. These trends have also contaminated the margins of the institution since prominent religious figures have voiced their desire to see the body rehabilitated in the Catholic dogma. They add that sexuality and a fully accomplished humanity were willed by God. Individual prayer, but also introspection and a quest for God in the deepest caves of human interiority, are encouraged by some, as are ecology and the protection of the earth as part of creation. The expression of free opinions which contradict Rome's unchanging regulations (for instance on compulsory clerical celibacy, the place of women in the Church etc.) has become commonplace. These examples clearly echo tendencies identified in non-Christian or partially Christian circles, albeit adapted to the Catholic framework.

The cult of information and communication which resulted from Celtic Tiger Ireland's entry into the late modern world dealt a deadly body blow to the Church at the very time when revelations of child abuse came to the fore. Its culture of secrecy and cover-up was exposed and media attacks had an extremely damaging effect on the Church's credibility and power. This is not to say that religion in general has suffered from the exponential growth of media power and the internet. The Catholic Church and Catholic lay groups are present on the World Wide Web, sometimes in unexpected ways, through online confession services for instance. But the internet is particularly helpful to New Religious Movements which actually rely on it for their expansion and survival. Such is the case of movements like the Fellowship of Isis, for instance, which came into being thanks to the internet. Cyber religiosities have also contributed to the internationalization of Irish neo-paganism, which seems to be stronger on the web than in real life. An unexpected consequence has been the reappraisal of the nature of religion and in particular its collective and participatory dimension. Besides, religious messages are now unexpectedly conveyed by popular singers or groups. MTV, the radio, YouTube and iTunes have become sources of inspiration or identification for young people in need of identity in an increasingly fragmented society. Sinéad O'Connor or the Cranberries, but also U2, fed the Celtic Tiger generation of young people with a cocktail of freely defined or interpreted religious notions, which may have contributed to the autonomy of the self but also to the mood of freedom, relativism and disrespect for dogmatic Churches that is generally associated with the Celtic Tiger.

As noted above, a superficial analysis of data would seem to indicate that the Celtic Tiger only marginally affected religiosity in Ireland. However, in terms of values and beliefs, the 1990s and the following decades witnessed spectacular changes that can safely be ascribed to the side-effects of economic transformations. Nevertheless it is as yet unclear if consumer values are identifiable in the choice of religious affiliations in the past twenty years. In his analysis of the evangelical movement in the Republic of Ireland, Mark Noll argued that it 'exploited the new competitive marketplace, where the ability to draw a crowd and attract attention for a "product" was beginning to count more than deference to traditional patterns of "consumption" as provided by the established Church' (Noll 1997, pp. 33–36). It has become commonplace to use marketplace rhetoric to analyse religious phenomena, as if religions were no different from other 'products'. The fact that it may not be so induces a critical examination of the bases of such an approach, a must in our attempt to assess the impact of the Celtic Tiger on religiosity in Ireland.

It emerges from what has been said above that the Irish religious situation is much more complex than the classic secularization theory would have us believe. Some of the developments undergone by Ireland fit in the pattern, others do not. From a historical point of view, Ireland features among the modern states in which 'the disappearance of an ontic dependence on something higher' has been replaced by 'a strong presence of God' in the national identity. According to Taylor, such states may be defined as secular on grounds that they experienced a 'shift from the enchanted to the identity form of presence that set the stage for the secularity of the contemporary world' (Taylor 2004, p. 193). Vincent Twomey, while lamenting the disappearance of the 'profound faith' (Twomey 2003, p. 31) which characterized the Irish tradition, is aware that the politicization of Catholicism may very well have stood at the origin of secularization:

> As a civil religion, transcendent faith tends to become immanent, the bond that binds the nation together ..., and so the Church serves the nation rather than transcending it. Nationalism, even with a Catholic face, runs the risk of becoming 'the angel of the nation' ... who sets himself up against God. (Twomey 2003, p. 33)

Whatever the origins of what Twomey calls 'the ultimate cause of the implosion of the public face of the Church' (Twomey 2003, p. 33) over the past decades, religious matters have tended to be more and more restricted to the private sphere. 'Over the course of my political career', former Taoiseach Bertie Ahern said in 2008, 'I have observed a growing hesitation in public debate to refer to religion, the churches, issues of faith and belief, and sometimes even to acknowledge the very fact of the impact on our culture and institutions of the historical contribution of the church communities'. To him, there has been 'an attempt to exclude matters of faith and religious belief from the public debate and confine them to the purely personal, with no social or public significance' (Ahern 2008). Secularization and subjectivization in turn led to pluralization, relativism, personalization and the drop in religious practice, all of which have been identified as correlates of secularization (Tschannen 1992).

Unbelief, however, hardly decreased during Celtic Tiger years, and the rise of New Religious Movements evidenced the need for re-enchantment. The secularization hypothesis could not account for this phenomenon. To Paul Heelas, it needed 'to be put in its place – a place where it serves to complement explanations of growth' (Heelas 2006, p. 13). Commenting on the view that 'an intense desire for meaning and quest for spiritual experience' were perceptible in contemporary Ireland, Don O'Leary suggests that the rational choice theory of religion (also called supply side theory or religious market theory) may help understand this finding, which, to some extent, challenges the secularization hypothesis (O'Leary 2012, p. 238). Following the pioneering works of Stark, Finke, Iannacone and Bainbridge in the 1980s and 1990s, the supporters of this thesis argue that, far from causing secularization and religious indifference, pluralism stimulates competition and religious vitality. They believe that, if demand for religious goods is constant, supply varies; and, the more varied the supply of religious goods, the more vibrant religiosity is. Consumers are free to make a choice between different products and make a rational decision based on the principle of rewards and costs. Jeffrey Haden offers the following interpretation:

> Religious economies consist of firms, products, consumers, market shares and penetration, competition, regulated and unregulated economies, monopolies and so on. Anchored in rational choice, participation in religion is a voluntary activity. Religious organizations compete for members, albeit under different conditions in different cultures and historical periods. (Stark and Bainbridge (1987) 1996, p. 8)

Borrowing from this theory, Carmen Kuhling understands the contemporary Irish market in terms of competition between 'religious institutions which used to have a monopoly status' and other religious forms (Cosgrove et al. 2011, p. 214), and she emphasizes 'the rhetoric of consumer economics' which has found its way in religious discourse. In the same way, Don O'Leary sees *à la cartism* as an avatar of the cost-reward principle. People tend to reject the components of religion which they find too difficult to cope with and go for benefits that particularly appeal to them. He continues to say that, in the long run, only religions that prove able to adapt to the tastes of consumers will have a chance to survive (O'Leary 2012, p. 239). Jagodzincki and Greeley go further when they compare 'the competitive market place' of Northern Ireland and the traditionally monopolistic situation in the Republic, and reach the conclusion that competition stimulated religious commitment and preserved orthodoxy in the North, while devotional levels dropped as a result of the monopoly status of the Catholic Church in the South

(Jagodzincki and Greeley 2004, p. 8). Yet, however attractive this approach may be, it might be misleading to carry it too far.

The rational choice theory has come under severe criticism in recent years for both theoretical and empirical reasons. The use of economic concepts to describe religious phenomena has been criticized, as has the cost-benefit model. Measures used to assess religious competition have been contested and results have proved inconsistent. The theory appears to provide a satisfactory explanation for the American religious market but proves disappointing when applied to Europe. A comparison between all nations in the world leads Norris and Inglehart to conclude that there is no correlation between pluralism and participation. Writing in 2005, they argued that in the case of Catholic post-industrial socie-ties 'the situation is actually reversed, with the highest participation in Ireland and Italy where the Church enjoys a virtual monopoly, com-pared with more pluralist Netherlands and France where churchgoing habits are far weaker' (Norris and Inglehart 2005, p. 10).

They further suggest that the rational choice thesis is weakened by the fact it takes no account of cultural and socio-economic factors, and they convincingly argue that updating the secularization theory may be sufficient to make sense of apparently paradoxical developments. In their view, the impact of inheritance on religious commitment must not be overlooked: countries whose very national identity was shaped by a given religion are more likely to be influenced by traditional habits and beliefs, even when religious practice has dropped and contemporary Churches have lost their former power. Whatever the historical imprint, however, changing circumstances induce a secularization process, which progressively makes values and traditional allegiances wane. Evidence shows that this holds true for Celtic Tiger Ireland.

Norris and Inglehart also emphasize and clarify the link between religiosity and economic development. What matters is not only the level of economic growth but the distribution of national resources. Inequality fosters high levels of religiosity. Data collected in the hype of the economic boom (2002) exposed Ireland as one of the most blatantly unequal post-industrial societies as well as one of the most religious. They concluded:

> Despite all the numerous possible explanatory factors that could be brought into the picture, from institutional structures, state restrictions on freedom of worship, the historical role of state-church relations, and pat-terns of denominational and church competition, the levels of societal and individual security in any society seems to provide the most persuasive and parsimonious explanation. (Norris and Inglehart, 2005, p. 12)

A complementary interpretation of Celtic Tiger religiosity in Ireland, but one which in no way invalidates Norris and Inglegart's 'secure secularization theory', is that which suggests Ireland has entered the 'post-secular age'. In an oft-quoted speech delivered at the inauguration of structured talks with Churches, faith communities and non-confessional bodies in February 2007, Bertie Ahern condemned 'the aggressive secularism which would have the state and state institutions ignore the importance of [the] religious dimension. Ireland shares in the inheritance of over two thousand years of Christianity', he said, 'this heritage has indelibly shaped our country, our culture and our course for the future'. It was not true to say, he added, that religious belief, religious identity and the role of religion has been shrinking. Consequently, 'governments which refuse or fail to engage with religious communities and religious identities risk failing in their fundamental duties to their citizens' (Ahern 2007). These comments showed how religion was back in the public sphere as in the rest of Europe. Even if the Irish State may have never succumbed fully to secularization, Ireland's evolution arguably fits in the pattern described by Klaus Eder when he defines post-secularism thus:

> During secularization, religion did not disappear *tout court*. It simply disappeared from the public sphere. In other words the voice of religion was no longer audible, having become a private matter. Today religion is returning to the public sphere. This is what I call post-secularism. (Bosetti and Eder, 2006)

But Bertie Ahern made it clear that the Irish government did not wish 'to recreate a special or privileged relationship with any denomination or creed'. It simply meant to deal with 'the multicultural reality' of contemporary Ireland (Ahern 2007). It may therefore be argued that the import of migrant religions as a result of the economic boom at least partly resulted in the emergence of post-secularism in the Republic of Ireland. In this perspective, the target is clearly more political than religious since what is fundamentally at stake here as in the rest of Europe is the integration of immigrants and the preservation of social peace.

Tom Inglis has noted that Ireland both conformed to, and diverged from, the Western model in terms of its approach to religion (Inglis 2008). Indeed the Irish case both illustrates and challenges universal interpretations of religious evolutions, ultimately invalidating all coherent mutually exclusive theories. From an international perspective, Ireland therefore proves an extremely interesting case study. One of its specificities was the brutal acceleration induced by the Celtic Tiger, which made possible a live analysis of transformations that were very slow in the rest of the Western world. The connection between increased affluence and religious evolution was highlighted as a result, but what emerged was the contrasted picture of a nation both attached to its inherited values and eager to modernize. Yet a page in the history of the country has irremediably been turned. It is unlikely religion will ever recover the privileged position it once had in Ireland in spite of attempts on the part of Catholicism to recover some of the lost ground. The Celtic Tiger favoured and accelerated religious changes by giving Irish people confidence in themselves. Affluent Ireland became fully European and global and conformed to the late modern ethos of the Western world. This influenced religiosity and the religious identity of Ireland in a complex and largely unexpected manner. Barely palpable spirals of interrelated causes and effects with endless ramifications broke the traditional equilibrium, and it is unclear which new coherent pattern (if any) will emerge from the present situation. Inconsistencies in the figures about irreligion are emblematic of the wide range of possibilities for the future in a new economic context. Let us hope that reason and good will as embodied in the post-secular approach will prevail, to make the future successfully multicultural and tolerant.

Works cited

Ahern, Bertie (2007) 'Speech by An Taoiseach, Mr Bertie Ahern T.D. at the Inauguration of the Structured Dialogue with Churches, Faith Communities and Non-Confessional Bodies in Dublin Castle, on Monday. 26 February 2007', available: www.taoiseach.gov.ie/index.asp?loclD=558&doclD=3257 [accessed 2 August 2012].

Ahern, Bertie (2008) 'Address by An Taoiseach, Bertie Ahern T.D., at a Reception for Churches and Faith Communities in the Structured Dialogue. Tuesday, 22nd April', available: www.taoiseach.gov.ie/eng/News/ Archives/2008/Taoiseach% 27s_Speeches_2008/Address_by_An_Taoiseach,_ Bertie_Ahern_T_D_at_a_Reception_for_Churches_and_Faith_Communities_ in_the_Structured_ Dialogue_Tuesday,_22nd_April,_2008.html [accessed 22 August 2012].

Bosetti, Giancarlo and Eder, Klaus (2006) 'Post-Secularism: A Return to the Public Sphere', Eurozine, available: www.eurozine.com/articles/2006–08– 17-eder-en.html [accessed 22 August 2012].

Cassidy, Eoin (2002) Measuring Ireland: Discerning Values and Beliefs, Dublin: Veritas.

Census 2011 Preliminary Report and Census 2006 Report (Central Statistics Office of Ireland), available: www.cso.ie/en/census/.

Census 2011, Statistical Tables – Profile 7 Education, ethnicity, religion, tables and appendices pdf (Central Statistics Office), available: www.cso. ie/en/media/csoie   /census/documents/census2011profile7/Profile%207%20

Education%20Ethnicity%20and%20Irish%20Traveller%20entire%20doc. pdf [accessed 22 August 2012].

Children of Artemis – Witchcraft and Wica (2008), available: www.witchbox. com/ [accessed 22 August 2012].

Cosgrove, Olivia, Cox, Laurence, Kuhling, Carmen and Mulholland, Peter (eds) (2011) *Ireland's New Religious Movements*, Newcastle upon Tyne: Cambridge Scholars' Press.

Eurobarometer – Social Values, Science and Technology (2005), ec.europa. eu/public_opinion/archives/ebs/ebs_225_report_en.pdf [accessed 22 August 2012].

EVS (2008) available: www.europeanvaluesstudy.eu/.

Global Index of Religion and Atheism (WIN-Gallup international poll) (2012), available: www.redcresearch.ie/wp-content/uploads/2012/08/RED-C-pressrelease-Religion-and-Atheism-25–7-12.pdf [accessed 22 August 2012].

Heelas, Paul (1996) *The New Age Movement: The Celebration of the Self and the Sacralization of Modernity*, Oxford: Blackwell.

Heelas, Paul (2006) 'Challenging Secularization Theory: The Growth of "New Age" Spiritualities of Life', *The Hedgehog Review* (22 March 2006), available: www.iasc-culture.org/THR/archives/AfterSecularization/8.12FHeelas. pdf [accessed 22 August 2012].

Inglis, Tom (2008) *Global Ireland: Same Difference*, New York and London: Routledge.

Irish Catholic Bishops' Conference (2010) *Religious Practice and Values in Ireland – A Summary of European Values Stud 4th Wave Data*, available: www.catholicbishops.ie/wpcontent/uploads/images/stories/cco_publications/ researchanddevelopment/evs_4th_wave_report.pdf [accessed 22 August 2012].

Jagodzincki, Wolfgang and Greeley, Andrew (2004) 'The Demand for Religion: Hard Core Atheism and "Supply-Side" Theory', available: www.agreeley. com/articles/hardcore.html [accessed 22 August 2012].

Keohane, Kieran and Kuhling, Carmen (2004) *Collision Culture – Transformations in Everyday Life in Ireland*, Dublin: Liffey Press.

Kuhling, Carmen (2004) *The New Age Ethic and the Spirit of Postmodernity*, New York: Hampton Press.

Mac Greil, Micheál (2009) *The Challenge of Indifference – A Need for Religious Revival in Ireland (Based on a National Survey of Religious Attitudes and Practices in the Republic of Ireland in 2007–2008)*, Dublin: Veritas.

Molloy, Dara (2009) *The Globalisation of God – Celtic Christianity's Nemesis*, Indreabhán (Co. Galway): Aisling Publications.

Noll, Mark (1997) *Turning Points: Decisive Moments of the History of Christianity*, Leicester: Inter-Varsity Press.

Norris, Pippa and Inglehart, Ronald (2005) 'Sellers or Buyers in Religious Markets?', available: www.iascculture.org/THR/archives/AfterSecularization /8.12HNorrisInglehart.pdf [accessed 22 August 2012].

O'Leary, Don (2012) *Irish Catholicism and Science: From 'Godless Colleges' to the 'Celtic Tiger'*, Cambridge: Cambridge University Press.

Partridge, Christopher (ed.) (2004) *New Religions: A Guide*, Oxford: Oxford University Press.

Stark, Rodney and Bainbridge, William (1996) *A Theory of Religion*, New Brunswick, NJ: Rutgers University Press.

Taylor, Charles (2004) *Modern Social Imaginaries*, Durham, NC, and London: Duke University Press.

Tschannen, Olivier (1992) *Les Théories de la sécularisation*, Paris: Droz.

Twomey, Vincent (2003) *The End of Irish Catholicism?* Dublin: Veritas.

Waters, John (1997) *An Intelligent Person's Guide to Modern Ireland*, London: Duckworth.

WIN (2012) available: www.wingia.com.

3

Shattered assumptions: a tale of two traumas

Brendan Geary

The focus of this book is on the recent unparalleled experience of prosperity of the people of Ireland, and the Icarus-like crash that occurred
in 2008, the consequences of which are still unravelling today. At
the same time as the Irish economy suffered from near collapse, the
Catholic Church was going through its own agonies, most specifically
as a result of the revelations related to the emotional, sexual and physical abuse of children, as revealed in the Ferns (2005), Murphy (2009),
Ryan (2009) and Cloyne (2011) reports, but, as has been discussed
elsewhere, also due to a longer process of change and adjustment in
Irish society *vis-à-vis* the power and influence of the Roman Catholic
Church. In this chapter, I wish to discuss these developments making
use of the psychological concept of trauma, benefiting from the work of
Ronnie Janoff-Bulman in her book *Shattered Assumptions* (1992) from
which I borrow the title of this chapter, and James Fowler's concept of
Stages of Faith (Fowler 1981). Fowler's model will be used to explore
the impact on religious adherence of the changes in Irish society over
the past half-century, and, in particular, the impact of the child sexual
abuse crisis.

Stages of faith

James Fowler posited that there are six distinct and recognizable stages of
faith development. His theory builds on the work of developmental psychologists such as Freud, Jung, Erikson and Piaget. As with other stage
theorists he suggests that there is a developmental continuum, which is
related to maturity, and that people can become stuck at different stages.
(See Margaret Placentra Johnston: Exploring Spiritual Development
website.) Fowler suggests that the capacity to trust underlies the whole
concept of faith and that this develops in infancy. His first stage,
typical of children from two to seven years of age, is when the imagination is formed; images of God, the devil, heaven, hell develop in the

child's imagination during these early years. During the second stage the child begins to sort out reality from fantasy; however, in line with the child's psychological development, things tend to be taken literally. Children invest a lot in rules at this stage. Fairness is important and children develop a belief that if you keep God's rules (don't sin) you will be rewarded. Some people remain at this stage throughout their lives. A lot of traditional Irish Catholicism was rule-based; moral behaviour was strongly related to adherence to Church discipline, especially in the area of sexual morality.

Fowler suggests that most people reach Stage 3, which he calls Synthetic–Conventional faith. It is non-analytical – therefore synthetic – and is characterized by conformity – therefore conventional, and this is achieved in adolescence. People at this stage find their identity in a particular society, Church and value system. They allow themselves to be influenced by the views of others; authority is invested in those higher up in the system, and majority opinion holds power for the individual. The symbols of the faith system are internalized, and individuals can have difficulty differentiating the symbol from the reality, or the values the symbol attempts to hold or represent. Attempts to demythologize the faith of people at this stage will meet with resistance and will be interpreted as a threat. Fowler notes that religions need to have many adherents who remain at this stage of faith development and that tel-evangelists have become expert at manipulating the 'secularized religious hungers' of people at this level of faith development (Fowler 1981, p. 164).

Fowler's fourth stage, which often begins in the early to mid-twenties, is characterized by critical reflection, where people begin to examine their faith. Since this can lead to people questioning, and possibly reject-ing, the faith system they are part of, it is understandably distrusted by institutional religion. This can be an exciting, but also frightening, time, as it involves the uncomfortable process of examining assump-tions, symbols and beliefs, which may have been strongly held, or simply unquestioned. The strength of this process is that people can arrive, after a period of reflection and critical examination, at a place of deepened personal commitment to their faith. The downside is that the process can remain largely cerebral. Fowler describes his fifth stage as 'Conjunctive Faith', where people move from an 'either/or' world (Placentra Johnston 2012) to embrace the complexity of a world where simplistic clarity is no longer available. This most often occurs around mid-life. Fowler's Stage 6 is described as 'Universalizing Faith', where compassion and understanding lead to the ability to live with serenity while taking a prophetic stance regarding injustice and the oppression of others. Fowler suggests that very few people reach this stage: those who do can be simultaneously attractive and disturbing.

The changed 'habitus' of Irish society

Inglis, in his book *Moral Monopoly* (1998), uses Bourdien's sociological analysis to explore the 'habitus' of Irish society. 'Habitus' is defined as 'a lasting, general and adaptable way of thinking and acting in conformity with a systematic view of the world' (Inglis 1998, p. 11). Irish Catholics knew the rules, regulations, expectations and limitations regarding what was considered permissible or desirable, to be allowed or discouraged. Arguably there were strong aspects of Fowler's Stage 2 in traditional Irish Catholicism. What was unique in Ireland (though post-Second World War Poland would offer comparisons) was the linking together of nationalism and the movement for independence that brought together a particular vision of an independent Irish State with Catholic morality. As noted above, symbols are very potent for people at Stage 3, and those who remain at this stage have difficulty separating the symbol from the reality. They tend to become defensive if they are challenged. Inglis notes that there was an informal consensus among politicians, bishops, priests and educators about the nature of Irish society, which lasted into the 1960s, and beyond.

A fundamental aspect of the 'habitus' of Irish Catholics was an acceptance of and support for Catholic orthodoxy in terms of dogma and moral, especially sexual, behaviour. Inglis suggests that the Church encouraged external conformity to aspects of Church practice and did not nurture an internalization of the ethical principles that supported these practices. External conformity is a characteristic of Stage 3. People at this stage are aware of how they are seen by other people and let these judgements affect their behaviour. When this loses its value – or is scorned – the faith and practice of people at Stage 3 are significantly undermined. To be a good moral person in Ireland meant adherence to the rules and regulations of the Catholic Church, and participation in the various practices of the faith. By contrast, Mary Kenny noted that currently, 'Among Dublin's smart set it seemed the kiss of social death to admit to being a practising Catholic' (Kenny 2012, p. 2).

Stage 3 faith development and Irish Catholicism

As long as Irish society accepted the 'habitus' described by Inglis as a guide to values and behaviour, adherence to the requirements of the Catholic Church would be strong. However, as Irish society became more secularized, people gave their allegiance to other institutions, like the media, and their values were more and more influenced by the commercialism and consumerism associated with the Celtic Tiger. Peter Costello, born in the 1950s, writes of his own generation:

> Many of my friends went to weekly confession. While I was riddled with doubts and hesitations about many aspects of religion, they happily conformed. Come the modernisation of religion, by the 1970s they conformed again. When the country was religious, they were religious: when the country ceased to be religious, they happily ceased to be religious – with a great sense of relief on the half of those erstwhile penitents. Now they felt they had nothing to be penitent about. My doubts lingered on. (Costello 2012, pp. 35–36)

Costello describes well the conformity that characterizes Stage 3 faith. Significant changes in Irish culture led to adjustments in the behaviour and loyalties of people whose faith development had remained at Stage 3.

Fowler suggests that there are a number of critical events or experiences that can lead to the breakdown of this stage. These include 'clashes or contradictions between valued authority sources', and 'the encounter with experiences of perspectives that lead to critical reflection on how one's beliefs and values have formed or changed' (Fowler 1981, p.173). The recent experiences of Catholics in Ireland have led to serious clashes between the authority of the bishops, the Pope and the Vatican, and the fundamental values of care for children, institutional transparency and honesty in the public domain. There has also been a profound clash between the Church and the media, which the Church is ill-equipped to handle. The revelations of profound discrepancy between public teaching and private practice in the sexual lives of high-profile members of the clergy, followed by the child sexual abuse scandals, have caused many Catholics to reflect critically on their religious beliefs and how they were formed. For some, this can be a gateway to the next stage, where values are internalized and individuals take more seriously their own responsibility for their beliefs, attitudes and choices. For others, the need for security and conformity is transferred to a different authority. In Ireland, this was the Ireland of the Celtic Tiger, which was also shown to have feet of clay.

Fowler suggests that some people manage the transition to Stage 4 in their early twenties, others do so in their thirties or forties, though it is usually more difficult at this stage as it involves letting go of previously strongly held views. The transition involves looking critically at the assumptions that have been held until that point. He suggests that the transition is frightening and disorienting, and brings 'loss, dislocation, grief and even guilt' (Fowler 1981, p. 180). This is similar to the language used to describe the experience of trauma. One of the most famous lines uttered in the crisis was when Brian Lenihan said, 'We all partied'. In this simple line we can hear a sense of the loss of the good times, a feeling of guilty collusion in what went on, and the disorientation that came afterwards, like a hangover, when the party came to an end. Some commentators have also noted that Irish Catholics colluded in the clerical system and did not want to hear about the abuse of children. Not everyone abused, but many people – including priests, religious and bishops – responded ineptly to the abuse when they became aware of it.

Fowler noted that for many people the abandonment of Stage 3 faith is the result of a loss of confidence in authority figures, often due to exposure of hypocrisy. Some people can work through the crisis to reach a more individualised 'mature faith', where the symbols of the faith and leaders are given less authority, and the individual takes responsibility for his or her own lifestyle, commitments and attitudes (Fowler 1981, p. 182). He suggests that this process can take from five to seven years. Many, though, complete only half of the journey. They abandon the faith – and institutions – of Stage 3, but do not continue to reach Stage 4. Many will transfer their allegiance to other sources of authority. The Ireland of the Celtic Tiger, with its promises of a better life, less clerical oppression, more personal freedom, increased affluence, better houses and more foreign travel, was an attractive new destination. As we know, this new source of authority also let people down. We will now turn to what happens when assumptions are undermined or shattered.

The shattering of assumptions

Trauma is normally conceptualized in terms of severity of assault: for example, we talk of a traumatic injury, with the implication that it has caused considerable damage requiring medical intervention and time for repair. From a psychological perspective, the most significant aspect is not severity so much as the threat to a person's assumptive world.

The phrase 'the Celtic Tiger' quickly became a way of describing not only the growing prosperity in the Irish economy but also the changed social context that developed in Ireland from the 1990s until the crash of 2008. The word 'Celtic' indicates that a sense of national pride and identity was part of the change, and the word 'Tiger' indicates the energy and pace of change – with a suggestion of the drivenness and aggression associated with the financial arrangements and property deals that generated the growth. The new Ireland was held together by a set of assumptions that were radically different from Catholic Ireland of the early twentieth century. The focus was on change rather than stability, secularization rather than religious fidelity, affluence rather than sacrifice and an international outlook rather than an insular and self-focused national identity. Religious practice was already in decline, and the Catholic Church no longer held a position of moral control. Inglis suggested that the media became the new arbiter of morality, and clergy, when they appeared on television, especially in the aftermath of sexual scandals, took the posture of confessor or penitent rather than moral authorities. This represents an extraordinary change in Irish society (Inglis 1998, p. 218).

The English writer Colin Murray Parkes coined the term 'assumptive world', which he described as: 'A strongly held set of assumptions about the world and the self ... learned and confirmed by the experience of many years' (Janoff-Bulman 1992, p. 5). People develop working models regarding the world and their place in it. The working model brings with it a set of behaviours, values and expectations, which, in a sense, becomes the oil that enables the self and society to function. The key feature of this 'assumptive world' is that it offers predictability.

Janoff-Bulman suggests that we live with three fundamental assumptions; that the world is benevolent, that the world is meaningful and that the self is worthy. She suggests that these beliefs (or something like them) are at the core of each person's assumptive world, and that events that challenge, undermine or show these assumptions to be false in any way can lead to trauma. I wish to suggest that the assumptions supporting the Celtic Tiger and the influence of the Irish Catholic Church had found a similar role in Irish people's psyches, and that, when these assumptions were experienced as false, the response was similar to people experiencing trauma.

The economy

John Horgan, in the final paragraph of his biography of Mary Robinson, President of Ireland from 1990 to 1997, wrote:

> Ireland is no longer the picturesque backwater beloved of Hollywood, or the supplicant with a begging bowl at the door of its richer European neighbours. It is a country where economic growth is increasing at an unprecedented rate, even as the political problems connected with the distribution of that wealth remain. (Horgan 1997, p. 219)

This paean to the new Ireland highlights the power that this new identity had ones the Irish psyche. Irish people had trusted that the politicians were looking after their interests, and that the banks, with their complex financial deals, worked with probity and integrity. This trust was shattered when the Tiger economy was shown to be based on unsustainable levels of borrowing, overinflated property values and questionable financial structures and deals. It was this collapse of confidence, and shattering of the assumptions of political responsibility and fairness, that led to the experience that I am describing as traumatic for the Irish people.

The Church

The shock to the Church was perhaps even more severe. As Inglis has shown, the Catholic Church achieved a position of prominence and power in Irish society that was unparalleled in the modern era (Inglis 1998). It should be noted that Inglis's book was written before the revelations of the four reports mentioned in the opening paragraph. Inglis writes that 'the bonds of censorship which the Church had tied around sex were *shattered*', that 'since the 1980s the Church's monopoly on discourse about sex has been *broken*' (Inglis 1998, p. 157), that 'decline in practice has been *dramatic*' (Inglis 1988, p. 209) and that 'the institutional Church is literally *dying off*' (Inglis 1998, p. 213) (my italics). Mary Kenny has written articles with titles such as 'The End of Catholic Ireland' (Kenny 2012) and 'Is Ireland Divorcing from the Catholic Church?' (Kenny 2011). She asks if Irish Catholicism is 'unravelling' (Kenny 2012, p. 1), and suggests that an older generation of Irish Catholics would find 'astonishing the acidly anti-clerical views expressed in the Republic' (Kenny 2011, p. 1).

Madeleine Bunting, an English journalist, suggests that the current model of authority in the Church is 'imploding,' and quotes Timothy Radcliffe, OP, who wrote that this model is 'struggling', 'creaking' and groaning' (Bunting 2011, p. 25). This language indicates a sense of seriousness, urgency and severity that could be felt as traumatic, both for the leaders and for many of the faithful. Archbishop Diarmuid Martin of Dublin said recently that the Church was at breaking point (Rogers 2012), and Brendan Hoban, one of the leaders of the newly established Association of Catholic Priests, described it as 'shell-shocked' (Hoban 2012, p. 63) an image taken from the experiences of soldiers in the first World War that would now be described as Post-Traumatic Stress Disorder.

The effects of the shattering of assumptions

In the context of the Celtic Tiger, the whole population (with the exception of a few rich individuals) was vulnerable, and in the Church, not only the victims of abuse but also the faithful, who had put their trust in priests and bishops, and in the probity and credibility of the Church and its ministers, were left feeling exposed. It should also be said that many priests, bishops and religious were victims of the failure of the system to cope with the sexual abuse of children.

Traumatic events affect the whole system and lead to a questioning of the paradigms that have served people up to that point. For Irish people, the paradigm of the morally superior Irish State, bound together by ties of faith, culture, Irish language and nationalism (Hederman 2009), with a historic role as victims of an oppressive British (Protestant) State, came tumbling down at the same time as anti-British feeling was decreasing. The Church, whose ministers had been the defenders of the poor for centuries, were now exposed as oppressors too, who, according to the Murphy Report (2009), were more concerned with the protection of priests and brothers, and the Church's assets and reputation, than with care for victims. They appeared to have no awareness, or, worse, no concern for, the effects of abuse on children, parents and their families, as well as the impact of the abuse and its cover-up on the fabric of Church and society. The Church, which preached love and compassion, was shown to have lacked empathy towards the 'little ones' who were supposed to be its special care. The Church, which set itself above the people and the institutions of the State, had fallen to the point where it could be criticized in the same sentence as other institutions which were seen to have failed the people: 'The main institutions of the State – government, church, banks, the judiciary, the professions etc. – are regarded by many Irish people with loathing' (Logue 2012, p.14).

When people are traumatized they often feel helpless. This helplessness can show itself in a passive acceptance of the changed situation of victims, as if nothing can be done. This appeared to be the case for many victims of abuse until RTE took the courageous decision to broadcast the television programme *States of Fear* (2009), which proved to be the catalyst that led to many victims coming forward. As well as that, in the previous decade there had been a number of cases of child sexual abuse that had been reported in the media. This, of course, all occurred in a context already challenged by the revelations related to Bishop Eamonn Casey and Fr Michael Cleary. John O'Donohue wrote:

> Then the utterly unthinkable: the explosion in the sanctuary. A psychic bomb went off; a bomb that had been unknowingly assembled for years

from materials produced by the denial of the feminine, forced celibacy, power, loneliness and sublimated politics of desperation. That psychic bomb was the Bishop Casey event. The country woke to *Morning Ireland* that had a story that would put a dimension of the 'assumed Ireland' forever out of reach. (O'Donohue 2006, p. 464)

I refer once more to the language used: 'psychic bomb', 'explosion', 'assumed Ireland'. The Irish Church that rejoiced in its moral superiority, its influence over education, health and public policy, that had plentiful vocations, dedicated missionaries and a thriving church life, was seen to have a shadow side that was shocking and that touched the neuralgic issues of sex and power that were to hasten its loss of influence and status. O'Donohue continues in his article as follows:

A society is a fascinating system. Somehow, it manages to embrace and integrate intense extremities of difference and still function as a creative and unfolding unity. Often the ground that allows such a flow of interaction and change is an assumed intuition or ideal that remains latent. These quiet ideals are the tenuous yet enduring tissue of togetherness. When they suffer severe injury and irrupt into visibility torn and destroyed, they inflict a huge wound on trust, respect and hope. (O'Donohue 2006, pp. 464–465)

The assumptions that created the 'togetherness' of Irish Church and society have been shattered at the same time. As O'Donohue suggests, such a wound brings with it a loss of the trust, respect and hope necessary to hold the fabric of Church and society together. The loss of respect for the Church – with the loss of fear of its censure and spiritual penalties – was a significant rupture in the delicate tapestry of Irish society, playing, as it did, such a crucial role in the self-identity, values, aspirations and approved behaviours of the people. This leads to profound disillusionment that has been evidenced in the strikes and protests that followed the collapse of the economy, and the outpouring of anger and scorn on bishops and Church leaders through the media.

Another indicator of the change can be seen in McWilliams's book *The Pope's Children*. One of the remarkable things about this book is that, despite its title, there is little reference to the Catholic Church, apart from a discussion of the social importance of First Communion celebrations and the change to an individualized New Age, ersatz, 'Celtic' spirituality. He also includes priests in the group of 'Status losers', in the Irish society of the Celtic Tiger (McWilliams 2005, p. 126). This new spiritual awakening sometimes exists in parallel with traditional faith (as can be seen in the bookshops and items for sale in retreat and health centres), and in other ways it is taking people in a different, more individualized and self-focused direction. The traditional Catholic faith discouraged any focus on the self, which was seen as sinful and unworthy (worth came from fidelity to the Church's teachings and practices). Time and energy should be devoted to the care of others. The conformity that was given to the Church has now been given to the secular and materialistic culture of Irish society. Fowler's Stage 4 of faith development, on the other hand, often begins with critical thinking, leading to reflection and critique of the assumptions and beliefs that the person accepted uncritically up to that point.

Recovery

For people to recover from trauma they need to create a valid assumptive world. They can do this by reimaging their world or by attempting to retreat to the past. For the Irish State, recovery will involve the long, slow process of achieving financial stability, crafting and passing legislation to regulate banking, establishing boundaries between developers, bankers, media and politicians, and the regaining the confidence of the Irish people.

The process for the Church will be more difficult. The Irish people have no choice but to be citizens, unless, like generations before them, they choose to emigrate. The Catholic faithful, however, can stop attending Mass, officially leave the Church or join another religious community. Evangelical Churches and the Church of Ireland have seen an increase in membership in recent years that is not unrelated to disenchantment of many people from the Church of their birth.

When people are traumatized, there is a natural impulse to protect the self. This can be done through denial of what has occurred, and through the process of emotional numbing, leading to a kind of paralysis, which reveals itself in an inability to make important decisions and move forward. If we look at the current leadership of the Irish Church, many commentators spoke about the visit of the bishops to Rome in 2009 to meet Pope Benedict XVI. While no one knows what happened behind closed doors, the visual image of the bishops in two rows, listening to the Pope addressing them and criticizing them for their failures, looked like adults being scolded. This did not present an image of a group of men who had the energy or vision to solve their problems.

Until the appointment of Bishop Crean to the diocese of Cloyne in November 2012, six of the twenty four Irish dioceses were without a bishop for three years after the publication of the reports on clergy sexual abuse of children. Cardinal Brady, the Archbishop of Armagh, by all accounts a good, compassionate, pastoral man, is considered to be compromised as a result of his involvement in taking notes from a victim of child abuse when he was a young priest, and not automatically informing the parents or secular authorities (Agnew 2012, pp. 4–5). He continues in office despite pressure to resign. Monsignor Eugene Martin of Derry Diocese was appointed as coadjutor archbishop on 18 January 2013. Archbishop Diarmuid Martin of Dublin, admired by the media and respected by victims of clerical abuse, appears to have lost the confidence of many of his priests (*The Tablet* 6, 2012) and possibly the Vatican (Vatican Insider 2012). At an institutional level, this reflects a Church that is traumatized, as shown, among other things, by a period of paralysis at the level of leadership. With the three recent appointments (including Brendan Leahy as Bishop of Limerick on 5 February 2013) it appears that new leaders are now being appointed to lead the Irish Catholic Church.

The response of the Vatican has been to attempt to reimpose order and control. This can be seen in the visitation to the Irish seminaries, where it was reported that the visitators were particularly interested in the notes and power point slides used in the teaching of moral theology (Claffey 2011, p. 16). They also wanted to re-establish a clear boundary between seminarians and secular students (*The Tablet*, 2012a). Hoban (2012) wrote that the statement released after the report of the Visitators noted 'a certain tendency among priests, Religious and laity to hold theological opinions at variance with the teachings of the Church'. The document suggests that this 'requires particular attention, directed principally towards improved theological formation'. Despite a response to a question by Archbishop Diarmuid Martin saying that Rome was not going to get involved in 'heresy-hunting', within a short period a number of well-known priests were informed that they had been censured or silenced (Hoban 2012, pp. 90–91).

Further evidence that the Vatican and bishops see the solution in a return to orthodoxy and the 'habitus' of the past is revealed in a sermon delivered by Archbishop Charles Brown (2012) at the closing Mass of the National Novena, Knock, on 22 August 2012. He identified a number of signs of hope. These included the tens of thousands of people who attended the Eucharistic Congress in Dublin, an ordination to the priesthood, thousands of pilgrims who climbed Croagh Patrick on Reek Sunday, with hundreds going to confession, and hundreds of young people kneeling in adoration at Clonmacnoise, praying the rosary and sharing their joy and excitement. While these can be seen as signs of hope, it is also evident that they are all illustrations from Ireland's Catholic past, and do not reflect any attempt to wrestle with the traumatic experience that has shattered the cosy world of Irish Catholicism. Frawley-O'Dea, writing of the hierarchy's inability to mourn and how this is preventing healing in the Church, notes that healthy mourning requires a 'renegotiated engagement with the real and the possible' (Frawley-O'Dea 2012). She suggests that attempts to restore the past are a form of denial, where mourning is refused.

From a psychological perspective, recovery comes from the hard work of facing and integrating the traumatic wound. It requires innovation and transformation. People need to know that they can make a difference. This is difficult in the Church as channels for participation in decision-making are closed to all but a small group of clergy. Those who survive trauma have to live with the painful truth that their assumptions were illusory. In their recovered world, they have to live with disillusionment – and move on. Church leaders will not inspire confidence in those shaken by the abuse crisis if their only solution is lots of public confession and apology from bishops and priests, followed by a large dose of devotional practice and religious obedience.

Hoban writes about finding a new voice and searching for new meaning (Hoban 2012, p. 65). The language traditionally used by the Church in its public statements will not be sufficient to meet the challenges of a people whose critical reflection has moved beyond the arid legalisms and 'bland statements' of the past (O'Brien, 2010). Writing prior to the publication of the Visitators' report, Patrick Claffey wrote, 'The fear is that what will be presented in the end will be a document couched in what many will see as the usual turgid Vaticanese that will inspire little confidence or hope' (Claffey 2011, p. 5). The response of many commentators to the report when it was published was one of disappointment and of an opportunity missed.

Psychologists consider a capacity to live with ambiguity as a sign of maturity. People who move to Stage 5, which is characterized by a capacity to live with complexity and paradox, are able to hold together valued aspects of earlier stages, while being open to truth in other traditions and worldviews. Their faith is suffused with compassion, and they hold structures and symbols more lightly. The same is true of people who move beyond traumatic events. They integrate what remains of value from the past in the light of the traumatic event(s). This can lead to Fowler's sixth stage, where, to quote Julian of Norwich, 'All shall be well, and all manner of thing shall be well'. Such 'Universalizing' faith is reached by few individuals, but remains the goal to be aimed for. This goal can unite fidelity to a religious tradition with a universal attitude of respect and compassion for all. Such attitudes can be seen in some of the victims of the abuse crisis who can move to a place where their suffering is held, honoured and integrated, and they can speak with compassion and not bitterness.

Conclusion

The collapse of the Tiger economy and the revelations of clergy child sexual abuse, along with the exposure of the inconsistency between the morality preached by some Church leaders and the reality of their lives, has deeply shaken Irish society. Human beings live with a set of assumptions that develop through childhood and adolescence, which enable them to function meaningfully in society and the Church. When these assumptions are shattered, the effect can be a profound disorientation, and feelings of anger, loss and disillusionment. Denial and numbing are often the first reactions, but these are not healthy in the long term. Recovery requires a painful integration of the traumatic event with a more mature appropriation of important values, leading to a holding together of vulnerability and loss, with the confidence to move forward.

The Irish Catholic Church had already lost its position of unchallenged authority in the eyes of many Irish Catholics. This loss was hastened by the revelations of abuse. Church leaders lost much of their credibility, and their role has been taken over by a media with a different set of values. Many Irish people transferred their allegiance to the values and promises of the Celtic Tiger, only to find that these too were illusory. James Fowler suggests that the majority of believers – and Ireland was a land noted for religious belief – remain at a stage of faith characterized by conformity, until their faith is shaken by a crisis, often related to issues of authority. Many Irish people were already in the process of transferring their allegiance to the new Ireland of the Celtic Tiger. This was hastened by the abuse crisis. Some Catholics may respond by moving to a more personal, reflective, stage of faith. Others will simply abandon the Catholic Church as another failed institution.

There are clearly signs of hope for those who wish to return the Church to the 'habitus' of the past, as well as for those who wish to invest energy in creating an Irish Church where people's voices will be heard in a spirit of dialogue, where teaching on issues of sexual morality and clerical authority will be examined with the hope of change, and a renewed spirituality will be built on more than devotional practice. John O'Donohue noted in this regard: 'The old maps and their faded geographies no longer offer much' (O'Donohue 2006, p. 467). Indeed, recovery from trauma requires the courage to venture to new lands, and not only to return to the tried, but perhaps no longer true, ones.

Those who have experienced the shattering of assumptions in the

Irish Church and economy have gone through bitterness and need to find a new truth, in terms of the State and religion, which integrates their experiences and gives them hope. In Fowler's terms, the crisis could be an opportunity for people to grow to a more mature stage of faith. There are many priests, religious and lay people in Ireland who are involved in this process, but the bishops, following the Vatican's lead, seem to want to maintain a Stage 3 Church, where the people are obedient, devout, support the practices of the faith and do not raise their voices in criticism. The allegiance given to the Church appears to have been transferred to the new Ireland which has been shown to have feet of clay. This is a potentially dangerous time for Ireland, but it is also an opportunity to forge a new Ireland, based on values that the people share, with leaders who are worthy of the trust placed in them. It remains to be seen whether or not the Church can learn from processes of faith development and healing from trauma to help establish a more mature, adult, renewed and humble Church, or will try to retreat to a smaller, tighter version of the Church that existed before the crisis.

Works cited

Agnew, Paddy (2012) 'An Ever Widening Divide', *The Tablet*, available: www.exacteditions.com/read/tabled/12-may-2012–31168/4/2/ [accessed 25 August 2012].

Brown, Charles (2012) 'The Future of the Church in Ireland', available: www.irishcatholic.re/content/papal-nuncio-archbishop-brown-future-chruch-ireland [accessed 5 October 2012].

Bunting, Madeleine (2011) 'The Catholic Church Is Still in Crisis, But It Is Still Able to Influence and Inspire', *The Guardian*, p. 25.

Claffey, Patrick (2011) 'Rome's Wider Remit', *The Tablet*, 12 March, pp. 16–17.

The Cloyne Report (2010) *Report by Commission of Investigation into Catholic Diocese of Cloyne*, available: www.justice.ie/en/JELR/Pages/Cloyne_Rpt [accessed 7 October 2012].

Costello, Peter (2012) 'The Not-So-Secret Sayings of Jesus: What the Catholic Church Meant and Means to Me', in Littleton, John and Maher, Eamon (eds), *Catholicism and Me*, Dublin: The Columba Press, 33–41.

The Ferns Report (2005) *The Ferns Report*, presented by the Ferns Inquiry to the Minister for Health and Children, available: www.nochildsbehindleft.org/docs/Ferns_Report.pdf [accessed 7 October 2012].

Fowler, James (1981) *Faith Development*, San Francisco: Harper and Row.

Frawley-O'Dea, Mary Gail (2012) 'Hierarchy's Inability to Mourn Thwarts Healing in Church', available: ncronline.org/news/accountability/hierarchys-inability-mourn-thwarts-healing-church [accessed 5 October 2012].

Hederman, Patrick (2009) 'The Leader Interview with Patrick Hederman, Abbot

of Glenstall', *The Limerick Leader*, available: www.limerickleader.ie/inter
view/The-Leader-Interviewwith-Patrick-Hederman.5378997.jp [accessed 5
October 2012].

Hoban, Brendan (2012) *Where Do We Go from Here? The Crisis in Irish
Catholicism*, Ballina: Banley House.

Horgan, John (1997) *Mary Robinson*, Dublin: The O'Brien Press.

Inglis, Tom (1998) *Moral Monopoly: The Rise and Fall of the Catholic Church
in Modern Ireland*, Dublin: University College Press.

Janoff-Bulman, Ronnie (1992) *Shattered Assumptions*, New York: Free Press.

Kenny, Mary (2011) 'Is Ireland Divorcing from the Catholic Church?',
The Telegraph, available: www.telegraph.co.uk/news/worldnews/europe/
ireland/8663451/Is-Ireland-divorcing-from-the-Catholic-Church.html
[accessed 10 August 2012].

Kenny, Mary (2012) 'The End of Catholic Ireland', *The Guardian*, available:
www.guardian.co.uk/commentisfree/belief/2012/aug/08/end-of-catholic-
ireland [accessed 25 August 2012].

Logue, Brendan (2012) 'Leadership Needed to Mend Our Sorry State of
Delusion', *The Irish Times*, 20 September, p. 14.

McWilliams, David (2005) *The Pope's Children: The Irish Economic Triumph
and the Risk of Ireland's New Elite*, Dublin: Cull and Macmillan.

The Murphy Report (2009) *The Commission of Investigation Report into
Catholic Archdiocese of Dublin*, available: www.dacoi.ie [accessed 7 October
2012].

O'Brien, Breda (2010) 'Staying with a Shambolic Church Because I Believe in
the Message', *The Irish Times*, available: www.irishtimes.com/newspaper/
opinion/2010/0213/ 1224264352076.html [accessed 5 October 2012].

O'Donohue, John (2006) 'Before the Dawn I Begot You', *The Furrow*,
September, pp. 463–473.

Placentra Johnston, Margaret (2012) 'James Fowler's Stages of Faith
Development', available: www.exploring-spiritual-development.com/James
FowlersStages.html [accessed 5 October 2012].

Rogers, Stephen (2012) 'The Church Is at Breaking Point', *The Irish Examiner*,
available: www.irishexaminer.com/ireland/church-is-at-breaking-point-mar
tin-185855.html [accessed 6 October 2012].

The Ryan Report (2009) *Report of the Commission to Inquire into Child
Abuse*, available: www.childabusecommission.com/rpt/pdfs [accessed 7
October 2012].

States of Fear (2009) RTÉ, April–May.

The Tablet (2012a) 'Maynooth Seminarians To Be Set Apart', 21 January, p. 31.

The Tablet (2012b) 'Martin's Relations with Priests "Close to Breakdown"', 23
March, p. 33.

Vatican Insider (2012) 'Archbishop Martin of Dublin Snubbed from Vatican
Abuse Symposium', available: vaticaninsider.lastampa.it/en/homepage/the-
vatican/detail/articolo/papa-pedofilia-irlanda-simposio-pope-pedophilia-ire
land-symposium-papa-pedofilia-irlanda/ [accessed 25 August 2012].

4

'Tendency-wit': the cultural unconscious of the Celtic Tiger in the writings of Paul Howard

Eugene O'Brien

> Books, education, learning, these things have their place in the life of young men, of course. But not in yours. Because you are an élite ... Many of you will go on to play rugby for clubs and form new alliances. A good number of you will meet a fellow at your new club who will get you a highly paid, yet unfulfilling, job that requires you to wear a suit – perhaps in a bank or some other such financial institution – where you'll open envelopes for fifty or sixty thousand pounds a year. Others will discover that the inability to spell the word lager is no hindrance to getting a job as a rep for a major brewing company if they happen to sponsor your team. Some of you will go on to manage your father's business. (Howard 2004, pp. 159–160)

These words were spoken by Father Denis Fehily, a character in *The Miseducation Years* by Paul Howard, one of a series of novels featuring the adventures of an upper-middle-class character called Ross O'Carroll-Kelly. Fehily is the headmaster of the fictional Castlerock College, an exclusive private Catholic school on the (affluent) south side of Dublin, and he makes it very clear that he is speaking to members of a socio-cultural elite. He appears in a number of the books in the series, all of which are supposedly dictated by the fictional main character, Ross, to the author, Paul Howard. This pseudo-confessional mode is relevant in the context of this reading of the books as evocative of the Celtic Tiger.

There are ten books in the series to date. *The Miseducation Years* (Howard 2004 – originally privately published) describes Ross's last two years at Castlerock College and his Leinster Senior Cup victory. *The Teenage Dirtbag Years* (Howard 2003a) sees Ross in his first year in a sports management course in UCD. *The Orange Mocha-Chip Frappuccino Years* (Howard 2003b) shows us Ross leaving home and working for his friend J.P.'s father as an estate agent. *PS, I Scored the Bridesmaids* (Howard 2005) deals with his marriage to his long-term 'portner', Sorcha. *Should Have Got Off at Sydney Parade* (Howard 2006a) deals with the birth of Ross and Sorcha's daughter, Honor, and

Ross's participation in his new nightclub, Lillie's Bordello. *The Curious Incident of the Dog in the Nightdress* (Howard 2006b) tells of Ross's discovery that he has an eight-year-old son called Ronan, living on the North side. *This Champagne Mojito Is the Last Thing I Own* (Howard 2008a) deals with his fall from grace as his father goes to prison and Ross is forced to take up paid work, while Sorcha finally leaves him. There are numerous intertextual references throughout the books, including the titles, which reference *The Miseducation of Lauryn Hill, Teenage Dirtbag, Adrian Mole: The Cappuccino Years, PS, I Love You* and *The Curious Incident of the Dog in the Night-time* respectively. *Mr S and the Secrets of Andorra's Box* (Howard 2008c) deals with his new job as the rugby coach of the Andorran national team and also with his attempts to cope with separation from Sorcha and Honor while *NAMA Mia* (Howard 2011) conflates the National Asset Management Agency and the Abba song 'Mama Mia', and, like his 2012 book *The Shelbourne Ultimatum*, it deals with an Ireland suffering the effects of austerity in the wake of the Celtic Tiger.

The characters speak in a specific idiolect. The writing is phonetic, as the spelling attempts to mirror the Southside Dublin accent that is spoken by practically all of the main characters. Thus, the vowel changes stress the pronunciation so we get 'orm' for 'arm' and 'hort' for 'heart', as well as rhyming slang: 'jo' is a taxi ('jo maxi' – an Irish television programme); 'chicken's neck' is a cheque; 'jack' is the story (jackanory), and 'saucepan' stands for a kid (saucepan lid) (Howard 2008b). Allied to this is the punctuation of almost every fourth sentence with the phatic term 'roysh', and acronyms like 'TMI' (too much information), all of which combine to provide a very particular mode of discourse in these books. Through this phonetic spelling, and very specific usage of acronyms and rhyming slang, he is able to isolate this specific, affluent social group through how they speak as well as through what they are actually saying. The notion of accent as a social stratifying device is something with which we are all familiar, but it has seldom been used in fiction to such telling and highly humorous effect.

The humour is pervasive and works on a number of levels, with some stock comic characters. Rugby dominates the books, with Ross's full name being 'Ross Kyle Gibson McBride O'Carroll-Kelly', a name encompassing some of the greatest Irish rugby players (Jackie Kyle, Mike Gibson and Willie John McBride). Ross is sexist, a snob, politically incorrect, extremely vain, insensitive to the feelings of others, easily duped and self-obsessed – but Howard makes us actually like him by taking the reader into Ross's confidence. Generically, the style is that of the first-person fallible narrator, and the technique of all the books is to use the voice of the narrator to undercut himself. One can see traces of the work of Brett Easton Ellis in these books, specifically in terms of the attitudes of a financial elite to those outside that elite world.

Howard's work is immensely popular, and has not been the subject of a lot of academic criticism, being strongly aligned to popular culture as opposed to high culture. As Pierre Bourdieu has noted, 'taste classifies, and it classifies the classifier' (Bourdieu 1984, p. 6), so possibly Howard's critique of the Celtic Tiger is a little too close to the bone for those academics and reviewers who were part of the entire process. I would argue that the whole idea of high culture is in need of interrogation. In the first place, any system or structure is not monadic in that it exists and operates differentially – for there to be a system of high culture there must be one of low culture (and the adjective 'low' is the technically correct term in this context, as it is the binary opposite of 'high', but it has been attenuated for the purposes of political correctness into the less pejorative term 'popular'). As Bourdieu has noted, each position in the field of high culture, or in a particular canonical system, 'receives its distinctive value from its negative relationship with the co-existent position-takings to which it is objectively related and which determine it by delimiting it' (Bourdieu 1993, p. 30).

As is argued elsewhere in this book, high cultural representations of the Celtic Tiger have been quite rare, and Howard's work is one of the very few sustained representations of this period in fiction. I would suggest that it is through such fictional representations that the 'real' of this period can be accessed. Humour, according to Sigmund Freud, can be 'purposive', and he goes on to define this purposivity in terms of its 'tendency' to run 'the risk of ruffling people who do not wish to hear it' (Freud 1922, p. 128). Howard's work is an example of such tendency-wit. Even the rhyming slang has an exclusionary quality to it, as those who are part of the elite group are aware of the rhyming significations, while those who are not part of this group are not, and are left at an epistemological disadvantage. In all of these books, it is very much a case of an elite talking to itself, with little room left for interaction with any other social class. Freud has noted that crises or trauma are often not signified in ordinary social discourse:

> We designate that form by the term 'repression'. It is characterized by the fact that it excludes from consciousness certain former emotions and their products. We shall learn that tendency-wit itself is capable of liberating pleasure from sources that have undergone repression. (Freud 1922, pp. 205–206)

I would suggest that the trauma of the whole financial collapse, the plummeting of property prices and the catastrophic level of debt in

Ireland was so intense that a collective emotional repression has taken place, which explains why there have been so few systemic consequences of this whole affair in Ireland. The inability to confront what has happened through discussion that might have led to understanding, and the ensuing imperative towards repetition of previous actions, has been the on-going trope of the Irish response to the crisis – and one could see the plethora of economic and political analyses of the period as a signifier of this trend. Governments have repeated poor decisions of previous governments; bankers and auditors, who were unable to see what was happening, remain in power and still offer guidance despite their bad advice; the culture of secrecy, borrowed from the private-sector obsession with not allowing competitors access to information, is still operative and, perhaps most worryingly, the mistakes made by Japan in a parallel situation, which resulted in a moribund economy for some ten years, are being repeated in Ireland. For Freud, compulsive action is 'a repetition of what is forbidden' (Freud 1918, p. 86), and he sums it up in the terms 'fixation to the trauma' and 'repetition-compulsion'. He gives the examples of a man who has had a long-forgotten mother-fixation in his childhood, but who will later 'seek for a woman on whom he can be dependent, who will feed and keep him', and of a girl who 'was seduced in early childhood' who may in later life 'orient her later sexual life towards provoking such assaults over and over again' (Freud 1939, p. 122). Such compulsive repetitions serve to mask our access to the root cause of the problem, to what I term the 'real'.

I am using this term in the sense coined by the French thinker Jacques Lacan, who notes that most of our dealings with others are conducted through language, or what he terms the symbolic order of meaning, where words signify according to accepted cultural codes. Owing to legal and societal constrictions and strictures, information is very often not fully signified in the symbolic order. For Lacan, the 'real' refers to the world beyond language, to that which cannot be symbolized in language, it is 'what resists symbolisation absolutely' (Lacan 1991, p. 66); it is therefore that which is 'without fissure' (Lacan 1988, p. 97). It hints at what lies beneath the symbolic order, things that have an effect, but that cannot be said: 'when discourse runs up against something, falters, and can go no further ... that's the real' (Lacan 1990, p. xxiii), one can take the example of the minutes of a fractious meeting, when the symbolic order never accesses the real emotions of the actual meeting; yet it is the real effects of the arguments and ill-feeling that will continue to influence the people in that organization for a long time to come.

There has been a lot written about the period in terms of political and economic studies, but there has been no attempt to understand the underlying factors that allowed Ireland to feel that it had somehow inverted and destroyed the global economic models and that growth would be on-going. No one has been charged with fraud or malfeasance; no one lost their job or pension because of incompetence; and a certain socio-cultural elite (colloquially termed 'the golden circle') has remained insulated from the effects of the recession and the budgetary austerity. I would argue that this is due to what can be termed societal repression, as we have been very reluctant to face the 'real' of this crisis, and I will further argue that it is through Howard's tendency-wit that we have some chance of understanding the cause of the failure of the Celtic Tiger.

To exemplify what I mean by the real in this context, I would like to look at the events of 29 September 2008, when the chief executives of Allied Irish Bank and Bank of Ireland looked for a bank guarantee from the Taoiseach Brian Cowen and the Finance Minister and a small group of advisers and higher civil servants. This guarantee was based on the idea that the banks had a liquidity issue; hence it was granted. All deposits were guaranteed unconditionally, and this was sanctioned by an incorporeal cabinet meeting in the small hours of that morning, when the remainder of the cabinet were contacted by phone and confronted with a *fait accompli*. What this meant, in actuality, was that the taxpayers, the private citizens, the ordinary people of Ireland, under the guise of their own relatively small savings accounts of up to €100,000 being protected, in fact were now burdened with the debts of the banks, debts which, it would soon become clear, were cataclysmic.

The fact that senior bankers at best did not know the true state of the liquidity of their institutions on the night of 29 September, when they met the then Minister of Finance Brian Lenihan, and at worst blatantly lied about the state of the banks, has never really been addressed. They spoke of a liquidity crisis when in fact what was at issue was a solvency crisis. Regulation was non-existent, a point made in a report by Klaus Regling and Max Watson: 'it appears clear, however, that bank governance and risk management were weak – in some cases disastrously so' (Regling and Watson 2010, p.6). Given the genre involved here, that of a government report, and the generally nuanced and carefully chosen symbolic tenor of such discourse, this is a damning indictment of the structures of management in private banks, specifically Allied Irish Bank, Bank of Ireland and Anglo-Irish Bank. This final bank was the cause of much of the problem owing to its reckless lending, which resulted in a €1.5 billion bail-out for it and full guarantees for all bondholders, secured and unsecured, in all banks. The result was national bankruptcy, the need for a financial bail-out from Europe, and a rise in unemployment to some 400,000 people. Four to five years later, the Irish public sphere is still shell-shocked. In the light of this behaviour, Alain Badiou's gnomic remark that 'the State does not think' (Badiou 2005, p. 87) becomes clearer. By this he means that the State seldom has a philosophy; instead it has a pragmatic system through which it enacts the necessary performatives which make it a State. The symbolic order of the State, unwilling to face the traumatic consequences of this catastrophe, resorts to repetition, but Lacan says that 'what is refused in the symbolic order re-emerges in the real' (Lacan 1993, p. 13).

In terms of accessing the 'real' of what has happened in Irish society over the period of the Celtic Tiger, we do not say that the bankers involved in the infamous bank guarantee are liars and cheats who have conspired through stupidity and greed to destroy an economy. Howard, however, cuts to the quick as, when it is revealed that there is 'a hundred grand missing' from Ross and Sorcha's current account, it is Ross who says 'I, er ... well, I bought a couple of apartments. In Bulgaria' (Howard 2008a, p. 219). Here the casual ease with which property, the ultimate commodity fetish of a certain class of people during this period, is bought encapsulates, more than any government report, the 'real' of this time.

We do not point to the stupidity of the sovereign taking on the private debt of speculators and capitalists. Instead, the symbolic order chooses its words far more carefully. So in a reply to a government committee, the chief executive of the National Asset Management Agency, which was set up to manage grossly over-valued property whose mortgage debts could not be paid, said that 'the information given by banks did not turn out to be the reality':

> Brendan McDonagh chose his words carefully. He did not call the banks liars or cheats – he said that 'a lack of awareness and denial ... was prevalent' – but the implication was clear: Ireland's bankers, who remain in business because the State saved them from collapse, have lied to the government and its agencies from the very beginning of this financial crisis and they have kept lying all the way through. (Ruddock 2010, p. 10)

The real of the situation is only addressed by the reporter, Alan Ruddock, who sees it as implied. The real questions arising – why are the Irish people paying for the bankers folly?; why are people who lied to the government and NAMA not in jail?; why are many of the same people on the boards of the banks, on whose watch these events took place, still on the same boards four years later?; why has it taken so long to bring charges of fraud against a very small number of banking executives?; why has our society been so passive in its acceptance of all of this, and why has there been no understanding of how all of this happened? – have not been addressed.

I would suggest that this is because the 'real' of the situation has never been assessed. It is resistant to explanation, but there are ways that it can be accessed: 'in the symbolic order, the empty spaces are as signifying as the full ones' (Lacan 2006, p. 327), and there are instances where:

> the signifier – which has fallen silent in the subject – first makes a glimmer of signification spring forth at the surface of the real, and then causes the real to become illuminated with a flash projected from below its underpinning of nothingness. (Lacan 2006, p. 468)

I think that the novels by Paul Howard are just such a glimmer of signification. The lack of regulation that was so formally referred to in the Regling and Watson report, and also in the comments by Brendan McDonagh, speak to a sense of an elite at work in the Irish financial and political spheres. What was lacking was any sense of responsibility to the future and to the Irish State. The responsibility of the bankers on the night of the bank guarantee was to themselves and to their organization; the same was true of the developers and of the government, who gave a guarantee which included all bondholders and all creditors. Their responsibility was to the elite figures of global capital as opposed to the people who elected them. Private debt, incurred by venture capitalists and senior debt and bondholders, has been transferred to the public, and the present Fine Gael–Labour government, which decried this guarantee in opposition, promptly renewed it in government: another example of repetition compulsion. There is a strong sense of an elite ensuring that errors of other members of that elite are borne by the rest of the population, and there is no major difference between either government in terms of action (or one might say inaction) on ensuring that people who ventured their capital in the hopes of profit should now take responsibility for their losses: the colloquial terms for this being 'burning the bondholders'. Again, this sense of disbelief that such a catastrophe can happen is captured in a scene where Ross discovers that his father, Charles, is about to go bankrupt:

> My body just goes totally numb – and we're talking totally. It's in my old man's name – my BMW Z4, my beautiful, black BMW Z4 …
>
> Hennessy nods, like he understands what I'm going through here. Then he goes, 'I have to ask you for the keys. I'm supposed to surrender them today …'
>
> As I'm handing them over, all I can think to say is, 'Dude, what the fock

am I going to do for, like, money?' and Hennessy's like, 'I'm sorry if this sounds a touch old-fashioned, but have you considered working?'

I sink back into the seat and go, 'Fock, things really are that bad.' (Howard 2008a, p. 220)

Work, like responsibility, or a sense of ownership of debt, is very much for other people, who are seen as like exhibits or a different form of life. Thus when Ross visits his father in Mountjoy Jail, he speaks of the people he sees like beings from another planet. Referring to a major shopping centre in Henry Street, Dublin, Mountjoy is 'like the Ilac Centre, but with focking bors on the windows. We're talking Adidas everything and Lizzy Duke Bling and it hums of, I don't know, defeat – defeat and desperation and Lynx' (Howard 2008a, p. 5). These are the people who belong in prison, not the likes of Charles, or Sean Fitzpatrick, or the CEOs of banks who lied to the government about the liquidity and solvency of their banks. In a radio interview on RTE before the details of Anglo-Irish bank were released, Fitzpatrick stated that 'Anglo-Irish Bank is a very well-capitalised bank' (www.youtube.com/watch?v=kD6jobUqyjg), and on 29 September 2008 Merrill Lynch, advisers to the Irish government, said that 'all the Irish banks were well-capitalised' (http://www.rte.ie/news/2010/0716/banks.html). Yet these people were all being paid huge salaries for their expertise, and have suffered no consequences for the appalling nature of that advice and financial stewardship.

Such a level of societal dysfunction is frightening, as generally there is a sense that people who are in charge of political and financial systems are paid their very large salaries because they are competent; to face the fact that they are not, and that the people who might replace them are similarly incompetent, is a truly appalling vista, and this is why it is repressed. In terms of repression, Freud has made the point that:

> Owing to the repression brought about by civilization many primary pleasures are now disapproved by the censor and lost. But the human psyche finds renunciation very difficult; hence we discover that tendency-wit furnishes us with a means to make the renunciation retrogressive and thus to regain what has been lost. When we laugh over a delicately obscene witticism, we laugh at the identical thing which causes laughter in the ill-bred man when he hears a coarse, obscene joke. (Freud 1922, p. 147)

Humour, then, according to Freud, is one way of accessing the real which has been masked by repetition and avoidance. In terms of the real of the situation, we are back in the dressing room of *The Miseducation Years*, where the notion of elite who will be forever cossetted from the consequences of their actions is vividly set out across the series. It is often through fiction that the real is accessed, and 'the true aims at the real' (Lacan 1998, p. 91), and I would argue that it is by looking at events through the fictive lens that aspects of the real will become clear. Before we look at the fiction, it is salutary to look at the fact that, before he resigned, and keeping in mind the questionable financial practices that were to be found in Anglo-Irish bank, the CEO, Sean Fitzpatrick, called, in 2008, for the government to 'cut services, cut wages, and increase "competitiveness"' (Kerrigan 2010). In other words, despite the fact that his bank would soon be a causal factor in the collapse of the Irish economy, he was suggesting that the best possible reaction to any financial downturn would be to punish those on lower incomes.

Ironically, or perhaps not, this is exactly what the government did, introducing swingeing budget cuts in the Irish economy in successive budgets, while ensuring that the banks were fully capitalized and paying back all of the senior and junior bondholders. While not overtly stated, what happened here is precisely the sense of loyalty to an elite group that was spelled out by Father Fehily at the beginning of this chapter. This is the real parallel of Paul Howard's fictive universe, where the focus is on the affluent inhabitants of Dublin 4, who speak a very different language to the ordinary Irish people, and whose loyalty is very much to their own class as opposed to the general public sphere. Through a very distinct use of a phonetic spelling, Howard is able to catch this through the different idiolect spoken by these affluent Southsiders.

> The harsh-sounding 'ar' sound is softened to become 'or'. Thus, harsh becomes horsh. Arts is Orts. The bar is the bor. The car is the cor. The *Star* is a newspaper read by poor people. (Howard 2008a, p. 71)

While this is humorous in terms of delineating a specific upper-middle-class accent, it is another signifier of an elite group with its own identifying matrices. The accent, of course, is one such matrix. The insertion of phatic markers in speech is another: so many of Ross's sentences are concluded with the term 'roysh', which is a phonetic version of 'right', a term which is often used as a modifier, but which also acts as a badge of identity of the elite cited at the beginning of this chapter.

Ross is a prototype of this community; he has been brought up in affluence, and is devastated when his father loses everything after being convicted of tax fraud: 'the money, the cars, the boat, the golf-club membership, the apartments in Villamoura, the box at Leopardstown' (Howard 2008a, p. 219). He is a synecdoche of a social class privately educated, affluent and responsible only to its own idea of itself. His attitude to money is very much that of a certain social elite in the days of the Celtic Tiger:

I call into the old pair's gaff, though I really don't know why I focking bothered. Actually, I do. My cor insurance is due, roysh, and there's no way I'm paying three Ks out of my own pocket for it. But I still called to see them, roysh, yet all the old man wants to know about is, like, how Sorcha is and how's that grandchild of theirs coming along. (Howard 2006a, p.25)

Ross sees his parents, despite his low opinion of them, as an unending source of money. He puts up with his father's conversation here only in order to get him to write a cheque for him, and is appalled that his father has changed the combination of the family safe. We find out that this is because:

'€5,000 went missing from that very safe a month ago.' I'm like, 'It didn't go missing. I took it,' and he stops mid-dial, suddenly looking all worried, puts the phone down and goes, 'You took it? But why?' and I'm there, 'Does it matter?' and he's like, 'Oh, I, em, suppose not.' (Howard 2006a, p.27)

It transpires that Fionnuala, Ross's mother, had blamed their Italian cleaning girl, Maria, for stealing the money and she was subsequently sacked, with Charles making some comments on the 'Italians and their lack of moral fibre. Changing sides in wars and so forth' (Howard 2006a, p.27).

The interesting response from both father and son to this treatment of an innocent person is paradigmatic of the attitude that has seldom been voiced in the literature of the Celtic Tiger. Ross is thinking about his need for a new phone, as he has had his present one for 'three months now' (Howard 2006a, p.27), while Charles is equally cavalier:

'still, hey ho, I'm sure she'd have stolen something eventually,' and he picks up the phone again and dials a number as he's saying this, roysh, he whips open his drawer, pulls out his chequebook and writes me a chicken's neck for four Ks, no questions asked, after leaving me standing there, listening to his crap for, like, twenty minutes. So I grab it off him, give him the finger and, like, get the fock out of there. (Howard 2006a, p.28)

This tendency-wit cuts to the real of the social unconscious of the Celtic Tiger. Banks who have been bailed out by the taxpayer have routinely flouted the pay cap as senior executives are given packages beyond the €500,000 limit set by the government. However, the same government is hiring advisers whose own salaries breach the government-imposed pay cap of €90,000. In a recent cost-cutting move, the Irish health service executive (HSE) suggested cutting home help and home-carer allowances, while consultants earn salaries of some €220,000. Rather than burning the bondholders, the current government is merely repeating the golden circle system of its predecessors, cutting the weak and the vulnerable and hoping that things will get better. The attitude of the recession-proof elite here is best encapsulated by the 'hey ho' of Charles, as opposed to a number of government reports, expert groups, position papers and policy documents.

Howard describes the real of this cultural elite in a mock-travel guide to south Dublin:

> Bathed by the warm currents of the Gulf Stream and the North Atlantic Drift, South Dublin has a hot, humid climate, not unlike that of the Cayman Islands, with whom Southsiders share a natural affinity. Add in the 365 days of guaranteed sunshine per year and it's not difficult to see why houses here are changing hands for the equivalent of the GNP of a small, backward country, such as Albania, Chad ... or the rest of Ireland. South Dublin is still technically part of the Irish Republic, although to all intents and purposes it is a sovereign state unto itself, with its own language, rituals and customs. Prosperity has accelerated the progress towards full secession, which, it is predicted, could take place before the year 2020. South Dublin is not only the cradle of the Celtic Tiger, it is also a land rich in cultural diversity, where barristers live next door to stockbrokers, where judges live next door to stockbrokers, where judges live next door to businessmen and where heart surgeons live side by side with brain surgeons. (Howard 2008b, p. 11)

Here the satire offers access to the 'real' of the socio-cultural elite in Ireland. This sense of entitlement that is never made overt in State or organizational documents is clear here. As with the earlier comment about the *The Star* being a 'newspaper read by poor people' (Howard 2008a, p. 71), there is a sense that a social contract has been torn up, a perspective which is reinforced in terms of South Dublin being seen as a sovereign state in itself. Any sense of a community is non-existent and this has been clear in the utterances of the elite. Sean Fitzpatrick, widely seen as one of the architects of the financial meltdown, when asked about how Ireland could cope better with recession, 'called on the Government to reduce corporation tax and tackle the "sacred cow" of universal child benefit, State pensions and medical cards for the over-70s' (O'Brien 2008). Fitzpatrick clearly lost his sense of irony along with everything else in the debacle of Anglo-Irish Bank, but his comments offer a rare glimpse into the mindset of the people at the very top of the Irish financial system.

Like Ross and Charles, it is always someone else's fault, and someone else should take the blame and the pain. That someone whose reckless financial practices had contributed to ruin the country and ultimately brought about a loss of sovereignty should seek to claw back the 'sacred cow' of child benefit and remove benefits from single mothers reinforces my point. The same can be said of the recently mooted cut to home care services while consultants' fees remain untouched, or the complete inability of this government, and previous governments, to levy any form of wealth tax. While golden circles gambled money and lost, it is the people at the bottom of the *socius* who bear the brunt of the suffering, though, of course, this is never stated in government documents, which always talk about sharing the burden equally. The mantra 'we all partied' during the Celtic Tiger years is used to make people feel that austerity is the correct policy, though it is those in poorer areas who bear the brunt of these policies.

In this respect, the fictive social comments of Charles O'Carroll-Kelly enunciate the real through their tendency-wit:

> 'On teenage mothers – they should be forcibly sterilized to ensure they don't produce any further burdens on the State,' and of course that gets a big laugh, even from me, because we all remember him saying that.
>
> 'On the National Lottery – an ingenious way of giving poor people dole money and then taking it back from them again. On heroin – God's way of culling the package holiday classes ...'
>
> 'On the hospital crisis – if these so-called patients can afford cigarettes, scratch-cards and Sky Television, they can afford private health insurance. What's wrong with sleeping on a hospital trolley anyway? Think of it as a bed with wheels ...'
>
> 'On Travellers – I don't know why they call them Travellers. The ones on the Sandyford Road have been there for fourteen years. They never travel anywhere.'
>
> 'On the Hill of Tara – why is something worth keeping just because it's old? If I'd adopted the same attitude to my Lexus GS 430, well, then I would never have driven the Lexus IS 300. And you can quote me on that.'
> (Howard 2008a, p. 21)

In terms of tendency-wit, there would seem to be very little difference between the fictive Charles and the all too real Sean Fitzpatrick. Charles gives voice to a real that is generally occluded in the symbolic order of the cultural elite; he is voicing an aspect of the real of the Celtic Tiger *mentalité*, namely the 'withering away of the Hegelian-Durkheimian view of the state as a collective authority with a responsibility to act as the collective will and consciousness, and a duty to make decisions in keeping with the general interest and contribute to promoting greater solidarity' (Bourdieu 2005, p. 11).

Freud has noted that 'the realm of jokes has no boundaries' (Freud 1920, p. 199), and it is in humour that the repressed 'real' of the Celtic

Tiger can be made to return. Like dreams, jokes use the same techniques of condensation, indirect representation, and displacement. But unlike dreams, which are unintelligible, asocial and opaque in terms of motivation, joking is highly social, is quickly understood and explicitly exposes the underlying thought in defiance of accepted modes of conscious expression. The real of the Celtic Tiger was a fracturing of the social contract by class-based elites who were free from the consequences of their actions. In a country where home help is cut while consultants are paid obscene levels of salary; where governments repeat the errors of the past and break their own austerity-driven pay ceilings; and where election promises habitually scatter like confetti at a wedding, I would argue that the real is better expressed by the opening words of Fr Denis Fehily than by any of these compulsive repetitions.

Works cited

Badiou, Alain (2005) *Metapolitics*, London: Verso.

Bourdieu, Pierre (1984) *Distinction: A Social Critique of the Judgment of Taste*, translated by Richard Nice, Cambridge, MA: Harvard University Press.

Bourdieu, Pierre (1993) *The Field of Cultural Production: Essays on Art and Literature*, translated by Randal Johnson, Cambridge: Polity Press.

Bourdieu, Pierre (2005) *The Social Structures of the Economy*, Cambridge: Polity Press.

Finucane, Marian (2008) 'Interview with Anglo Irish Bank Chairman, Sean Fitzpatrick', *The Marian Finucane Show*, RTÉ Radio1, 4 October 2008, available: www.youtube.com/watch?y=kD6jobUqyjg [accessed 20 October 3012].

Freud, Sigmund (1918) *Totem and Taboo: Resemblances between the Psychic Lives of Savages and Neurotic*, translated by Abraham Arden Brill, New York: Moffat.

Freud, Sigmund (1920) *Interpretation of Dreams*, London: Allen and Unwin.

Freud, Sigmund (1922) *Wit and Its Relation to the Unconscious*, translated by A. A. Brill, London: Kegan Paul.

Freud, Sigmund (1939) *Moses and Monotheism*, translated by Katherine Jones, London: The Hogarth Press and the Institute of Psycho-analysis.

Howard, Paul (2003a) *The Teenage Dirtbag Years*, Dublin: O'Brien Press Ltd.

Howard, Paul (2003b) *The Orange Mocha-Chip Frappuccino Years*, Dublin: O'Brien Press Ltd.

Howard, Paul (2004) *The Miseducation Years*, Dublin: O'Brien Press Ltd.

Howard, Paul (2005) *PS, I Scored the Bridesmaids*, Dublin: Penguin Ireland.

Howard, Paul (2006a) *Should Have Got Off at Sydney Parade*, Dublin: Penguin Ireland.

Howard, Paul (2006b) *The Curious Incident of the Dog in the Nightdress*, Dublin: Penguin Ireland.

Howard, Paul (2008a) *This Champagne Mojito Is the Last Thing I Own*, Dublin: Penguin Ireland.

Howard, Paul (2008b) *Guide to South Dublin: How to Get by on, Like, €10,000 a Day*, Dublin: Penguin Ireland.

Howard, Paul (2008c) *Mr S and the Secrets of Andorra's Box*, Dublin: Penguin Ireland.

Howard, Paul (2011) *Nama Mia*, Dublin: Penguin Ireland.

Howard, Paul (2012) *The Shelbourne Ultimatum*, Dublin: Penguin Ireland.

Kerrigan, Gene (2010) 'Harney Didn't Create Chaos on Her Own', *Sunday Independent*, 14 March.

Lacan, Jacques (1988) *Seminar 2 The Ego in Freud's Theory and in the Technique of Psychoanalysis 1954–1955*, edited by Jacques-Alain Miller, translated by Sylvana Tomaselli, Cambridge: Cambridge University Press.

Lacan, Jacques (1990) *Television: A Challenge to the Psychoanalytic Establishment*, translated by Rosalind Krauss, Denis Hollier and Annette Michelson, New York: Norton.

Lacan, Jacques (1991) *Seminar 1 Freud's Papers on Technique 1953–1954*, translated by John Forrester, New York: Norton.

Lacan, Jacques (1993) *Seminar 3 The Psychoses*, translated by Jacques-Alain Miller, London: Routledge.

Lacan, Jacques (1998) *Seminar 20: On Feminine Sexuality: The Limits of Love and Knowledge Encore*, edited by Jacques-Alain Miller, translated by Bruce Fink, New York: Norton.

Lacan, Jacques (2006) *Écrits: The First Complete Edition in English*, translated by Bruce Fink in collaboration with Héloïse Fink and Russell Grigg, London: Norton.

O'Brien, Tim (2008) 'Bank Chief Calls for "Brave" Budget', *Irish Times*, 6 October.

Regling, Klaus and Watson, Max (2010) *A Preliminary Report on the Sources of Ireland's Banking Crisis*, Dublin: Government Information Services.

RTÉ News (2010) 'Government Was Warned over Bank Guarantee', *RTÉ News*, 26 July, available: www.rte.ie/news/2010/0716/banks.html [accessed 20 October 2012].

Ruddock, Alan (2010) 'Don't Bank on This Lot to Come Clean on Their Own', *Sunday Independent*, 18 April.

5

Popular music and the Celtic Tiger

Gerry Smyth

Sing when you're winning

On 14 June 2012, the Republic of Ireland soccer team was comprehensively beaten 4–0 at the UEFA Euro Football Championships by the eventual winners, Spain. During an on-the-pitch post-match interview for the UK's ITV network, the Irish midfielder Keith Andrews praised the quality of the opposition as well as the 'brilliant' support of the Irish fans, who continued *en masse* to sing 'The Fields of Athenry' throughout the final minutes of the match. Coverage then returned to the studio where the former Republic of Ireland and Manchester United player Roy Keane (working as a regular analyst for the station during the competition) was invited to comment. He was, as is his wont, livid:

> I think the players, and even the supporters, they all have to change their mentality. It's just nonsense when players speak after the game about how great the supporters are. Listen, the supporters want to see the team doing a lot better and not giving daft goals away like that. So, no, listen, I'm not too happy with all that nonsense ... I know that we're a small country and we're up against it, but let's not just go along for the sing-song every now and again. (www.youtube.com/watch?v=1hB7ErOuH-s)

Four days later, the Republic played Italy in its final group-stage match; the team was again well beaten, capping off a thoroughly miserable performance at the competition. Before kick-off, however, television cameras sweeping the Irish sections of the crowd halted momentarily on a group of fans holding a medium-sized Irish tricolour on which the words 'Can We Sing Now Roy?' had been written. As imminent defeat loomed towards the end of the match, 'The Fields of Athenry' once again featured strongly as part of the televisual soundtrack.

The virtual exchange between Keane and (some of) the Irish fans rehearses in symbolic form (some of) the issues attendant upon the rise and fall of the Celtic Tiger. Keane's determination to win (for which he was noted as a player); his insistence on challenging established 'mentalities'; his resistance to Ireland's traditional fate as 'happy-to-be-here losers' – all these resonate strongly in terms of an Irish generation which grew up in a context of sustained economic success and cultural confidence. At the same time, Keane's explicit indictment of those who 'just go along for the sing-song', his joyless response to the 'entertainment' on offer and his description of Andrews's comment as 'nonsense' – all this seems out of kilter in some respects with the general 'party' atmosphere that characterized the Tiger years, as well as with a widespread impression of the Irish as good sports.

I find it interesting that this exchange took place in terms of different evaluations of the role of music in relation to Irish identity. For Keane, it appears that music is a distraction from the reality of competition; after all, it's not 'the sing-song' that he resents, but the discrepancy between singing and performance in the Irish experience. The sensible thing is to 'sing when you're winning' – hence, the famous terrace chant. The Irish response is 'nonsense' because it flies in the face of this apparently natural logic, and because it smacks of a traditional 'mentality' in which we could only sing whilst inevitably succumbing to the better endowed and the better prepared.

The designers of the 'Can We Sing Now Roy?' banner appear to have embraced an alternative reality with reference to an alternative logic – one organized in relation to ideas of performance, community participation and a readiness 'to be' in the moment. Whereas Keane was affronted by the willingness of the Irish fans to continue singing in the face of ignominious defeat, it might be argued that the music itself was apparently an indication that those fans were in fact already 'winning' in terms of a different logic, a different reality, a different game – one from which Roy Keane, with his 'winning' mentality, would always be excluded.

In some senses, this is a very old debate in so far as it rehearses an opposition which has been troped in numerous different ways and contexts throughout Irish history. In another sense, however, it stands as a very modern (or perhaps 'postmodern' would be better) exchange, one that resonates strongly in terms of the on-going troubled response of contemporary Irish popular music to the Celtic Tiger.

Uncertain economics

Some people like to date the onset of Ireland's decisive entry into the modern world from U2's appearance on stage at the Live Aid concert in London on 13 July 1985. That performance certainly represented an iconic moment in modern Ireland's developing sense of what it was and what it could be. If I had to choose one moment to mark the onset of a new dispensation in modern Irish history, however, one text through which to observe the emergence of a new paradigm for modern Irish identity, I would have to opt for 19 November 1991, the date on which U2 released their seventh studio album, *Achtung Baby!* That this event occurred nearly three years *before* Kevin Gardiner's famous article naming the Celtic Tiger is indicative of music's extreme sensitivity with regard to paradigmatic shifts within the systems (including the economic system) that comprise any given national formation.[1]

Achtung Baby! represented the sound of a band growing up, leaving home and embracing everything that the modern world had to offer in the way of sensory, intellectual and emotional stimulation (Smyth 2001, pp. 159–87; Smyth 2005, pp. 196–102). This was a radical gesture for two reasons: firstly, because up until that time U2 had deliberately and self-consciously traced the conscience of the nation from which it emerged; and, secondly, because that same nation had been characterized by circumspection – not to say restriction – in precisely those areas with which the band was now looking to engage. After a decade and more in which the limits of U2's musical questing had been set by discourses of 'expression', 'authenticity' and 'truth', on *Achtung Baby!* the band courageously broached the possibility of a new aesthetics – one organized around ideas of uncertainty, performativity and the moral compromises attendant upon living in the modern world. In short, *Achtung Baby!* dramatized the existential stand-off between success and failure before the Celtic Tiger rendered that dilemma a reality for Ireland itself.

U2 continued to pursue this line throughout the 1990s and into the new millennium, each new release offering (amongst other things) an indication of the directions in which Ireland's moral compass was likely to swing in response to rapidly changing circumstances. This was an effect, moreover, of both sound and words – which is to say, the themes engaged by Bono in his role as singer, and the music through which those themes were articulated and explored by the remainder of the band and the production team. Taken together, the prevailing ethos of

---

[1] In *Noise: The Political Economy of Music*, Jacques Attali writes: 'Music is prophecy. Its styles and economic organization are ahead of the rest of society because it explores, much faster than material reality can, the entire range of possibilities in a given code' (Attali 1985, p. 12).

the music is *uncertainty* with regard to all the ideas and the values that once sustained a particular view of the world. In a typically postmodernist coup, however, that very quality *can* (as the title track from 1993's *Zooropa* puts it) 'be a guiding light' – indeed, in the absence of any other credible mechanism, it *must* be (Clayton et al. 1993).

I would like to suggest that the quality of 'uncertainty' as encountered in the music of U2 during the 1990s is a direct analogue in the cultural or emotional sphere of ideas relating to 'mobility', 'flexibility', even 'deregulation', in the economic or political sphere.[2] Beyond issues concerning the relations between the different spheres of activity comprising contemporary society, however, such a suggestion raises difficult questions – many of which turn on the difference between those small words *can* and *must*. Did the Republic embrace Tiger economics because back in the early 1990s there was no other game in town, and because, after decades of economic underperformance, those in power owed it to the nation to pursue 'success' at whatever cost in other areas of national life? Can we, from a post-crash perspective, really blame those who failed to find the 'certainties' in an uncertain world, or to ditch with such alacrity such 'certainties' as were already in place? Was the Celtic Tiger – its rise, short reign and ignominious demise – unavoidable in the 'light' of wider shifts in the global organization of capital? Is 'uncertainty' – once so sexy and attractive – now entirely tainted, a sign of moral turpitude and cultural decadence? And if so, how long will it remain so?

In retrospect, U2's view of the benefits of 'uncertainty' (when translated into politico-economic discourse) turned out to be overly optimistic. It may be simply tautological to say that postmodern capitalism is a good thing when it works in your favour; nevertheless, it is a bitter lesson in logic and rhetoric that everyone in Ireland has been obliged to learn.

Not 'bad'

Like anyone born in the 1950s or early 1960s, the individual members of U2 had experience of pre-Tiger Ireland, and this has coloured their response to, and engagement, with the kind of country that emerged during and since the 1990s. After all, the band had grown up and come to maturity in a very different country – an Ireland of the 'Troubles', of

---

[2] In *The Condition of Postmodernity: An Enquiry into the Origins of Cultural Change*, David Harvey defined postmodernism with reference to 'the emergence of more flexible modes of capital accumulation and a new round of "time–space compression" in the organization of capitalism' (Harvey 1989, p. vii).

determined clerical power, of cultural conservatism, social polarization, political venality and economic malaise. This was the country described in 'Bad' in terms of 'desperation, dislocation, separation, condemnation, isolation, desolation' – an island of police and priests, heroin and emigration, moving statues and attritional war (Clayton et al. 1984). The experience of living in such a time and place afforded the band an ironic perspective on the supposedly new, supposedly 'real' Ireland that followed hard on the heels of *Achtung Baby!* and *Zooropa*.

U2 anticipated the Celtic Tiger, and in some senses provided a language with which to begin to approach and articulate the new moral and socio-economic dispensation. They were never *of* the Celtic Tiger, however, in a way that a band like The Script so clearly were. This Dublin three-piece were part of Ireland's end-of-the-century baby boomer generation, members of an elite 'Expectocracy' (McWilliams 2005, pp. 52–67) which has been educated in, and inculcated with, a range of values and opinions vastly different from those of their parents. This is something, moreover, that is apparent in every aspect of the band's identity: lyrics, music, iconography and ethos.

Like U2 before them, on their eponymous debut album The Script tried to bridge the gap between local and general frames of reference. There are recognizable Irish allusions, such as the husband who 'hits the jar' in 'Together We Cry', and the 'Guinness' and 'Grafton Street' of 'Before the Worst' (O'Donoghue et al. 2008). At the same time, the album comprises songs detailing a range of generally downbeat perspectives (pain, regret, guilt, loss) that are not nation-specific. The 'man who can't be moved' may be standing on a corner in Dublin; but he is just as likely to be in Newcastle or Glasgow or Cardiff, or indeed in Boston, Sydney or Toronto. In this regard, The Script were merely working within in a long tradition of 'Irish popular music-makers' who have tried to negotiate the conflicting forces operating within that very designation.[3]

But what really signals The Script as a popular musical articulation of the Celtic Tiger is the *sound* of the music – which is to say a studio-honed, blue-eyed R&B, the signature element of which is Danny O'Donoghue's rich, supple voice and his highly stylized vocal delivery. Other Irish acts had broached this sound previously, most notably the Dubliner Samantha Mumba in her short-lived career of the early 2000s. It is the sound of a generation that grew up listening to Destiny's Child, Justin Timberland and Christina Aguilera; for whom the discourses of

---

[3] See Smyth (2005, pp. 30–45) on the pattern which saw an early generation of Irish popular musicians (such as Rory Gallagher, Van Morrison and Thin Lizzy) seek their success in the UK and elsewhere.

American hip-hop and rap were entirely conventional aspects of the international musical soundscape; and for whom the elaborate vocal techniques evolved from earlier popular music traditions (most centrally, soul) represented the 'natural' context within which to develop a vocal interpretation.

Irish bands had been playing soul and related genres since the 1960s. The story of Belfast youth's grieved reaction to the death of Otis Redding in 1967 is well known, and the city's close identification with that particular brand of African-American popular music must surely have influenced Van Morrison's later description of his own music as a kind of 'Irish soul'.[4] Later still, the fictional Commitments purveyed a brand of Dublin soul, and tried to make common cause with the genre's ideological and iconographical roots in working-class pride and social exclusion (Doyle 1987; Smyth 2009, pp. 65–83). As in the case of the American originals, however, these sources are related to, but different in a number of key respects from, the version of R&B that began to emerge during the 1980s and became such a powerful influence on global popular music during the last decade of the millennium – the same decade that saw the emergence of the Celtic Tiger.

Of course, The Script are not a *real* R&B band (whatever that might mean). They are in fact entirely typical in so far as shades of many different popular genres and styles (even U2) may be identified in their music. Certainly, however, some of the core attitudes and assumptions of R&B have seeped into the musical, lyrical and iconographical identity of the band. Once there, they cross-fertilized with a cluster of attitudes and assumptions born of the Celtic Tiger – born, that is to say, living in a society powered by what seemed at the time like an unstoppably successful economy. One might refer to this as a 'structure of feeling', a 'mentality', an 'ideology', a 'politics of truth' or some other designation; the point is that a society infuses the culture it produces in a myriad of explicit and implicit ways; and the Celtic Tiger infuses the sound of The Script in ways that they would hardly acknowledge and would in truth probably wish to deny.

In short, the *sound* of The Script is the *sound* of the Celtic Tiger – even when the band are singing about 'bad things'. The various 'failures' articulated by the various protagonists on the first album, for example, are belied by the ideology of expectation and attainment that underpins

---

[4] In Nuala O'Connor's *Bringing It All Back Home: The Influence of Irish Music*, Morrison is quoted as claiming 'that soul music originally came from Scotland and Ireland' (O'Connor 1991, p. 6). I am grateful to the poet Gerald Dawe for the story regarding Belfast's response to the death of Otis Redding.

the music itself. It is the sound of success pretending to fail. It is interesting to note, for example, that 'the man who can't be moved' is only playing the part of a homeless person, with his sleeping bag, his cardboard and his politely recalcitrant attitude towards the police. In fact, he is 'not broke', only broken-hearted; there is a hole in his heart but not in his shoes. The girl jumps on an aeroplane to stay with friends in London; the guy speeds through the dark streets in his car looking for her; the music surges, perfect in its texture and in its resonance. The generation which won tells a story about failure, and wins again.

The Script was released on 8 August 2008, a few weeks before Brian Cowen's government declared the Republic to be in recession. We all know what happened after that.

Dreams and songs to sing

The particular song which called forth Roy Keane's ire deserves some consideration. 'The Fields of Athenry' is a modern ballad written in 1979 by Dublin singer-songwriter Pete St John. It's set during the Great Famine (1845–50), and tells the story of a man named Michael who is transported to Australia after being caught stealing food for his starving family. The song was already familiar to Irish record-buyers through versions by artists such as Danny Doyle and Barleycorn before a version recorded in 1983 by Paddy Reilly became, for no immediately apparent reason, an Irish musical phenomenon, catching the ear of the record-buying public and staying in the national record charts for over a year.

Since then the song has continued to grow in fame and familiarity. Not unexpectedly, many recording artists have attempted to capitalize on its popularity by recording versions in a wide range of styles.[5] More interestingly and more significantly, 'The Fields of Athenry' has been adopted and reproduced in a wide range of public contexts – especially sporting events. These days one may hear it sung at rugby matches, soccer matches and Gaelic Athletic Association matches; in Glasgow and Galway, Dublin and London, New York and Boston. In England 'The Fields of Anfield Road' forms the melancholy backdrop to Liverpool Football Club's fading glory. Alongside the almost equally ubiquitous chant of 'Olé, Olé, Olé', St John's composition was heard during the London Olympics as the euphoric soundtrack to Katie Taylor's memorable victory in the Women's Lightweight Boxing competition. The fact

---

[5] 'The Fields of Athenry' has featured in the stage shows of international artists such as Bruce Springsteen and Take That.

is that 'The Fields of Athenry' has assumed a protean profile within the international soundscape which is far above and beyond either its original context or the various attempts to capture it in textual (that is, recorded) form.

The emergence of 'The Fields of Athenry' as an Irish sporting anthem seems a strange development, especially when one considers the tragic nature of the story it relates. A multitude of nineteenth-century Irish woes are covered in three shortish verses, including poverty, hunger, subjection, separation, loneliness, imprisonment and transportation. To describe such a song as 'downbeat' would be understated; it is in fact a litany of Irish 'failures' – political, personal, cultural, economic. The piece is 'traditional' in terms of its musical discourses, certainly, in as much as it *sounds* like an Irish ballad. But it is also traditional in terms of its subject matter: a typical 'Irish' story of dispossession and defeat. St John employs an interesting image to expedite the pathos of the narrative: young lovers dreaming and singing (real or metaphorical) songs. With the disappearance of her dreams along with her husband, however, the character of Mary is left with no songs to sing other than the lament that is 'The Fields of Athenry'. As pointed out above, all this seems a long way removed from Celtic Tiger Ireland and its fetishization of success in the forms of acquisition and conspicuous consumption. The question is: how did this very traditional ballad come to occupy the role it does in contemporary Irish popular culture at this particular time?

A number of possibilities suggest themselves. Firstly, it may be observed that it is usually only the chorus that is sung at these public sporting events; the verses, wherein the worst of the depredations are recounted, tend to be beyond either the ability or the ambition of large-scale spontaneous choirs such as the one that sang continuously for nearly ten minutes at the end of the Spain–Ireland game mentioned at the outset of this chapter. The opening word may be 'low', but it is in fact sung on one of the highest notes of the melody, and this creates an oddly uplifting effect which belies the downbeat lyric. Added to this is the fact that the melody as a whole always repairs to the major key in which the song is set; so, whereas the lyric offers only 'hope' as the one positive element within a landscape of despair, the melody brings the community of singers (and listeners) 'home' in a way that's both predictable and comforting. The contradiction between melody and lyric, and the semiotic predominance of the former over the latter in performance, may be one of the reasons why 'The Fields of Athenry' has been so enthusiastically adopted by a range of Irish and Irish-related sporting audiences.

Secondly, and related to this, there is the fact of the song's amenability (which it shares with most ballads) to potentially unrestricted unison performance: this means that as many people as wish to can join in. Of course, this is in the nature of modern sports-fan culture: there is no room for individual expression within a singing (or chanting) crowd. In this respect, crowd singing belongs to a form of premodern (or pre-modernist) cultural expression in which the community, rather than the individual, constitutes the Subject of meaning. In this respect, we might say that 'The Fields of Athenry' represents a form of communal vernacular culture which is at odds with modernist individualism, and this has helped it accrue a kind of residual value within a cultural economy in which the old and the new, the imagined past and the imagined future, existed alongside each other as powerful influences. It's this effect which qualified Celtic Tiger Ireland to be described as a 'postmodernist' society, one in which history (past, present and future) operated as an active element within the lives of all its constituent members.

So, in some sense, crowd-based unison performance of 'The Fields of Athenry' represents a form of nostalgia for an imaginary pre-Tiger Ireland. It's a way of showing that we have not forgotten who we are, or where we've come from, or what has gone into our historical development. But such is, as ever, an anxious strategy because the very performance acknowledges and confirms an ineluctable difference between then and now, between an ideal (imaginary) event located somewhere else in time and space, and the one that's occurring now, here, in the present. Irish fans were widely commended for the prolonged duration of their singing in the face of inevitable defeat by Spain. There is a sense, however, in which all those repetitions of the chorus of 'The Fields of Athenry' represent a kind of hysterical response to trauma – not the trauma of immediate sporting defeat but the trauma of separation (rehearsed again and again with every repetition) from the community's formative experience.

OMG you guys!!!

One piece of music that did not feature in the repertoire of the Irish fans at the UEFA 2012 competition was 'Put the Green Cape On', a charity single released by the pop phenomenon known as Jedward. This was a remix of 'Lipstick', the song with which that group represented Ireland at the Eurovision Song Contest in 2011. Written by the Irish radio DJ Colm Hayes, the new lyric extols the virtues of the Irish football team, and invites the listener to join an army of green-caped super-supporters in order to put 'Europe on the run' and help Ireland win the competition. The minor key and high tempo give the record a martial feel which is in keeping with the lyric's mock-heroic pretentions. The vocal is a highly modified unison performance by the two singers which relies for effect not on traditional performance values of 'interpretation' or 'expression' but on studio-honed editing, especially in the areas of timing and tuning.

There was no sign during the team's three games at UEFA 2012 of 'Put the Green Cape On' replacing either 'The Fields of Athenry' or the traditional chant of 'Olé, Olé, Olé' (which it references in its own lyric) as a performance option for Irish fans. This may have been because the song was not conducive to mass performance, but it is more likely to have been a reflection of the distance between the aesthetic values of (Irish) football and the particular kind of popular music with which that particular group is associated. The fact is that Jedward tend to polarize opinion in Ireland, with the majority tending towards a negative esti-mation of their worth as performers and as representatives of modern Irish identity. And yet, there are qualities in their music, in their image and even in their composite personality which suggest something of the essence of the Celtic Tiger (even though they emerged only after the demise of that phenomenon). Indeed, from the perspective of modern Irish society 'Jedward' ask more questions of us than we could ever ask of them.

'Jedward' is the name assumed by identical twin brothers John and Edward Grimes, born ten minutes apart in Dublin in 1991. They first emerged into public view in 2009 when they appeared on the British talent show *The X Factor*. Although they did not win, the brothers won the support of Irish impresario Louis Walsh (who featured as judge and mentor on the show), and under his management they have gone on to develop a strong media presence in both Ireland and the United Kingdom. At the time of writing Jedward have, amongst other things, released three albums, represented Ireland at Eurovision on two occa-sions and appeared on numerous television programmes, including their own daytime children's show. The twins' semiotic signatures – extended blond quiff and 'OMG!' salute – are ubiquitous, like a colourful rash all across television, radio and internet. Like it or not, dear reader, we are all to some degree or other inhabitants of 'Planet Jedward'.

I remarked above that the sound of The Script *is* the sound of the Celtic Tiger; as an addendum it might be observed that the soul of Jedward *is* the soul of the Celtic Tiger – young, brash, loud, four eyes focused firmly on the prize, 'talented' principally in the ability to exploit all available systems (tax laws on the one hand, technology on the other) in pursuit of the underlying goal. One senses a canny intelligence behind all the posing and the inane chatter; if this is partly the presence of Louis Walsh, the influence of two well-educated, middle-class, highly focused young men should not be discounted. Growing up in the era of hugely successful Irish pop acts such as Boyzone and Westlife, Jedward's ambitions were further expedited by the advent of mass-market 'Talent TV' and so-called 'Celebrity' culture – genres for which the twins might have been invented.

There is at the same time a kind of hollowness at the heart of the Jedward enterprise, one which echoes the society that produced them, and which produces a kind of anxiety that is above and beyond the mere antipathy their work excites in so many. John and Edward never really 'say' or 'sing' anything; their words are always 'exclaimed' or 'quoted' in a kind of faux-American accent, with an affected intonation as if every enunciation were of seminal significance. One of the effects of this is to create the impression that there is no distance between the reality the boys inhabit and the various realities into which they project themselves as singers and personalities. The anxiety arises in the first instance from the listener's uncertainty as to whether this is ironic or 'real' – that is, whether the imaginary quotation marks constitute the reality within which 'Jedward' exist, off screen as well as on, off mic as well as on. And if 'Jedward' are real, does this extend to the society that produced them, as well as to the subjects – you, reader, as well as I – that have an investment of some kind or degree in that society?

To employ a different metaphor, Jedward's mask is maintained only with an effort that becomes increasingly obvious the more one is exposed to them. This creates a mood of hysteria – one in which the listener or watcher is implicated – as if everything is constantly on the brink of collapse, and only perpetual movement (of body and language) and a kind of willed ignorance can keep the whole edifice from imploding on its own essential absence. Such an image brings us back once again to the Celtic Tiger.

Conclusion

One of the lines in 'Put the Green Cape On' exhorts the reader to 'forget the bank bail-out'. No doubt that is precisely what the travelling Irish fans were attempting to do; although how people from a country in deep recession managed to pay for travel, accommodation, subsistence and tickets, and what they faced when they returned, are matters worth considering. In the meantime we might observe that this particular line represents a moment of acknowledgement between the world of popular culture – in particular, the world of popular music – and the economic realities which determine all our lives. Such moments were once rare enough in contemporary Ireland. For the majority of people, after all, popular music is that to which you turn precisely in order to forget about such realities. Popular music appears to remind us that humankind does not live by bread alone, and that there are species of emotional and spiritual experience which remain impervious to merely material concerns.

The truth was always very different, of course. Indeed, I would contend that there is no area of popular culture that is more mediated by economic reality than music; as a consequence, there is no area of popular culture that is more politically sensitive than the music that is consumed by the mass of the population. As Jacques Attali has written: 'Music, the quintessential mass activity, like the crowd, is simultaneously a threat and a necessary source of legitimacy; trying to channel it is a risk that every system of power must run' (Attali 1985, p. 14). The burden of this chapter has been that it is precisely in the channelling of its popular music, and in the various risks (aesthetic, psychological, material) attending such an activity, that the reality of the Celtic Tiger and its aftermath continues to be most fully and most sensitively engaged.

In an article written during the heyday of the Celtic Tiger, I offered a definition of music (following Attali) as the political organization of noise. 'We ignore music at our peril,' I claimed, 'for at the same time as it affords us the most accurate impression of *how things are*, it offers us the most enabling impressions of *how things might be* – for good *and* bad, in sickness *and* in health' (Smyth 2004, p. 10, original emphases). I claim no prescience (although the references to 'bad' and 'sickness' came home to roost sooner than probably anyone expected), but the main point holds good: U2 may have become tragically unfashionable; The Script may have discovered a new kind of Irish-American sound; 'The Fields of Athenry' may have been converted from sentimental ballad to sporting phenomenon; and Jedward may be nothing more than a bad joke. For those with ears to hear, however, somewhere amongst all this music may be discerned echoes of our recent past and our imminent future; somewhere amongst all this noise we should be able to get an idea of how we got where we are and of where we might be heading.

Works cited

Attali, Jacques (1985) *Noise: The Political Economy of Music*, translated by Brian Massumi, Manchester: Manchester University Press.

Clayton, Adam, Evans, Dave, Hewson, Paul and Mullen, Larry Jr (1984) *The Unforgettable Fire* [recorded by U2]. (Vinyl LP and CD) London: Island.

Clayton, Adam, Evans, Dave, Hewson, Paul and Mullen, Larry Jr (1993) *Zooropa* [recorded by U2]. (CD) London: Island.

Doyle, Roddy (1987) *The Commitments*, vol. I of *The Barrytown Trilogy*, London: Minerva.

Harvey, David (1989) *The Condition of Postmodernity: An Enquiry into the Origins of Cultural Change*, Oxford: Basil Blackwell.

Hayes, Colm, Priddy, Daniel, Jensen, Lars Halvor and Larsson, Martin (2012) 'Put the Green Cape On'[recorded by Jedward]. CD single and digital download. Dublin: Universal Music Ireland.

Jensen, Lars, Larsson, Martin and Priddy, Dan (2011) 'Lipstick' [recorded by Jedward]. CD single and digital download. Dublin: Universal Music Ireland.

McWilliams, David (2005) *The Pope's Children: The Irish Economic Triumph and the Rise of Ireland's New Elite*, Dublin: Gill and Macmillan.

O'Connor, Nuala (1991) *Bringing It All Back Home: The Influence of Irish Music*, London: BBC Books.

O'Donoghue, Danny, Power, Glen and Sheehan, Mark (2008) *The Script* [recorded by The Script]. (CD) London: Sony.

Smyth, Gerry (2001) *Space and the Irish Cultural Imagination*, Basingstoke: Palgrave.

Smyth, Gerry (2004) 'Introduction: The Isle Is Full of Noises – Music in Contemporary Ireland', in Gerry Smyth (ed.) *Music in Contemporary Ireland: A Special Edition of the Irish Studies Review*, 12:1 (April), pp. 3–10.

Smyth, Gerry (2005) *Noisy Island: A Short History of Irish Popular Music*, Cork: Cork University Press.

Smyth, Gerry (2009) *Music in Irish Cultural History*, Dublin: Irish Academic Press.

6

'What does a woman want?': Irish contemporary women's fiction and the expression of desire in an era of plenty

Sylvie Mikowski

Perhaps one of the most spectacular side-effects of the new economic prosperity in Ireland in the 'Celtic Tiger' era was a shift in the balance of power between Irish men and women. Indeed, as of the 1990s, Irish women were given unprecedented control over their own lives and destinies. The election of Mary Robinson to the position of President of the Irish Republic in 1990 has been hailed by several commentators as one of the most significant events in the ushering of the country into the postmodern era. With the election of a woman president, Catholic Ireland raised itself to the same level of gender equity as some of the most advanced Western democracies, such as Britain, Germany or Sweden. As of the last decade of the twentieth century, and together with increased material affluence, Irish women have been granted the right to divorce (1996) and access to contraception (1992) and to abortion (2013). Parallel to this, Irish women began to escape the tight control of the Catholic Church over their minds and bodies. The rapid decline of the influence of the Catholic Church, resulting from the various sex scandals and cases of child abuse as revealed by (various) official reports, happened roughly at the same time as the sudden rise of the gross domestic product of Ireland and of the average income.[1]

As the Church held less obvious sway over the country, the doctrine of liberalism started to apply not just to the field of capitalistic venture, but also to the area of private, individual behaviour, where freedom of thought started to prevail over obedience to the dictates of religion and conservative morality. Moreover, while the secularization of Irish society entailed the loss of belief in religion as the founding principle regulating not just the life of the individual but also that of the family and of the whole society, the advent of the Good Friday Agreement in

---

[1] Real GDP grew by an average of 7.2 per cent per year in 1990–2000.

Northern Ireland in 1998 put an end to what remnants had survived of nationalist feelings in the Republic. The common dream of becoming 'a nation once again', which had been the focus of public life for so long, was given up and forgotten in favour of the struggle to attract more and more multinational companies. The nation which had risen up to the call 'ourselves alone' became one of the most globalized economies in the Western world, virtually selling itself and its workforce out to foreign capital. In this new, ultra-liberal Ireland, the individual was no longer 'the citizen', the stereotype of which was immortalized by Joyce's famous episode in *Ulysses* or by O'Casey in his play *The Plough and the Stars*, nor one of the flock who could be upbraided by the parish priest, but a potential consumer convinced that he/she can buy their way to happiness. By encouraging the rise of new needs, capitalism raises individual expectations, exacerbates the sense of a unique, separate self and creates the illusion of unlimited freedom of access to all forms of pleasures. The limits of human desire thus seem to constantly recede, and everybody is induced to take it for granted that the unattainable is in our reach.

But human desire, or 'jouissance', as Freud and Lacan have shown, are not meant to be ever fully satisfied, and because we are endowed with the capacity to use symbols, such as language, our destiny as human speaking beings is to be split from the moment we are separated from the maternal body, and to experience an incurable sense of lack, which language can only attempt to encompass. The more desire is offered as an attainable goal – as is the norm in our liberal, capitalist societies – the greater becomes the inevitable frustration, which can lead to all kinds of psychological disorders such as depression, neurosis, bulimia, anorexia, suicide, criminal drives and so on. The French Lacanian psychoanalyst Charles Melman has called this tendency 'the new psychic economy', which he defines as an utter dependency on the satisfaction of desires, no longer regarded as a mere possibility but as a right, and as complete devotion to the acquiring and the consumption of objects, which he explains is a consequence of the development of the new liberal society (Melman 2009, p. 17). As far as women are concerned, this dependency on the satisfaction of desire is complicated by the new freedom of choice regarding child-bearing, which can also be a source of further anxiety and frustration. In short, it seems that the question of women's desire, which Freud raised at the beginning of the twentieth century, in a letter to Marie Bonaparte quoted by his biographer Ernest Jones – 'What does a Woman Want?' (Jones 1988, vol. 2, p. 445) – is more relevant than ever in the context of ultra-liberal, secularized contemporary societies, such as the one Ireland has become today.

This chapter will deal with three Irish women writers – Deirdre Madden, Éilís Ní Dhuibhne and Anne Enright – who have published remarkable depictions of the effects of the new prosperity upon the psyche of their female characters, through new types of behaviours and also through new inner conflicts. In order to achieve this, they have borrowed either from the tradition of psychological realism or from that of the comedy of manners, following on the path of Jane Austen. Like Austen's novels, their books discussed here – Madden's *Authenticity*, Ní Dhuibhne's *Fox, Swallow, Scarecrow*, and Enright's collection of short stories *Taking Pictures* – can be said to combine traditional realism in the descriptions of the characters' *habitus*, social satire in the critique of the conventions and limitations imposed by contemporary society, and romance in the way they place relationships, love and marriage at the core of their plots. But the generic hybridity of the three fictional representations is not limited to a mix between realism, romance and satire: they can also be read as reflections on the role of art in the expression and the resolution of inner conflicts, either by staging characters claiming to be artists – such as Julia in *Authenticity*, or Anna Sweeney in *Fox, Swallow, Scarecrow* – or by attracting attention to their own literariness, as is again the case for Ní Dhuibhne's novel and for Enright's stories. Thus each of the three books forces the reader to wonder about the persistence of female desire in a world of material affluence, as it interrogates the nature of that desire, and foregrounds the role of art in its expression.

In her novel *Authenticity*, published in 2002, Deirdre Madden directly addresses the issue of material prosperity which she opposes to a moral, psychological and even aesthetic ideal, as is evidenced by the title. By locating her story in Dublin, in contrast to her previous works in which she evoked either rural Ireland (*The Birds of the Innocent Wood, Nothing Is Black*) or Northern Ireland, with its atmosphere of violence, as in *One by One in the Darkness* or *Hidden Symptoms*, Madden makes it clear that the capital of the Republic is the place where all the signs of the new social game are played out, and she is eager to capture them as accurately as possible, abiding by the code of realism in the most traditional fashion. Authenticity is primarily an issue she raises from an aesthetic point of view, embodied by her female protagonist Julia, a young budding artist, and her lover Roderic, an older man who has experienced the material comfort of domesticity but found himself unfit for it, because of his devotion to the higher demands of his artistic vocation. The cast of characters also comprises William, a well-off businessman going through an existential crisis, after which he decides to pursue his childhood dream of becoming a painter.

From the start, Julia stands for unconditional devotion to the gratuity of art, and she conveys the writer's preoccupations regarding representation, imitation and veracity through art. For instance, an early chapter of the novel accounts for Julia's artistic calling by an anecdote about her childhood, when her father gave her a book full of colour reproductions and the child 'stared and stared at these things, wondering how it was that they seemed more exact, more true, than the apples that grew in their orchard' (Madden 2002, p. 28). By thus suggesting that art is first and foremost about conveying a truth about the world around us, Madden claims her faith in the capacity of art – and therefore literary language – to reflect reality through the observation and the rendering of the most minute details of her characters' daily lives. Thus the description of Julia's room is meant to mirror her personality: as is traditional in a realist novel, it is introduced through the point of view of an outside observer, in this case William:

> Looking around, he could see that much else was like this, improvised and shabby: cloths not quite covering boxes that served as tables, a bookshelf constructed from planks and bricks, flowers in a cut-down plastic water bottle that served as a vase. Strangest of all, at the far end of the room were a few good pieces of antique furniture, including a hunting table and a wooden trunk. (Madden 2002, p. 55)

Julia's bohemian lifestyle, her utter lack of interest for the signs of material success or for the ownership of valuable objects, are thus firmly established. They are blandly contrasted to William's own domestic interior, which the reader is expected to disapprove of, in the wake of Julia's reaction to it:

> Left alone now, she had her first chance to look around at the room in which she was sitting. Everything in it, burnished and glowing, bespoke of money … Although she liked individual elements – the fine rugs, the delicate tables – the overall effect was stifling and oppressive. (Madden 2002, p. 70)

As a painter, Julia is a sharp observer of details such as colours, clothes or jewels, which allows her, in a typical Austen fashion, to situate people at first sight according to their social class, lifestyle and worldview. Once again, a moral judgement is attached to this description of concrete objects:

> To look at her confirmed what Julia had surmised: mid-thirties, sober suit and briefcase, wedding ring and a cluster of diamonds … And although the woman's life was alien to Julia – in many ways she was out of sympathy with the values that underpinned it – there was no denying its immense pathos. (Madden 2002, p. 64)

What Madden suggests is the way in which in a consumer society such as contemporary Ireland, objects and belongings are used to cover up people's real selves, their true feelings and hidden desires, and allow them to wear what Julia calls 'a social mask' (Madden 2002, p. 377).

The highly significant role granted to places, settings, interiors and objects is not unique to Madden's style of writing, as we find it also in Ní Dhuibhne and in Enright's books. For instance, Ní Dhuibhne makes the most of Dublin's new topography, as is evidenced by the role she attributes in *Fox, Swallow, Scarecrow* to the new 'Luas' – a fact already observed by Susan Cahill (Cahill 2011). Just as Austen was able to define her characters according to the sort of coach they were able to ride in, the Irish author regards the tramway as a contemporary sign of distinction: 'Travelling by tram, at least on the Green Line, had a bit of cachet. Being seen on it was not necessarily a bad thing, whereas being seen on a Dublin bus, even a most respectable bus like the 7 or the 11, was an abject admission of social and economic failure' (Ní Dhuibhne 2007, p. 2). Right from the beginning of the novel therefore, Ní Dhuibhne insists on the 'signs of distinction' which rule Irish society in the twenty-first century, in which money, and therefore class, have taken an unprecedented significance, just as in Austen's England at the turn of the nineteenth century, when the aristocracy was being superseded by the rising bourgeoisie, the class of merchants and entrepreneurs.

Likewise, in some of the stories in *Taking Pictures*, Anne Enright uses specific and sometimes ludicrous objects to define her characters' personalities: for instance, she is able to summarize a woman's life in a single phrase such as: 'She married the man she was supposed to marry, and she got the curtains she was supposed to get' (Enright 2008, p. 118), as if the aim of the woman's life had indeed been to be rich enough to decorate her house the way she wanted. She also uses certain places to suggest her characters' social aspirations and the frustrations they entail, as in the story 'Caravan', whose title, connoting exoticism and orientalism, clashes with the material reality of the mobile home rented by a young middle-class couple in the Vendée for the holidays: 'If he stooped to get a saucepan out from under the sink, their backsides would collide through the bathroom door. The van, she called it. Le tin can' (Enright 2008, p. 175). In *The Forgotten Waltz*, published in 2011, Enright also provides details describing the material environment of her characters, including prices, for example when the narrator-cum-protagonist mentions the house she has newly bought with her companion: 'The place was going up by seventy-five euro a day, he said, which was – he did the calculations under flickering eyelids – about five cents a minute' (Enright

2012, p. 14). This emphasis on prices, salaries, bank accounts, taxes is a feature shared by the three novels. In *Fox, Swallow, Scarecrow*, the protagonist's husband is a building contractor who spends his time buying and selling property with a view to making huge profit: '"I sold the place in Cork for forty million", he said. "That sounds like a lot", she said. "It cost me five million six years ago. So it is a lot," he said proudly' (Ní Dhuibhne 2007, p. 85). Again, Austen and the details she provides about the characters' annual income come to mind: '"Is he married or single?" "Oh, single, my dear, to be sure! A single man of large fortune – four or five thousand a year. What a fine thing for our girls!"' (*Pride and Prejudice*, chapter 1).

Of the three writers, Ní Dhuibhne is perhaps the one who uses the devices of literary realism – the creation of the referential illusion through allusions to extra-linguistic reality – in the most self-conscious manner, as when she has her character ponder over the fact that today place-names have been replaced by mere numbers on Irish roads: 'He loved it that places with names like Rathfarnham and Dundrum had now been translated to short numbers, like 13. It was like moving from a Thomas Hardy sort of landscape into a modern one, where a number – Route 3 – could evoke all sorts of memories and feelings' (Ní Dhuibhne 2007, p. 29). By making such allusions to literary works, Ní Dhuibhne suggests that the novelist today can only refer to a reality which itself is always already encoded, denying the existence of an 'authentic' world outside the text, to use an expression from Madden's novel.

The accumulation of details regarding brand-names, place-names, prices or objects in the three novels sometimes verges on excess, parody or caricature, pointing to the underlying satirical intention which brings them close to the typical Austenesque comedy of manners, by making good fun of the characters – even if it less true of Madden's novel. Now satire in Austen's novels mostly targets the institution of marriage, which she implicitly compares to a market where women are used as tokens of exchange, and which is meant to secure the reproduction of the difference between social classes. To the dictate of the 'good' marriage based on socio-economic criteria, the nineteenth-century authoress opposed true love and romance, providing her readers with the delight of a happy ending in the form of the fairy-tale union of the Prince Charming with Cinderella, even though she made a point of ending the story at the moment when the marriage actually began, evading the necessity of describing what marital bliss could be like. She was thus already introducing the idea that women cannot be satisfied with the material comfort or the social status provided by marriage and instead yearn for other types of satisfaction. This is what Sigmund Freud explained himself one century later in 'Civilized Sexual Morality and Modern Nervous Illness', a conference in which he described the 'mental disillusion and the physical deprivations' resulting from marriage as being conducive to neurosis (Freud 1908). The notion that the bourgeois marriage not only fails to make a woman happy but leads to mental disorder thus lies at the heart of Flaubert's masterpiece *Madame Bovary*, in which he stages the boredom and growing hysteria of a woman who seeks refuge in the world of her imagination, nourished by romantic literature.

Even if today marriage is no longer ruled by social and economic necessities, as was the case in Austen's time, conjugal life and its inherent constraints remain a cause of disillusion and anguish for Enright's, Madden's or Ní Dhuibhne's female characters. For instance, Anna in *Fox, Swallow, Scarecrow* has married a rich husband, but now feels like Emma Bovary – even though the more obvious intertext Ní Dhuibhne has based her novel upon is Tolstoy's *Anna Karenina*. Anna reflects on how boring her married life has become: 'Was that what marriage was like for everyone? How could they really know? People lied about those these things as a matter of course, to themselves and to their friends' (Ní Dhuibhne 2007, p. 91). The remedy in her case is to escape to an imaginary world: Anna is a half-successful writer whose favourite genre is fantasy, her models being Philip Pullman and J. K. Rowling. Then she meets Vincy and fancies she is living a fairy-tale Bovary-like romance, an indulgence for which she is severely punished by the writer, who has her lover killed in the most ludicrous manner at the end of the book. Marriage is also the butt of Enright's satirical vignettes in *Taking Pictures*, whose stories are populated by adulterous men and women, as well as by single men or women trying to find out what went wrong with their former relationships. Apart from the curtains already mentioned, Enright encapsulates the *mal de vivre* of one of her married female characters through her obsession for new carpets, symbolic of her incapacity to obtain what she wants from her husband: '"Five years", said Margaret. "Five years I have been trying to get carpets for the back bedrooms." "I know what you mean". "I mean, five years I've been trying to get to the shop to look at the carpet books to start thinking about carpet for the back bedrooms"' (Enright 2008, p. 142).

For Michelle, the protagonist of 'Caravan', the feeling of 'mental disillusion' is encapsulated by the holidays in the mobile home in the Vendée, a sure sign to her eyes that the fairy tale of an exotic journey into 'Neverland' has painfully failed: the narrator thought she and her husband were 'doing well' – an ambiguous phrase which plays upon the material or psychological meanings of 'well' – but the reality is different, as her husband forces her to acknowledge: '"We're not doing well", he said. "We're doing all right"' (Enright 2008, p. 175). In *Authenticity*, Madden also explores the trappings of domesticity, even though for her the disillusion stems less from the difference between genders than from the gap between what the characters witness of the businesslike, materialistic spirit of their time and the utter dedication demanded by their artistic vocation, which makes them unable to fit in. Thus Roderic the painter finds himself at odds with a wife who is too preoccupied with appearances and material comfort: 'She would begin some long discourse about getting the shutters painted or buying new bed linen or planning a dinner to which her family would be invited: domestic details that bored him so immensely his mind would simply close down and move on to a more absorbing object' (Madden 2002, p. 144). To the question 'What does a woman want?' raised by Freud, the two Irish women writers thus ironically answer: new curtains, or carpets, or bed linen, as if to parody their characters' seemingly insatiable longings.

Freud's answer to his own question however, was that what a woman wants is to become a mother. In her oedipal development, he argued, the little girl is supposed to go through a stage when she resents her mother and discovers that she is deprived of a penis, a lack, which, according to Freud, can be made up for only by the birth of a child: 'The feminine situation is only established, however, if the desire for a penis [*penisneid*] is replaced by one for a baby' (Freud 1933, p. 139). The theory has infuriated generations of feminists, but can be justified by the historical, cultural context in which Freud was writing, a context which continued to prevail in Ireland until the last decade of the twentieth century and which presented motherhood as the allegedly natural, 'biological' fate of women, a stereotype enforced by the combined forces of Church and State. But whereas today the pressure to procreate has become less oppressive and Irish women can decide if they want a child or not, writers like Enright, Ní Dhuibhne and Madden insist that motherhood, even when it is the result of a free choice, does not necessarily bring an answer to the question of woman's desire, a concept which was such an obsession of Freud's. Enright is perhaps the most forceful in this regard, staging young mothers overwhelmed with their new role, as in the story 'Shaft', in which the pregnant narrator is enclosed in an elevator with a stranger staring at her stomach, which starts her thinking about the immensity of the task of motherhood – a concern she cannot share with her husband:

> There was this guy looking at my stomach in the lift on the way up to the seventh floor one Tuesday morning when I had very little on my mind. Or

everything. I had everything on my mind. I had a new whole person on my mind, for a start ... I had all this to worry about, a new human being, a whole universe, but of course this is 'nothing'. *You are worrying about nothing*, my husband says. (Enright 2008, p.131)

In 'Yesterday's Weather', a young mother's weekend, during which she is meant to have 'a good time', is spoilt by the demands of her crying baby, leading to a major row with her husband: 'Mind you, his screaming sounded the same as every other night's screaming, she thought, so it was impossible to know how much he had been damaged by it all; by the total collapse of the love that made him' (Enright 2008, p.146). The 'damage' this young mother worries may have been done to her child is perhaps the damage done to her, in the sense that motherhood may reveal a painful contradiction with her true desire as a woman. Indeed, as Lacan has explained in response to Freud's theory of motherhood being what a woman wants, the satisfaction of being a mother must be distinguished from a woman's desire. He even argued that Medea was the archetype of the 'real woman' – another possible meaning of Madden's favoured 'authenticity' – because she went as far as killing her own children in order to remain true to her desire (Lacan 1966, p.761).

This does not mean that, for Lacan, woman's desire is less mysterious than it appeared to Freud, or less elusive and unsayable. Indeed, according to Lacan, woman is *'pastoute'*, which can be translated as 'not all' or/and 'not whole' (Lacan 1975), meaning that woman (but Lacan adds that *'la femme, ça n'existe pas'* – there is no such thing as woman (Lacan 1975, p.93)) does not situate herself entirely in the phallic function.[2] As a result, she is not entirely motivated by phallic 'jouissance', but has access to what he calls a supplementary jouissance, *'une Autre jouissance'*, but which is impossible for her to talk about, because there is no signifier to represent it, contrary to the phallus.[3] Lacan also distinguishes men's tendency to privilege 'having' (*'l'avoir'*) over 'being' (*'l'être'*), in relation to the phallus, which entails that men tend to favour action, leadership and achievement, whereas women are not so easily satisfied with social or material success – even though there are of course women who are. As the French Lacanian psychoanalyst

[2] 'when a speaking human being is situated under the banner of womanhood it is because he is founded on the fact of being not whole/all, he places himself in the phallic function' (Lacan 1975, p.93). All translations from French by the author.
[3] 'it is not possible to state whether a woman can say anything about it – if she can say what she knows about it' (Lacan 1975, p.95).

Colette Solers puts it, 'Feminine jouissance depends on no materiality and is satisfied by nothing which can be named' (Solers 2003, p. 145). As a result, a woman is liable to experience the symptoms of what Lacan calls '*un manque-à-être*', a 'lack of being', which can lead to all sorts of disorders.

Enright has her own way of pointing this unnameable desire when she has her characters repeatedly ask the same question: 'what do you want?', meaning both 'what do you wish' and 'what do you lack'. '"Oh, be careful what you want"', says her mother to the narrator in the story 'What you want', who tries to assess what she has obtained from life except 'her ups and downs' (Enright 2008, p. 152). Most of the female characters in *Taking Pictures* yearn for a part of themselves which they somehow lost on the way, and try to nurse their disillusions: 'Because I grew up with the same dreams as every other girl, but when the chips were down ... When the chips were down, I kept my head held high' (Enright 2008, p. 192), confesses the narrator of 'Until the Girl Died', whose husband has had an affair with a young girl. Many of Enright's characters feel haunted by the vague image of what they wished they had become, or what they fear they might become, like Michelle in 'Caravan' who sees the ghost of a woman sitting in the mobile home: 'There was something else about this woman: the set of her face; there was some other wreckage in her that Michelle did not yet recognise' (Enright 2008, p. 182). Here the word 'wreckage' seems to echo Lacan's notion of '*ravage*' which he discovers in the female psyche, and which he assigns alternatively to the men–women relationship or to the one between mother and daughter.[4] Enright's stories are full of examples of '*ravage*', the most striking one being perhaps the character of the anorexic in the story 'Little Sister'. Anorexia was analysed by Lacan as 'a hunger strike' directed against the anxiety-ridden image of an all-powerful, menacing morbid mother (Lacan 1984, p. 34).

Mothers indeed loom large in Enright's stories, such as in 'Honey', in which the protagonist is overwhelmed by a wave of desire after her mother has just died from cancer, as if this desire were finally given free rein after the disappearance of the menacing motherly figure:

---

[4] 'The Freudian rantings about the Oedipus complex whereby woman is like fish in water, and castration is a reality for her from the start (according to Freud), painfully clashes with the ravages which result for most women from their relationship with their mother, from whom as a woman she seems to expect much more substance than from her father – what goes wrong with him being secondary in this destructive process' (Lacan 2001, p. 465).

'She was ashamed of what she had felt as she stepped away from her mother's grave. That lightness – it was desire. And it was vast' (Enright 2008, p. 90). 'Ravage' in men and women's relationships, or to put it simply, troubled femininity, is also much of the subject of Fox, Swallow, Scarecrow, in which the neurotic Anna falls prey to romantic delusions which are never sufficient to appease her, even after she has obtained a child from her lover Vincy: 'She wondered why she was not feeling happy, now that she had got exactly what she had longed for' (Ní Dhuibhne 2007, p.278). Another 'ravaged' character in the novel is Kate, a young single woman who loses herself in work, and tries to convince herself that she is entirely satisfied by it: 'Did she like her job? She adored it. It was fabulous. Really really really hard work, twenty-four seven, it took everything you could give and she gave it everything she could' (Ní Dhuibhne 2007, p.66). But this tremendous display of energy fails to conceal Kate's 'manque-à-être' and she ends up a patient in a mental hospital after she suffers a major breakdown.

Even Julia, in Authenticity, presented by her lover as 'completely authentic' and 'solid' (Madden 2002, p. 34), and who indeed stands out against her two troubled male friends, experiences the attraction of another, unsayable jouissance: 'Once again the traffic drove past and a crowd began to gather, waiting to cross the road where she stood … And then it happened: whatever it was … Something had permitted her to glimpse behind reality' (Madden 2002, p. 324). Of course in Madden's view, Julia's yearning for another, unsayable reality is not a symptom of a troubled femininity but is a product of her artistic vocation, which is further evidenced by the description of the type of artefacts she creates: 'Julia's work consisted of a series of long wooden boxes, each sealed in front with a pane of glass … There was about all of them, he thought, a mysterious, elegiac atmosphere, each presenting a small, sealed, rather beautiful but utterly inaccessible world' (Madden 2002, p. 98). That 'sealed', 'mysterious', 'inaccessible world' inspiring nostalgia is strangely reminiscent of the lost maternal womb, which lies at the source of what Julia Kristeva, a literary critic and psychoanalyst, has called 'the semiotic', namely the type of language which does not strive after coherence and meaning but is close to the non-linguistic, non-grammatical form of communication preceding entrance into the symbolic order (Kristeva 1974). Julia, whose mother died when she was still a child, has thus found in art a means of expressing her desire to return to an initial state of perfect harmony and contentment, denied and repressed by the demands of society.

But Madden also makes it clear that art for her female character is a form of resistance against the surrounding materialism, hence the emphasis on Julia's 'authenticity', her 'solidity' and 'reality', all terms used to describe her. Roderic admires how she holds on to her integrity: 'You're determined to be absolutely true to your own vision. It's one of the things I admire most about you' (Madden 2002, p. 230). On the contrary, Anna in *Fox, Swallow, Scarecrow* tends to use art as a means of evading the reality of her desire, as well at achieving social recognition, a lack of authenticity for which she is punished by failure and even plagiarism, when one of her best friends steals her manuscript from her. Through the description of the numerous book launches which Anna attends, and the literary people she meets, the writer also draws a sharply critical portrayal of the way in which art and literature in Ireland today may be enslaved to the dictates of the market economy and the pursuit of a social status. Ní Dhuibhne's own strategy to resist the commodification of art and the perversion of 'authenticity', in *Fox, Swallow, Scarecrow* is parody, which takes the form of citation (Tolstoy, Thomas Hardy, C. S. Lewis, J. K. Rowling, Philip Pullman etc.) but also of the parody of the bourgeois romance of adultery which her protagonist Anna desperately wants to be the heroine of. Another strategy Ní Dhuibhne has used is the introduction of supernatural or marvellous elements in the story, which all resort to traditional Irish folklore; their effect is not just to mock and contradict the bourgeois realist writers' claim to verisimilitude but also to point at the irrational, the fantasized and the imaginary parts of the characters' and the readers' unconscious fears, desires and anxieties, which society, especially a materialistic, profit-driven one, ignores and represses. Anne Enright's own strategy is hinted at by the very title she gave to her collection of stories, *Taking Pictures*. Indeed, she confronts the reader with very striking or incongruous images, which point at the unsaid, the unrepresentable and the repressed in the characters' lives. In 'In the Bed Department' for instance – in which, as is common in Enright's writings, she plays on the literal and the figurative meanings of the words – the construction of an escalator in the department store where the protagonist works materializes the idea that her life is full of 'ups and downs', but is also evocative of the flux of images – or the Freudian *fort–da–* released by the unconscious, especially through art, dreams or puns. In 'Honey', it is the image of a swarm of bees which helps the female protagonist face the reality of her desire: 'The bees were bristly and soft … She watched them until she could no longer tell them apart. Then she started to cry … That lightness – it was desire. And it was vast' (Enright 2008, p. 89).

That women tend to remain true to their desire, or 'authentic', in the words of Madden, however vast, unsayable, mysterious or even mystical, as Lacan suggested,[5] that desire may be, and this despite or beyond the satisfactions of material comfort brought about by a liberal economy based on the pursuit of profit, money and power, or the freedoms afforded by a secularized society, is what these 'Celtic Tiger' novels and stories tell us. But beyond a sort of anthropological survey of Irish woman in the twenty-first century, the three writers demonstrate how art and literature can resist the commodification of all human needs and feelings, and oppose 'the new psychic economy' defined by Charles Melman at the beginning of this paper.

Works Cited:

Austen, Jane (2002) *Pride and Prejudice*, originally published 1813, Harmondsworth: Penguin.

Cahill, Susan (2011) *Irish Literature in the Celtic Tiger Years 1990–2008: Gender, Bodies, Memory*, London: Continuum.

Enright, Anne (2008), *Taking Pictures*, London: Jonathan Cape.

Enright, Anne (2011), *The Forgotten Waltz*, London and New York: Norton.

Freud, Sigmund (1908) 'Civilized Sexual Morality and Modern Nervous Illness', available: www.scribd.com/doc/76620596/Civilized-Sexual-Morality-and-Modern-Nervousness-Freud [accessed 14 September 2012].

Freud, Sigmund (1965) [1933] *New Introductory Lectures on Psychoanalysis*, ed. James Strachey, New York: Norton, 1965.

Jones, Ernest (1988) *La Vie et l'œuvre de Sigmund Freud*, Paris: PUF.

Kristeva, Julia (1974) *La Révolution du langage poétique*, Paris: Editions du Seuil. Tel quel.

Lacan, Jacques (1966) 'Jeunesse de Gide' ou la lettre du désir', in *Ecrits*, Paris: Seuil.

Lacan, Jacques (1975) *Le Séminaire, Livre XX: Encore* (1972–1973), Paris: Seuil, 'Essais'.

Lacan, Jacques (1984) *Les Complexes familiaux dans la formation de l'individu*, Paris: Navarin Editeur.

Lacan, Jacques (1994) *Le Séminaire Livre IV, La relation d'objet*, Paris: Editions du Seuil.

Lacan, Jacques (2001) *Autres écrits*, Paris: Editions du Seuil.

Madden, Deirdre (1986) *Hidden Symptoms*, London: Faber and Faber.

Madden, Deirdre (1988) *The Birds of the Innocent Wood*, London: Faber and Faber.

Madden, Deirdre (1996) *One by One in the Darkness*, London: Faber and Faber.

[5] 'Isn't this "jouissance" one experiences but knows nothing about what sets us on the path to ex-sistence? And why not interpret one side of the Other, the godly side, as if it were born out of feminine jouissance?' (Lacan 1975, p.98).

Madden, Deirdre (2002) *Authenticity*, London: Faber and Faber.

Melman, Charles (2009) *L'Homme sans gravité, jouir à tout prix (Entretiens avec J. p. Lebrun)*, Paris: Denoël.

Ní Dhuibhne, Éilís (2007) *Fox, Swallow, Scarecrow*, Belfast: Blackstaff Press.

Solers, Colette (2003), *Ce que Lacan disait des femmes*, Paris: Editions du Champ Freudien.

7

Topographies of terror: photography and the post-Celtic Tiger landscape

Justin Carville

The title of this chapter is a sort of homage to Luke Gibbons's examination of eighteenth-century landscape aesthetics and Romanticism in
Ireland (Gibbons 1996). In the essay from which the title is borrowed,
and in several other subsequent publications, Gibbons has examined
those moments when the collision of cultures brought about by the violence of colonialism has stimulated the complex intersection of aesthetics and politics in philosophical thought, literature and the arts (Gibbons
2001, p. 206). In the same vein as Gibbons has explored the aesthetic
philosophy of what might be termed the colonial sublime in Ireland,
this chapter examines the visual rhetoric of the neo-liberal sublime of
the landscape during and after the Celtic Tiger period. Unlike Gibbons,
however, who draws on Edmund Burke's displacement of the centrality
of vision and the sovereignty of sight – then dominant in the tradition of
European aesthetic philosophy – in deference to the less empiricist and
more affective power of words (Gibbons 2006, pp. 6–7; pp. 104–107),
I argue in this chapter that recent Irish visual culture, and in particular
contemporary photography, provides a unique perspective on the tumul-
tuous impact of the collapse of global capitalism on the Irish landscape.
My aim here is not to claim a privileged position for the visual over the
textual, or to get drawn into the post-structuralist argument that the
photographic image cannot escape the control that language has over
its cultural operations. Nor, I might add, is this chapter concerned with
a reductive debate on the photographic image's privileged access to the
real. The photographic image's 'more' or 'less' *realistic* representation of
the social hardships brought about by the economic failure of the State
than other cultural forms, is not what is at stake in recent Irish photography. What I aim to do in this chapter, rather, is to reclaim a place for
a critical visual culture in general, and for the photographic image in
particular, in the cultural politics of the Celtic Tiger and its aftermath.

The focus of this chapter is on a series of photographic works which
are part of what I identify as a larger topographical turn in recent Celtic

and post-Celtic Tiger photography during and after the Celtic Tiger period. In the spirit of W. J. T. Mitchell, I see this 'turn' not as a designation of a dominant or unique theme threaded throughout contemporary photographic art but as a cultural practice that has emerged as an emphasis at a particular moment of crisis that is a turning point in Irish history (Mitchell 1994a, pp. 11–34; 2005, pp. 348–349). Somewhat conversely, following critics of the historical specificity of the term postcolonialism, what I identify as post-Celtic Tiger photography does not designate photographic practices solely attuned to the aftermath of the Celtic Tiger. While not wishing to eschew the clear rupture of the illusion of the Celtic Tiger myth inaugurated by the Irish government's bail-out of the Irish financial system with the Bank Guarantee scheme in 2008, or indeed issues of historical classification, I want to emphasize the tensions, resistances and conflicts with global capitalism that emerge as a topic in Irish photography during the Celtic Tiger years. In the interest of clarity then, a more precise explanation would be that what I identify as 'post' does not simply designate what comes after the Celtic Tiger, but rather what cultural collisions emerge out of its inauguration as an economic phenomenon in 1994 (Keohane and Kuhling 2004). The topographical turn of post-Celtic Tiger photography, as I conceptualize it, thus refers to an intervention into the cultural politics of the Celtic Tiger itself, an intervention that does not seek to document change but, following Walter Benjamin's theorization of the dialectical image in commodity fetishism, envisions the cracks, fissures and ruins of global capitalism's Irish journey before its spectacular collapse (Benjamin 1986).

The topographical turn

In 1995 Dublin's Gallery of Photography staged the first showing of a touring exhibition *The Lie of the Land* featuring the work of six contemporary Irish photographers. The show, curated to coincide with the shift from a makeshift exhibition space to Ireland's first purpose-built gallery of photography – itself an example of the country's changing economic fortunes – proposed a new perspective on photography's cultural imaginings of Ireland's social landscape. Against the backdrop of shifting perceptions of Irishness in the context of globalization, the exhibition identified each of the six photographers as bringing a new visual grammar to their individual exploration of the emerging complexities of place and identity in contemporary Ireland. In the accompanying exhibition catalogue, Fintan O'Toole observed that the work of the photographers inserted itself into the space between representation and reality to expose the tensions between two Irelands, one that was 'geographical', a bounded space with geological contours and borders, the other which was 'demographic', a disjointed network of subjectivities, aspirations, memories, dreams, absences and losses in a constant state of flux between the physical geography of the island and its diaspora across the globe (O'Toole 1995). These two Irelands posed their own set of difficulties, but while the geographic Ireland could be 'pictured', although somewhat problematically, as the contemporary configuration of a fixed, stable sense of an Ireland, the latter 'demographic' Ireland was outside the field of vision and the representational capabilities of mechanical pictorialization, and as a result had to be 'imagined'. As O'Toole outlined this crisis of representation, it was the fissure between the geographic and demographic Irelands that had to be imagined which revealed that the 'map of Ireland is a lie', and the photographers in the exhibition explored this 'lie' to reimagine Ireland as a geographically open and culturally porous site of contested identities, experiences and histories. As he noted on the problem of the demographic:

> Existing as it does, imaginatively, it is always open to the possibility of being re-imagined. As such, it poses a constant threat to the first Ireland. It questions its pictures of itself by showing that they are merely one strand from a range of possibilities that happened to develop within the frame of the island of Ireland. (O'Toole 1995, unpaginated)

The tension between the geography of the island that can be pictured, and its boundlessness, which is recalcitrant to the normative processes of pictorialization, itself suggests an inherent limitation to what photography can adequately represent within its own bounded geometric frame. Photographs frame their subjects by cutting other parts of the world around them out, every photograph always leaves behind an un-pictorialized excess which is visually absent but that the viewer nevertheless knows is still out there beyond the pictorial frame. But clearly for O'Toole, what the photographers in the *Lie of the Land* exhibition offered was a counterpoint to the arena of imagery – verbal, textual and visual – that projected a unitary geographical representation of Ireland, an oblique view of the cultural politics of geography that exposed the connections, contradictions and conflicts woven into the relations between place and identity.

From the perspective of hindsight, it is difficult now not to see the particular emphasis of Ireland's diasporic global relations in the exhibition as nostalgic. The politics of diasporic identity seem positively benign in comparison to the transnational flows of global capitalism – then not perceptible enough to the opticality of photography – which have further embedded cultural identity into the conflicted relations of place and globalization, and have now resulted in a new wave of geographic and cultural dislocation. The exhibition and the responses to it, do, however, initiate some threads of inquiry worth pursuing about the role of photography in 'the psychic investments we make in vision and image' to borrow Kevin Robins's phrase (Robins 1996, p. 5), not least of which is the anxiety generated through the sense of boundlessness of the photographic images' geographical imaginings of Ireland as place.

It is not clear if *The Lie of the Land* was conceived as the culmination of an ascendant culture of photographic practice, a retrospective of sorts of a prevailing movement in contemporary Irish photography, or as a new dawn, a departure-point for an emergent style of photographic art addressed to the growing political and cultural complexities of modern Ireland and its place in the world. What is apparent, however, is that its title gestured towards the myth of the centrality of landscape to contemporary Irish photographic culture. While Anthony Haughey's *The Edge of Europe* series turned briefly to the depopulated landscape of the Blasket Islands in the exploration of migration, it did so only from a distance which only served to obfuscate the pastoral as a remote experience (Haughey 1996). The work of the other photographers in the exhibition bore little relation to 'the land' as it resonated in the visual culture that O'Toole identified as being threatened by the cultural imaginings that exposed the incoherent network of global relations of place and identity. The landscape may have existed as a social and cultural sphere of experience in much photography from that period but rarely as a subject for the camera's lens in itself. This did not prevent O'Toole from highlighting the myth of the pastoral hidden in the pictorial renderings of the Irish landscape, a cultural lacuna which the photographers featured in *The Lie of the Land* exposed through their aesthetic effacing of the normative ocular clarity of the photographic image:

> But the landscape lied about itself. It concealed all sorts of absences, especially the absence of those who disappeared. Irish emigrants were removed, not merely from Ireland to elsewhere, but from the land to the city. And their absence from the landscape is what made it possible for them to disappear from the emergent culture of modern Ireland. In the absence left by emigration, the aesthetics of emptiness took hold. Empty wilderness is seen as innately more noble, and infinitely more worth looking at, than ordinary urban existence. (O'Toole 1995, unpaginated)

Something more than the aesthetics of emptiness is at work here in the pictorial concealment of the cultural loss that casts its shadow across the landscape. While the loss of tradition and community brought about by emigration and the acceleration of modernity can easily be incorporated into narratives of cultural memory and mourning that fill the empty landscape with an aestheticized sense of pathos, the visual regime of global capitalism sees this emptiness from an entirely different perspective. This is a significant point for understanding the emergence of a topographical turn in Irish photography after the staging of the *Lie of the Land* exhibition. While much creative endeavour and intellectual labour had been expended on the aesthetic ideology of the empty landscape as projecting the presence of absence – of tradition, heritage and community – to ameliorate the sense of cultural dislocation brought about by modernity and emigration, global capitalism's logic of rationalizing space through the visual envisions that same empty space as a site of future development (Harvey 1989). As Mitchell observes on the ideology of landscape in the Western pictorial tradition, the semiotic characteristics of landscape and the narratives of collective history and memory they create are conducive to the discourse of visual imperialism: 'Empires move outward in space as a way of moving forward in time; the "prospect" that opens up is not just a spatial scene but a projected future of "development" and "exploitation"' (Mitchell 1994b, p. 17). While the emptiness of the Irish landscape as a semiotic marker of the history of colonial violence might be imbued with Romanticism in a process of reclaiming the picturesque as an aesthetic imperative for a national visual culture as David Brett has suggested (Brett 1996, p.48), the empty landscape devoid of presence carries no such sentimentality in the visual imperialism of global capitalism.

In the midst of the Celtic Tiger period, and some years after *The Lie of the Land*, a number of photographers began to explore the physical manifestation of the economic intervention into these empty spaces by speculative development and the unifying spatial logic of global capitalism. This marked a return to the Irish landscape in Irish photography, but not in the oblique style and aesthetic obscurity of the photography identified by O'Toole as providing imaginative geographies of Ireland's 'incoherent networks' of place and identity. This attention to globalization's reconfiguring of space in Irish photography was accompanied by a visual practice largely orientated around that most artless of photographs, 'the document'.

By 'document' I do not mean documentary, although some of the photographers that I would associate with the topographic turn would categorize themselves within this genre. What I mean by the document, rather, is a very particular type of photographic image produced as a result of a methodological practice of pictorial regularity. Since photography's invention in the nineteenth century, photographic documents have been an important part of global visual culture. However, because they have largely been a feature of institutional and institutionalizing visual practices in science, criminology, archaeology and anthropology, they have tended to remain hidden away in archives and rarely come to the attention of the wider public. Most people are familiar with the look of these documents and have a sense of their function, but as they tend to be banal and visually dull, pay little if any attention to such photographs (Edwards 2006, pp. 12–39). This, in a sense, is precisely the aim of the photographic document, namely to appear visually unobtrusive. Its main characteristics tend towards pictorial clarity over artistic style, its emphasis of ocular plainness and lack of creative embellishment serving as a technical code for its objectivity.

While the photographic document is aesthetically minimal, its pictorial clarity is indented to convey vast amounts of information to the viewer. One role of the photographic document in the sciences for example has been as a type of pure visual epistemology, a sort of material example of the cliché 'seeing is knowing'. In this sense then, the photographic document is an accurate depiction of something, a transparent window on to the world that is descriptive in its visual representation of objects and people, rather than being interpretative. As it is designed to be descriptive in its pictorial representation of peoples, places and objects, the photographic document is also frequently patterned by its repetitive regularity. Many uses of the photographic document in the sciences, anthropology and the law operate through established methodological procedures which ensure that the pictorial clarity of the image is accompanied by a rigorous, repetitive process in the production of the image to confirm that it retains a technical similarity to other photographic documents.

These characteristics of the photographic document are a feature of what I identify as a topographical turn in Irish photography during the Celtic Tiger years. They are what William Jenkins described in relation to the emergence of photography of the suburban and industrial landscapes in 1970s America, as a type of image 'reduced to its topographic state, conveying substantial amounts of visual information but eschewing entirely the aspects of beauty, emotion, and opinion' (Jenkins 1975, unpaginated). Martin Cregg's series *The Midlands* evidences this topographic approach to the Celtic Tiger's configurations of the new landscapes of housing development and post-agricultural commercial warehouses (Cregg 2009). Cregg's photographs, constructed through the frontal straight-on direction of the cameras lens before the scene it frames, provides a transparent depiction of the object devoid of any aesthetic distraction. His series of empty houses from what have now colloquially become known as 'ghost estates', and the prefabricated vacant units of industrial parks, are almost

Figure 1 Dara McGrath, *N11 Kilmacanogue*, from the series *By the Way*, 2002. © Dara McGrath

planar in their repetitive depiction of the façades of the built environment that fill the pictorial space of the photograph.

The attention to the rectilinear details of urban and suburban development, and the visual description of the surface features of the Celtic Tiger marked upon the landscape through the photographic document, are only one feature of the topographical turn in Irish photography. Some photographers have employed technically less rigid strategies to represent the shifting contours of Ireland's landscape as it began to be re-wrought by the abstract spatial practices of globalization. Although not tied to the pictorial regularity of the photographic document, this work is no less rigorous in its visual depiction of the changing contours of Ireland's topography. What perhaps differentiates these photographers is that their visual strategies are more self-consciously analytical in their depiction of the harsh linearity marked by an emerging suburban sprawl. Dara McGrath's *By the Way* for example, scrutinized the emergence of new spaces that appeared in between the sites of new and existing urban and suburban developments (McGrath 2003). These spaces,

Figure 2 Martin Cregg, *The Manor, Scramoge, Co. Roscommon*, March 2008, from the series *Midlands*. © Martin Cregg

what the French Surrealists referred to as 'Terrain Vague' and what have recently been described as 'Edgelands' (Farley and Roberts, 2011), are the margins between the 'conceptualized' spaces of planners (Lefebvre 1991, p. 39), that although not diagrammatically mapped on paper are still spaces that connect people socially to place.

Despite the variations in visual strategies between photographers such as McGrath and Cregg, what both share is an orientation toward the changing topography of Ireland, not as recurring subject or a style, but as an intervention into the visual culture of the Celtic Tiger itself. For all its seeming passivity in following the methodological regularity of the document, Cregg's series, no less than McGrath's, exposed the yawning gap between the image of economic prosperity and its hollow, material façades scattered across the midlands and suburban Dublin. Significantly, both Cregg's and McGrath's series had begun to expose the fractures of the embrace of neo-liberal economics and the Celtic Tiger's reconfiguration of the Irish landscape in the uniform image of globalized space before the economic crash. It is, perhaps, because such an appalling vista could not be 'imagined' that the quiet exposure of the *terra infirma* of the Celtic Tiger landscape represented in Irish photography was not at the time recognized as envisioning its spectacular collapse. But what the topographical turn in Irish photography now confronts the viewer with, I want to suggest, is a 'sublime historical experience' to borrow F. R. Ankersmit's term (Ankersmit 2005), an image of impending catastrophe which the viewer is both distanced from, and yet seeks to overcome, through the epistemological weight and pictorial clarity of the photograph. The terror of the topography that photography confronts the viewer with is precisely this tension between the loss of the past that has been ruptured by the economic collapse of the Celtic Tiger, and the potential of its recovery through the visual form of the photograph. To tease this out a little further I want to examine two recent examples of post-Celtic Tiger topographical photography, Anthony Haughey's *Settlement* and David Farrell's *Banamaland*.

Late photography and sublime historical experience

Anthony Haughey's *Settlement* and David Farrell's *Banamaland* are two recent and, in the case of Farrell, ongoing projects on that most culturally resonant of post-Celtic Tiger topographies, the 'ghost estate'. First coined as a term by the economist David McWilliams in 2006 to describe the development of swathes of vacant housing across rural Ireland as a result of government tax schemes (McWilliams 2006), ghost estates have become twenty-first-century Ireland's 'empty landscapes' that instead of being filled with the aesthetics of loss and longing, are a terrifying spectre of the collapse of the property bubble that the collective consciousness would like to erase from its memory.

Haughey's photographs are a series of partially built houses and deserted construction sites taken between sunset and sunrise. Each image reduces the landscape to the rectilinear forms of the arrested development of scaffold-clad structures bathed in the artificial light that with the Celtic Tiger increasingly pollutes even the remotest peripheries

Figure 3 Anthony Haughey, *Untitled*, from the series *Settlement*, 2011. © Anthony Haughey

of rural towns. The use of light in the photographs, the combination of a descending darkness and an emergent luminosity, has, of course, its own sublimity, its own psychic affect of anxiety and apprehension (for much earlier discussion of the sublime see Burke 1990, pp. 132–135). This aesthetic friction of light, however, is overlaid with a more frightening tension that is intensified through the temporal logic of photography. Like that transitory moment between dusk and dawn, photography captures the uneasiness of a moment that is 'becoming', that fleeting instant when the past is about to unfold into the future. Haughey's photographs, in the combination of the ambient light that envelops the half-built landscape and their animation of the temporal anxiety of the contingent moment of the past and what is becoming, provide an 'unsettling' perspective of the post-Celtic Tiger landscape.

David Farrell's *Banamaland* comprises a vast survey of the ghost estates that have become the spiralling depreciated assets of the National Asset Management Agency. Systematically surveying ghost estates in each of Ireland's twenty-six counties, Farrell's series does not attempt to visualize the totality of the post-Celtic Tiger landscape (the shift-

Figure 4 David Farrell, *The Waterways, Keshcarrigan, Leitrim*, from *An Archaeology of the Present*, 2012. © David Farrell

ing terrain of economic uncertainty renders such a project impossible). Instead the methodical survey provides a series of fragments that comprise a vast archive of the archaeological remnants of a future speculated upon by endless development. Patterns emerge in the depictions of elaborate entrance gates to housing estates never commenced, and the corporate hoarding and banners around uncompleted developments that announce utopian futures for relocated families and communities. The concrete slabs of foundations and unclad frontage to buildings also provide detailed examples of how the division of labour and subcontracting has marked the post-Celtic Tiger landscape with a rough unevenness that ruptures the smooth spaces of the manicured gardens and bright-rendered façades that appeared in the property porn of estate agent brochures, property supplements and advertising hoardings. Such visual illusions of a suburban arcadia are part of the visual regime of the Celtic Tiger (Slater 1998, pp. 28–29) that fuelled property speculation through deception of the eye. At a time when there is a compulsive desire for the archive to yield the origins and responsibility for the nation's economic collapse, a moment of 'archive fever' as Derrida describes it, what is troubling about Farrell's photographic fragments of the illusion of property speculation is its endlessness, its refusal of a closure of the past and an opening out to a future yet to come (Derrida 1998, pp. 68–69 and pp. 90–91).

Haughey's and Farrell's projects bring their own distinctive topographic style to the representation of the post-Celtic Tiger landscape. Both are examples of what has been termed 'late' or 'cool' photography (Campany 2003 and Wollen 1997), a practice that eschews the depiction of events *in medias res*, 'in the midst of the action'; instead it favours a more forensic detachment of the event's aftermath. Yet the individual projects have their own technical and aesthetic codifications of the post-Celtic Tiger landscape, and different ocular perspectives or what might be termed 'geographical imaginings' of Ireland at a particular turning point in its history. While acknowledging these differences, I want to propose a way of examining these examples of topographical photography collectively as a visual experience of the historical geography of the Celtic Tiger and its aftermath.

Photography, I want to suggest, is a type of history. By identifying it as a type of history, I do not mean that it operates as a visual narrative of the past or functions epistemologically as a pictorial repository of historical knowledge. Photographs, as John Tagg reminds us, 'are never evidence of history', they are not passive reflections of the past transferred to the geometric surface of paper, nor are they a transparent window on to the world, 'they are themselves the historical' (Tagg 1988, p. 65). If, as Tagg suggests, photographs are the historical, photography then might be best identified as a type of historical experience. Ankersmit has noted that in Western history experience of the past has been repressed in favour of a historiography that posits an objective reality of how a 'people in the past experienced their world', a world that remains beyond the 'grasp and influence' of the historian (Ankersmit 2005, pp. 3–4). Against this he proposes the emergence of 'historical experience', a shift in perception from a 'timeless present' to 'a world consisting of things past and present' that raises the conscious awareness of a sense of loss with a break with the past (Ankersmit 2005, p. 9). For Ankersmit and the philosopher Eelco Runia (2010), at moments of radical discontinuity that break the normative trajectory of history – the French Revolution, the Second World War and, we might add in the context of this essay, the collapse of global capitalism – sublime historical experiences emerge out of a wish to stand outside the past as if it were an objective thing accompanied by a desire to overcome the past's historical distance by accessing it through historical knowledge. Following Burke's description of the sublime as 'tranquillity tinged with terror' (Burke 1990, p. 123), Ankersmit proposes that the sublimity of historical experiences originates from the paradoxical emotions of distance and close proximity, love and loss, and the desire to distance ourselves from a traumatic event whose terror we are never the less drawn to (Ankersmit 2005, pp. 317–368). For Runia, this sublime historical experience is more intensified with discontinuities in the recent past where people struggle to understand and even repress their role in a traumatic past in which they themselves had been active participants (Runia 2010, p. 3).

This later conception of sublime historical experience is particularly resonant for a culture that has been convinced by the state of its collective responsibility for the lack of fiscal oversight and regulation, a narrative that provided for the acceptance of public liability for private debt. In this context of the desire to distance ourselves from the recent past of the excesses of the Celtic Tiger that is transformed into a constant and permanent presence in the photographic topographies of post-Celtic Tiger Ireland by photographers such as Haughey and Farrell, I want to take a theoretical leap of faith and propose the concept of sublime historical experience as a salient feature of the photographic image. Roland Barthes, who noted how photographs reminded him that what separated his role as viewer from the people and objects in the photographs he was looking at was 'History', explained this historical experience as the shifting, schizophrenic temporalities of photography (Barthes 1984, p. 115). The temporal perception of the photograph according to Barthes moves 'back from presentation to retention', its motionless state preventing the normal corruption of time so that the viewer becomes aware that what is pictured within its frame is 'without future' except as tragedy (Barthes 1981, p. 90). Discussing the portrait of Lewis Payne in his cell awaiting his execution he exclaims:

> I read at the same time: *This will be* and *this has been*; I observe with horror an anterior future of which death is the stake. By giving me the absolute past of the pose (aorist), the photograph tells me death in the future ... I shudder ... *over a catastrophe which has already occurred*. Whether or not the subject is already dead, every photograph is this catastrophe. (Barthes 1981, p. 96)

This temporal arrest of perception of an impending catastrophe that cannot be halted is nothing less than a sublime experience. To borrow from Burke's description of the suspension of the emotions in the sublime, the terror of the '*this will be* and *this has been*' of the photograph fills the mind so completely that it cannot conceive of any other possibility of experience (Burke 1990, p. 53). In Celtic and post-Celtic Tiger topographical photography, this temporal anxiety of the photograph's depiction of a catastrophe that 'has already occurred' has been combined with a spatial configuration of an on-going moment of an unbounded geography to produce an intense sublime historical experience of the collapse of global capitalism.

As O'Toole identified in relation to *The Lie of the Land*, there is an arena of photography that is mobilized to construct a unitary geographical representation of Ireland, a visually cohesive sense of place. Photographs, like other abstract spatial representations such as maps, plans and architectural drawings, play a significant role in how people come to know, experience and respond to the world. They do not simply function as representations, but are rather ways of seeing the world that contribute to what Edward Said termed 'imaginative geographies' (O'Toole 1998, p. 6) that structure how people come to understand and situate themselves in space and time (Schwartz and Ryan 2003). The visual repertoire of tourist photographs and picturesque landscapes that circulate through the print and broadcast media contribute to stable, coherent and unified geographical imaginings of Ireland. The Celtic and post-Celtic topographical photography of Haughey and Farrell, much like that in the *Lie of the Land* exhibition, ruptures this unitary geographical representation by confronting the viewer with a temporal precipice. The Ireland they visualize is unbounded in its complex networks of geography and place, but it is the disorientating temporality of the photograph which holds the viewer in front of a past that was a projected future which initiates the

topographies of terror of the post-Celtic Tiger period. In the representation of the half-built houses bathed in the ambient light of deserted
housing estates and the fragmentary forms of the remnants of the
construction boom, the viewer is faced with a past whose catastrophic
end is certain and whose terror cannot be denied. Unlike the visual
obfuscation and displacement of vision that Gibbons identifies with
Burke's colonial sublime (Gibbons 2010, p. 46), the topographical turn
of post-Celtic photography initiates this disorientating sublime historical experience through an optical clarity that stretches the capacity of
the eye so that 'vibrating in all its parts must approach near to the
nature of what causes pain, and consequently must produce an idea of
the sublime' (Burke 1990, pp. 124–125). The photograph 'fills the sight
by force' as Barthes exclaimed (Barthes 1984, p. 91), and its violence of
vision cannot be escaped.

Walter Benjamin has observed that the experience of modernity is
that 'capitalism will not die a natural death' (Benjamin 1999, p. 667).
It very nearly did but in its resuscitation its punishment was to bring
everybody else down with it for the audacity of exposing the limits of
global capital. In a landscape littered with historical ruins, Haughey's
and Farrell's topographies of terror confront the viewer with Ireland's
newest of ruins drawn down to earth, not through nature's power
of decay but through the speculative forces of capital. Many of these
topographies have been formed through a series of leaps of faith into
a future that seemed certain. Land was speculatively purchased on the
promise of re-zoning for development, houses purchased off plans and
mortgages offered on the future escalation of financial capital, its own
numerical infinity creating a sense of economic sublime. In the midst of
the catastrophe of Ireland's economic collapse, the prevailing political
philosophy is to move forward inexorably towards the future as if ignoring the trauma of the recent past, to ameliorate the collective wounds
that are marked upon the landscape as a constant mnemonic inscription
of a lost prosperity. The topographical turn in photography is an important intervention into the myth of the Celtic Tiger, itself a mass visual
deception through the digital manipulation and 'photo-shopping' of a
projected futurescape of commercial and domestic property. Series such
as Haughey's Settlement and Farrell's Banamaland, much like Cregg's
and McGrath's, reclaim the ruins of the Celtic Tiger as a strategy to
rescue them from the cultural amnesia that threatens to cloak them in a
misty dawn of another future. They confront the present with its own
short-sightedness in imagining a future without earning from the failures
of the recent past.

Works cited

Ankersmit, Frank (2005) *Sublime Historical Experience*, Stanford: Stanford University Press.

Barthes, Roland (1984) *Camera Lucida: Reflections on Photography*, London: Flamingo.

Benjamin, Walter (1986) 'Paris, Capital of the Nineteenth Century', in *Reflections: Lated by, Aphorisms, Autobiographical Writings*, translated by E. Jephcott, New York: Schocken, pp. 146–162.

Benjamin, Walter (1999) *The Arcades Project*, translated by H. Eiland and K. McLaughlin, Cambridge, MA: Belknap, Harvard University Press.

Brett, David (1996) *The Construction of Heritage*, Cork: Cork University Press.

Burke, Edmund (1990) [1756] *A Philosophical Enquiry into the Origin of our Ideas of the Sublime and Beautiful*, Oxford: Oxford University Press.

Campany, David (2003) 'Safety in Numbness: Some Problems of "Late Photography"', in Green, David (ed.), *Where if the Photograph?*, Brighton and Maidstone: Photoforum/Photoworks, pp. 123–132.

Cregg, Martin (2009) *The Midlands*, Dublin: Gallery of Photography.

Derrida, Jacques (1998) *Archive Fever: A Freudian Impression*, Chicago: University of Chicago Press.

Edwards, Steve (2006) *Photography: A Very Short Introduction*, Oxford: Oxford University Press.

Farley, Paul and Roberts, Michael (2011) *Edgelands*, London: Jonathan Cape.

Gibbons, Luke (1996) 'Topographies of Terror: Killarney and the Politics of the Sublime', *South Atlantic Quarterly*, 95:1, pp. 23–44.

Gibbons, Luke (2001) '"Subtilized into Savages": Edmund Burke, Progress and Primitivism', *South Atlantic Quarterly*, 100:1, pp. 83–109.

Gibbons, Luke (2006) *Edmund Burke and Ireland: Aesthetics, Politics, and the Colonial Sublime*, Cambridge: Cambridge University Press.

Gibbons, Luke (2010) 'Words upon the Windowpane: Image, Text and Irish Culture', in Elkins, J. (ed.), *Visual Cultures*, Bristol: Intellect, pp. 43–56.

Harvey, David (1989) *The Condition of Postmodernity: An Enquiry into the Origins of Cultural Change*, Oxford: Blackwell.

Haughey, Anthony (1996) *The Edge of Europe*, Dublin: Gallery of Photography.

Jenkins, William (1975) *The New Topographics: Photographs of a Man-Altered Landscape*, New York: International Museum of Photography, George Eastman House.

Keohane, Kieran and Kuhling, Carmen (2004) *Collision Culture: Transformations in Everyday Life in Ireland*, Dublin: Liffey Press.

Lefebvre, Henri (1991) *The Production of Space*, Oxford: Blackwell.

McGrath, Dara (2003) *By the Way*, Dublin: Draíocht Centre for the Arts, Blanchardstown.

McWilliams, David (2006) 'A Warning From Deserted Ghost Estates', available: www.davidmcwilliams.ie/2006/10/01/a-warning-from-deserted-ghost-estates [accessed 8 July 2012].

Mitchell, W. J. T. (1994a) *Picture Theory: Essays on Verbal and Visual Representation*, Chicago: Chicago University Press.

Mitchell, W. J. T. (1994b) 'Imperial Landscape' in Mitchell, W. J. T. (ed.), *Landscape and Power*, Chicago: Chicago University Press.

Mitchell, W. J. T. (2005) *What Do Pictures Want: The Lives and Loves of Images*, Chicago: Chicago University Press.

O'Toole, Fintan (1998) 'The Lie of the Land', in *The Lie of the Land*, Dublin: Gallery of Photography, unpaginated.

Robins, Kevin (1996) *Into the Image: Culture and Politics in the Field of Vision*, London: Routledge.

Runia, Eelco (2010) 'Into Cleanness Leaping: The Vertiginous Urge to Commit History', *History and Theory*, 49, pp. 1–20.

Said, Edward (1994) *Culture and Imperialism*, London: Vintage.

Said, Edward (2003) *Orientalism*, London: Penguin.

Schwartz, Joan and Ryan, James (2003) 'Introduction: Photography and the Geographical Imagination', in Schwartz, Joan and Ryan, James (eds) *Picturing Place: Photography and the Geographical Imagination*, London: I. B. Tauris, pp. 1–18.

Slater, Eamonn (1998a) 'The Lure of Colour', in Slater, Eamonn and Peillon, Michael (eds), *Encounters with Modern Ireland*, Dublin: Institute of Public Administration, pp. 27–36.

Tagg, John (1988) *The Burden of Representation: Essays on Photographies and Histories*, London: Macmillan.

Wollen, Peter (1997) 'Vectors of Melancholy', in Rugoff, Roger (ed.), *The Scene of the Crime*, Cambridge, MA: MIT, pp. 23–36.

8

Immigration and the Celtic Tiger

Bryan Fanning

Introduction

The lack of substantial opposition to, or even sustained political debate about, post-1990s immigration in the Irish case contrasted strongly with what occurred in several other European countries. The Republic of Ireland quickly and quietly transformed from a mono-ethnic nation State, one characterized by historical antipathy towards indigenous minorities such as Jews, Protestants and Travellers, into one with a comparatively large immigrant population (Fanning 2012). The speed with which this occurred owed much to the economic boom. Prosperity fostered the quiet transformation of Ireland but did not on its own explain the lack of political controversy about immigration and the absence of anti-immigrant politics even when boom turned to bust and the large-scale emigration of Irish citizens resumed.

Until the mid-1990s, boom Ireland had a long history of large-scale emigration, punctuated by a few short periods during which some members of the diaspora (former emigrants and descendants of emigrants) returned to live in Ireland. As the economy began to grow rapidly from the mid-1990s it became apparent that, left to themselves, the Irish abroad might not return in sufficient numbers to meet the demands of the Celtic Tiger labour market. The turn of the century witnessed pro active efforts by the Irish State to encourage the return-migration of the 1980s generation of well-educated and highly skilled emigrants. From 1999 to 2002 its Jobs-Ireland programme ran exhibitions in Britain, Europe, Australia, the United States and Newfoundland 'to inform Irish people or people of Irish descent of the employment opportunities in Ireland with a view to encouraging them to return' aimed at cherry-picking the diaspora (Hayward and Howard 2007, p. 50). When this pool became apparently fished out, the Irish State actively fostered immigration as a means of extending the life of the Celtic Tiger:

What began with a clear focus on the skilled Irish expatriates soon moved to include members of the Irish diaspora (particularly in Britain, but also in Europe and North America) then spread to welcome qualified non-nationals from Britain, EU member States, East European States (including Russia), and then English-speaking States (including India). Most immigrants, other than the returning Irish, came from outside the EU. (Hayward and Howard 2007, p. 51)

Between 1995 and 2000 almost a quarter of a million people (248,100) immigrated to Ireland. This amounted to an aggregate figure of 7 per cent of the total population as recorded in the 1996 census. About half were returned Irish emigrants. Some 18 per cent (45,600) came from the United Kingdom, 13 per cent (33,400) came from other EU countries and 7 per cent (16,600) came from the United States. 12 per cent (29,400) came from the rest of the world. From 2000 the inflow of non-Irish migrants exceeded migrants with Irish citizenship or with diaspora ancestry and therefore entitled to Irish citizenship. 18,006 work permits were granted to migrants from non-EU countries in 2000, 36,436 in 2001, 40,321 in 2002, 47,551 in 2003 and 34,067 in 2004.

A 2002 Equality Authority study *Migrant Workers and Their Experiences* provided a snapshot of how immigrant health workers were proactively recruited. Gloria, a Filipina nurse, had responded to a newspaper advert placed on behalf of an Irish recruitment agency. In the course of a day she was interviewed by a Filipino agency, then by an Irish agency and then by a panel of three nursing directors as one of a batch of fifty nurses. Her first interview was at 6.00 am, her second at 6.00 pm. At stage two the Irish agency gave information about the expectations of the hospital and nursing responsibilities. She was shown pictures of the hospital. At stage three, she was told to bring warm clothes because it would be cold in Ireland. Filipino interviewees reported paying recruitment fees of €1,000, the equivalent of one year of salary in the Philippines (Conroy and Brennan 2003). Other case studies examined in this study included migrants from outside the EU who had been trafficked into Ireland and migrants who could not speak English who were badly exploited by Irish employers because they did not have meaningful access to employment rights. A large number of case studies of the exploitation of such migrant workers have been collected by advocacy groups such as the Migrants' Rights Centre Ireland (www.mrci.ie).

When the EU enlarged in 2004, the Irish State decided to permit migrants from the ten new East European member states to live and work in Ireland without visas and in doing so immediately accelerated the pace of immigration. All other pre-2004 EU states except Sweden and the United Kingdom delayed doing so for several years. Between 1 May 2004 and 30 April 2005, some 85,114 workers from the new EU-10 were issued with Irish national insurance numbers. This amounted to more than ten times the number of new work permits admitted to migrants from those countries in the preceding twelve months (National Economic and Social Council 2006, p. 26). The 2006 Irish census identified 610,000 or 14.7 per cent of the total population as having been born outside the State and revealed that about 10 per cent of the population were non-Irish nationals. In Ireland immigrants are often referred to as 'non-nationals', a term that replaced 'alien' in legislation and official discourse. Census data identified a rise in the non-Irish national population from 419,733 in 2006 to 544,357 in 2011. The 2011 census identified 122,585 Poles living in Ireland. Polish had overtaken Irish as the second most commonly spoken language in the state (www.cso.ie).

The politics of immigration

Nobody could have anticipated such demographic change at the beginning of the Celtic Tiger period. Rising numbers of asylum seekers from the late 1990s resulted in the politicization of immigration for the first time in the history of the Irish State. Ireland's response to asylum seekers mirrored the wider EU 'Fortress Europe' one. Asylum seekers invoked rights under UN Conventions to seek refuge from their countries of origin. The barriers raised by receiving countries, including the Republic of Ireland, included not just laws against human trafficking but restrictions on the rights to work and social security. The policy of the Irish State, in effect, was to prevent asylum seekers from becoming embedded in Irish society. The asylum seeker issue was most heavily politicized in the Irish case between 1999 and 2004, by which time the numbers arriving per annum were in decline, owing to the impact of a range of deliberately punitive policies. In 2000 asylum seekers were removed from the mainstream social protection system and most social policy responsibility for them was handed over to the Department of Justice Equality and Law Reform (DJELR), the aim being that asylum seekers would be cordoned off from the rest of the population in terms of where they were required to live and in terms of the economic resources available to them. Because of the common travel area within the European Union, there was something of a race to the bottom in the treatment of asylum seekers whereby countries competed to be the least attractive destination for migrants seeking protections they were entitled to under the UN Convention on the Rights of Refugees.

A second phase of immigration policy followed on from this focus on asylum seekers. It culminated in the 2004 Referendum on Citizenship. It began with a legal challenge to a 1987 High Court interpretation (*Fajouou v. Minister of Justice*) of the Constitution. The 1987 ruling had blocked the deportation of non-citizens who had an Irish citizen child. The ruling had subsequently allowed for the regularization of a significant number of asylum seekers and other immigrants with Irish-born children. A DJELR 'policy decision' was made to begin to refuse leave to remain to asylum seeker families in the knowledge that this would trigger a further test case in the Supreme Court (O'Connell and Smith 2003, p. 25). In April 2002 the 1987 ruling was overturned in the High Court (*Lobe v. Minister of Justice*). On 23 January 2003 the Supreme Court upheld this ruling, in essence holding that the Irish citizen child of non-citizens could be deported with its parents unless the non-citizen parent agreed to be deported without their child. This ruling was effectively superseded by the June 2004 Referendum on Citizenship that removed the existing birthright to citizenship from the Irish-born children of non-citizens. Until 2004, Irish responses to immigration were to a considerable extent dominated by security perspectives, specifically influenced by the expanding remit of the DJELR for asylum policy, 'reception and integration' and 'immigration and naturalisation'.

In this context the near-simultaneous decision to remove visa requirements from the ten EU Accession States, which hugely increased the number of immigrants coming to Ireland, might seem surprising. Ireland had become radically open to immigration, but at the same time made it considerably harder for migrants to become Irish citizens. A neo-liberal approach to immigration, which welcomed migrants able to participate in the labour market and which rejected asylum seekers who were not permitted to work, somehow co-existed with citizenship policies that deepened distinctions between 'nationals' and 'non-nationals'.

Within Irish responses to immigration two sets of rules of belonging might be identified. One has pertained to ethnicity and was institutionalized within citizenship – Irish citizens being predominately white, Catholic and members of the same ethnic group. Eighty per cent of these voted in 2004 to remove the birthright to Irish citizenship from the Irish-born children of immigrants who were not of Irish extraction. The 2004 Referendum was portrayed by the government as a means to achieve 'common-sense citizenship', the idea being that Irish-born children had previously became Irish citizens at birth because of a loophole in the Constitution. The Referendum to some extent pitted 'nationals' against 'non-nationals' by fostering cognitive distinctions between an Irish 'us' and a non-national 'them'.

Yet at the same time, proposals to radically open Ireland to migrants from the new EU States, resulting in perhaps the greatest act of social engineering since the seventeenth-century plantations, provoked little or no political response. To understand why this was the case there is a need to distinguish between cultural and economic phases of nation-building. The former created and shored up ethnic conceptions of Irish identity. But the perception that cultural nationalism singularly failed to secure the economic welfare of Irish people after independence became deeply embedded and produced a new economic nation-building project that was several decades under way before it reached its apotheosis during the years of the Celtic Tiger.

New rules of belonging: why was large-scale immigration accepted?

After independence the dominant sense of what it was to be Irish drew heavily on a nineteenth-century cultural 'revival' that had itself con-stituted a modernization of belonging. Ernest Gellner's prerequisites for nationalism as a basis of social cohesion include mass literacy and school-inculcated culture along with a codification of the past into a national history (Gellner 1987, p. 15). What is referred to as the 'Irish-Ireland' phase of political nation-building persisted for several decades after independence. The Irish Free State became increasingly isolationist. Its education system was preoccupied with the intergenerational repro-duction of culture (Irish language) and religion (the Catholic faith). The postcolonial Ireland influenced by cultural nationalism was protection-ist and isolationist. However, for all that intellectuals such as Daniel Corkery in *The Hidden Ireland* (1925) idealized the Gaelic past as a template for the twentieth century or Eamon de Valera commended a rural frugal life as the ideal Irish one, such cultural nationalism came to be undermined by economic pressures.

Since the Famine in the 1840s, Ireland's population had fallen census after census. That of the whole island fell from 8,175,124 in 1841 to 4,388,107 in 1905. The first census undertaken by the Irish Free State (later the Republic of Ireland) in 1926 found its population to be under three million. Partly as a result of on-going emigration this population continued to fall until the 1950s and remained under three million until the beginning of the1970s. Although Gaelic was the language of cultural and political nationalism, English became the language of the Irish nation State. Linguistic utilitarianism flourished in the wake of the Famine partly because it was necessary for effective emigration. As outlined by Joe Lee:

A certain paradox was involved here. English was allegedly embraced as the reputed language of economic growth. When adequate growth failed to materialise, emigration became the alternative. Once again English was embraced as the reputed language of effective emigration. Thus both economic growth, and lack of economic growth, apparently encouraged the drift to English. (Lee 1989, p. 665)

Independent Ireland had a mostly rural economy that exported cattle and surplus population to England on the same boats. Between 1932 and 1938, de Valera waged and lost an 'economic war' with Britain aimed at breaking Ireland's dependence on the cattle trade and on the importation of manufactured goods. Various protectionist economic policies were tried and abandoned. From the 1950s the 'Irish-Ireland' nation-building project became contested by a developmental national project that both fostered an open economy and emphasized economic and human capital reproduction as utilitarian nation-building goals. Whilst the rhetoric of cultural nationalism persisted, it no longer influenced economic policy. The national interest came to be defined principally in terms of economic growth.

This shift in emphasis has been generally traced to the publication of *Economic Development* (1958), written by T. K. Whitaker, the civil servant in charge of the Department of Finance. The seminal Irish government/OECD report *Investment in Education* (1965) emphasized what Denis O'Sullivan referred to as a new 'mercantile' cultural trajectory (O'Sullivan 2005, pp. 272–274). *Investment in Education* made the case for educational reform to support the economic development objectives. The early developmentalists emphasized the need for individuals to internalize new rules of belonging. In 1964 Garret FitzGerald maintained that *Economic Development* and subsequent attempts at planning 'more than anything' provided a 'psychological basis for economic recovery' in so far as they helped to alter radically the unconscious attitude of many influential people and to make Ireland a growth-orientated community (FitzGerald 1964, p. 250). In influential academic accounts – exemplified by Tom Garvin's *Preventing the Future: Why Was Ireland So Poor for So Long?* – modernizers came to triumph over a history of economic failure, emigration and cultural stagnation (Gavin 2005, p. 170). For critics of these, developmentalism proposed a simplistic and uncritical narrative of progress towards social liberalism, secularism, meritocracy and economic growth. Meritocracy was a taken-for-granted objective in the expansion of education but what occurred within the new machinery of developmental social reproduction was often anything but (O'Sullivan 2005, pp. 272–274).

Investment in Education noted that some 82 per cent of Irish-born UK residents had left school aged fifteen or earlier. Those who emigrated during the 1950s and early 1960s were predominantly young, from agricultural backgrounds and from unskilled or semi-skilled labouring families. Even in the mid-1960s over two-thirds of recent male emigrants became manual workers. During the 1970s return migrants were predominantly aged between thirty and forty-four years. Available evidence suggests that just 28 per cent of male returners were unskilled manual workers (Rothman and O'Connell 2003, p. 53). For those unable to improve their skills abroad emigration was most likely a one-way ticket. Emigration in a sense came to be presented as developmental. It afforded those without the skills needed to find employment in Ireland the opportunity to become eligible for return. As put in 1987 by the then Minister of Foreign Affairs Brian Lenihan:

> We regard emigrants as part of our global generation of Irish people. We should be proud of them. The more they hone their skills and talents in another environment, the more they develop a work ethic in countries like Germany or the U.S, the better it can be applied to Ireland when they return. (cited in McLaughlin 2000, p. 332)

Such accounts, Jim McLaughlin has argued, presented migration as an expression of agency and enterprise, 'conceptualising the "new wave" emigrant as a geographically mobile *homo economicus* logically moving between one labour market and the other, the embodiment of an Irish enterprise culture'. What McLaughlin called the radical openness of Irish society became a two-way street whereby both large-scale emigration and large-scale immigration could be simultaneously presented as in the national economic interest. Within policy documents and popular discourse the same developmental rules of belonging came to be applied to both immigrants and emigrants as Ireland became radically open to migration in both directions. These emphasized human capital and utilitarian criteria, such as being able to speak English, rather than ethnicity or culture. Such forms of cultural capital are, in many respects, transnational, the product of generic processes of social modernization that can be seen to contribute a globalization of education and skills. From this perspective, Ireland's experience of high immigration during the Celtic Tiger era needs to be located within the globalization of education and labour markets.

McLaughlin's analysis emphasized the influence of neo-liberalism. Analyses of Irish social partnership – the compact between trade unions, the State and the private sector – have emphasized the emergence of a shared competitive corporatist agenda that came to endorse strategies aimed at promoting economic growth above other goals (Rhodes 1997,

p. 208; Fanning 2009, p. 143). A sociological analysis might emphasize changes in what Pierre Bourdieu (1985) calls cultural capital – the habits, attributes and dispositions that work to the advantage of individuals in specific social situations. Somewhat similarly Amartya Sen emphasizes the role of capabilities – the cognitive skills and forms of knowledge that enable individuals to flourish in particular social and economic contexts. From such perspectives some well-educated migrants who spoke English and who had acquired norms that would work in their favour in many Western countries could be seen to have advantages over some marginal members of the host society (Fanning 2011, pp. 3–14).

A 7 July 2005 interview in the *Irish Independent* quoted the chief executive of Oracle. one of the largest high-tech American multinationals in Ireland, who quipped that that Celtic Tiger prosperity and immigration went 'hand in paw'. Oracle reported $600 million profits in Ireland in 2004 and sales out of Ireland of $2.45 billion between May 2004 and May 2005. It employed around 920 people in North Dublin. Just 55 per cent of them were Irish, with 32 per cent from the rest of the EU and 12 per cent non-EU citizens. The non-EU proportion of the workforce was reported as growing rapidly. The focus of the interview was on the need to recruit migrant workers with skills that were in short supply in Ireland. This business case for immigration was accepted by other social partners, including the trade unions. In 2006 the National Economic and Social Council (NESC), the social partnership think tank, published a cost-benefit analysis of immigration prepared on its behalf by the International Organisation on Migration (IOM). *Managing Migration in Ireland: A Social and Economic Analysis* was primarily focused on labour market policy. The report strongly advocated on-going immigration as a means of sustaining economic growth: 'Immigration has been an important element in the economic and social development of Ireland … That migrant labour helped fuel and support the Celtic Tiger is indisputable' (NESC 2006, p. 6). Immigration was not the cause of the Irish economic miracle, but it can help to sustain the Celtic Tiger's economic growth. As Ireland grapples with the 'problem' of managing migration on its journey to an uncertain destination, it is important to remember that immigration reflects Irish prosperity. Despite the problems associated with managing immigration and integration, there are likely few Irish who would want to go back to the 'old days' in which emigration rather than immigration was the dominant theme (NESC 2006, p. 94).

Managing Migration argued that from the 1960s and 1970s government policies concerning trade liberalization and foreign direct investment began to improve the domestic economic situation and hence, eventually, reversed the net loss of population due to migration. Weak economic performance during the 1980s was accompanied by a net outflow of migrants, a trend that was reversed in the mid-to-late 1990s. Economic growth during the 1990s saw the rapid expansion of the labour force from about 1.4 million in 1994 to just over 2 million in 2005. This increased labour demand was met initially by Irish nationals who had been previously unemployed or outside the labour market, then by returning Irish migrants and, as these reduced as a proportion of in-migration, by non-Irish migrants; by 2004 Irish returners constituted less than 25 per cent of total immigrants. *Managing Migration* claimed that on-going immigration was likely to make Irish society more resilient and adaptive:

> With Irish growth rates and employment projected in the near future to follow the impressive trend set during the last decade, migration will certainly remain a key feature allowing the labour market to react to changes in demand and further boosting Irish competitiveness. As such, Irish unemployment is expected to remain low, especially compared to other EU countries. This will be a significant advantage to Ireland in the expanded European Union. (NESC 2006, p. 93).

In effect, the report endorsed large-scale immigration whilst suggesting that 'in the unlikely event of economic downturn' immigration levels could be controlled. However the kind of measures suggested (limiting work visas to areas of labour market shortage) could only ever apply to non-EU migrants (NESC 2006, p. xx). With respect to these, *Managing Migration* endorsed selection criteria based on education levels and skills. The report argued that following the example of Canada and Australia in setting language and educational criteria for admission would result in significantly improved integration outcomes. Immigrants would be expected to 'invest' in these factors prior to applying for entry. This would 'shift the burdens of settlement (i.e. the cost of public and private integration programmes) from the host country back to the would-be-immigrants, and shifts the locus of adjustment from the country of destination back to the country of origin' (NESC 2006, p. 14). In essence it was proposed to accept, where possible, only those migrants with the capabilities to adhere to developmental criteria.

Such responses to immigration expressed an institutional elite consensus (NESC was the policy organization of social partnership) that defined the national interest primarily in terms of economic growth. The politicians and economists on Irish radio programmes who dominated debates on social policy sometimes referred to the Republic of Ireland as 'Ireland PLC'. In this context debates on immigration and on the integration of immigrants focused mostly on the economy. In effect a migrant was deemed to be integrated if she was in paid employment.

But the same presumption held for Irish citizens. The expectation that those who became displaced from the economy should consider emigration applied to Irish citizens as much as to immigrants. Debates on the cultural implications of immigration attracted little interest outside academic and NGO circles. In Ireland culture, however defined, had long become relegated to the private sphere, and the economy had in effect become the public sphere.

Legacies and challenges

Perhaps the most transformative effect of the Celtic Tiger on Irish society has been how it fostered large-scale immigration. Expectations that the numbers of migrants living in Ireland would decline in the wake of the post-boom economic crisis were confounded by the results of the 2011 census. The population who arrived during the economic boom were better educated than the host population. Comparative data for 2001 on migrants living in Ireland at the time (of whom asylum seekers were a considerable proportion) found that just one OECD country (Canada) had a higher percentage of migrants with third-level qualifications (OECD 2007; Figure 5). An analysis of 2006 census data for Dublin found that migrants had increased overall educational levels in all electoral areas (Figure 6). In 2008 the labour force participation rate for immigrant adults was in excess of 90 per cent compared to 65 per

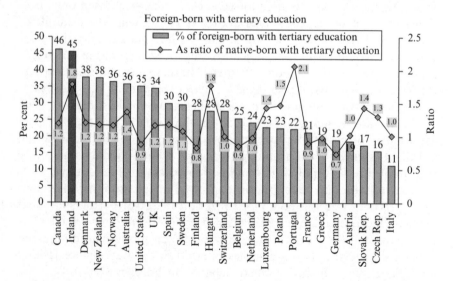

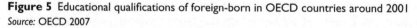

Figure 5 Educational qualifications of foreign-born in OECD countries around 2001
Source: OECD 2007

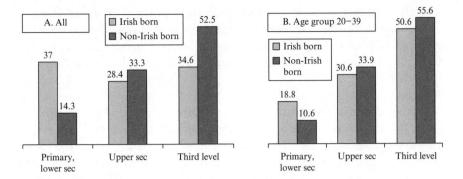

Figure 6 Educational profile of Irish/UK and non-Irish/UK born, Dublin 2006
Source: 2006 Census of Population 5% Sample of Anonymised Records (COPSAR); Source Fahey and Fanning (2010)

cent for the indigenous adult population (Government of Ireland 2008, p. 8). Yet, analyses of how migrants have fared in the Irish job market during the economic boom identified a tendency for migrants to obtain lower wages than similarly qualified members of the host population and disproportionately high rates of unemployment amongst black emigrants (Barrett, McGuinness and O'Brien 2008). Explanations have emphasized racism in the case of black immigrants who at the height of the boom were several times more likely to be unemployed than white people living in Ireland (O'Connell and McGinnity 2008).

There has been little concerted effort by the Irish State to promote the integration of immigrants. Following the 2007 general election, the Fianna Fáil and Green Party coalition government appointed a Minister of State for Integration policy. The first post-holder, Conor Lenihan (son of the aforementioned Brian Lenihan and brother of another government minister also named Brian Lenihan), exercised his brief with a considerable degree of apparent gusto, despite the lack of real government commitment, that later became clear, to the implementation of integration policies. In 2008 he launched a report, *Migration Nation*, outlining the government's integration vision. The report stated that Ireland had experienced large-scale immigration because of the strategy of developmental modernization that had been followed since the 1960s (Government of Ireland 2008, p. 8). Soon after the report came out Lenihan moved on to another government post. His two successors before the 2011 election introduced no further initiatives and the Office of the Minister of State for Integration was, in effect, wound down. Irish approaches to the integration of immigrants can be best summarized as benign neglect. But a thin conception of integration has also applied to Irish citizens. *Migration Nation* drew heavily on EU common basic principles of integration that emphasized economic participation and being able to speak the host country language. In the Irish case this meant that migrants would be expected to learn English, though no concrete measures to ensure this were set out in *Migration Nation*.

In this context the most crucial measure of integration is citizenship. Most of Ireland's immigrant population have by now lived in the country for several years. Sometimes these are referred to as the 'new Irish', but, given the cognitive and constitutional distinctions that exist between 'nationals' and non-Irish citizens, and given that only citizens can vote in general elections, change laws and alter the constitution, there is a case for making an analytical distinction between immigrants who have become Irish citizens and those who have not. The former, a relatively small but growing number, are empirically Irish – it says so on their passports. These mostly originate from countries outside the EU. The reason for this is that citizens of EU countries enjoy reciprocal rights to employment, social security benefits, rights to third-level education and free movement and therefore are less motivated to naturalize than migrants from outside the EU whose status in Ireland has often been more precarious. In the run up to the 2011 general election just 35,000 immigrants were entitled to vote.

It is a matter of huge concern that most of Ireland's immigrant population (544,347 in 2011) are not likely to become Irish citizens. More than ten per cent of the total population are likely to remain excluded from political representation and there will be little impetus to listen to or respond to their concerns. In recent years NGOs have campaigned to remove institutional barriers to the naturalization of immigrants who had applied for Irish citizenship. In 2009 an estimated 47 per cent of applications for citizenship were turned down when equivalent rates of refusal in the United Kingdom and Australia for the same period were just 9 per cent and in Canada just 3 per cent. There are indications that the Irish State has adopted a more proactive naturalization policy since the 2011 election. This has included the introduction of citizenship ceremonies, where more than twenty thousand new citizens were sworn in during 2012. Those who participated have chosen to be part of a society rather than just an economy.

During the Celtic Tiger era it was presumed that the integration of immigrants would be handled by the labour market. But a similar presumption applied to other members of Irish society. In Celtic Tiger Ireland the market was depicted as the main means of promoting social inclusion and social cohesion. Post-Celtic Tiger Ireland has seen the return of large-scale emigration and some return migration by migrants who were also displaced from the economy. If anything, the primacy of market rules of belonging – the presumption that to be part of Irish society one must be part of the Irish economy – became more apparent during the post-Celtic Tiger economic crisis. In this new social and economic context there seems to be little appetite for integration policies aimed at promoting social cohesion in a multi-ethnic Ireland. However, this is in keeping with the lack of emphasis on promoting social cohesion and social inclusion for the population as a whole. Immigrants who found themselves displaced from Ireland during the economic crash found themselves on the same boats and planes as Irish citizens displaced through unemployment from Ireland PLC. Immigrants who managed to remain in employment are, according to the prevailing implicit definitions, as integrated or socially included as any other such fortunate members of Irish society.

Works cited

Barrett, Alan, McGuinness, Seamus and O'Brien, Martin (2008) 'The Immigrant Earnings Disadvantage across the Earnings and Skills Distributions: The Case of Immigrants from the EU's New Member States in Ireland', *Working Paper No 236*, Dublin: Economic and Social Research Institute.

Bourdieu, Pierre (1985) 'The Social Space and the Genesis of Groups', *Theory and Society*, 14:6, pp. 723–744.

Conroy, Pauline and Brennan, Aoife (2003) *Migrant Workers and Their Experiences*, Dublin: Equality Authority.

Corkery, Daniel (1970) *The Hidden Ireland: A Study of Gaelic Munster in the Eighteenth Century*, Dublin: Gill and Macmillan.

Fahey, Tony and Fanning, Bryan (2010) 'Immigration and Socio-Spatial Segregation in Dublin, 1996–2006', *Urban Studies*, 47:8, pp.1625–1642.

Fanning, Bryan (2008), *The Quest for Modern Ireland: The Battle of Ideas 1912–1986*, Dublin: Irish Academic Press.

Fanning, Bryan (2009) *New Guests of the Irish Nation*, Dublin: Irish Academic Press.

Fanning, Bryan (2011) *Immigration and Social Cohesion in the Republic of Ireland*, Manchester: Manchester University Press.

Fanning, Bryan (2012) *Racism and Social Change in the Republic of Ireland* 2nd edition, Manchester: Manchester University Press.

FitzGerald, Garret (1964) 'Second Programme for Economic Expansion: Reflections', *Studies*, 53:211, pp. 233–252.

Garvin, Tom (2005) *Preventing the Future: Why Was Ireland So Poor for So Long?* Dublin: Gill and Macmillan.

Gellner, Ernest (1987) *Culture, Identity and Politics*, Cambridge: Cambridge University, Press.

Giddens, Anthony (1993) *The Transformation of Intimacy*, Cambridge: Polity.

Government of Ireland (1958) *Economic Development*, Dublin: Stationery Office.

Government of Ireland (1965) *Investment in Education*, Dublin: Stationery Office/OECD.

Government of Ireland (2008), *Migration Nation: Statement on Integration Strategy and Diversity Management*, Dublin: Stationery Office.

Hayward K. and Howard K. (2007) 'Cherry-Picking the Diaspora' in Fanning Bryan, (ed.), *Immigration and Social Change in the Republic of Ireland*, Manchester: Manchester University Press.

Lee, Joseph (1989) *Ireland 1912–1986*, Cambridge: Cambridge University Press.

McLaughlin, Jim (2000) 'Changing Attitudes to "New Wave" Emigration', in Bielenberg, A. (ed.), *The Irish Diaspora*, Harlow: Pearson, pp. 317–330.

National Economic and Social Council (2006) *Managing Migration in Ireland: A Social and Economic Analysis*, Dublin: Stationery Office.

O'Connell, Donncha and Smith, Ciara (2003), 'Citizenship and the Irish Constitution', in Fraser, Ursula and Harvey, Colin (eds), *Sanctuary in Ireland: Perspectives on Asylum Law and Policy*, Dublin: Institute of Public Administration.

O'Connell, Phillip and McGinnity, Frances (2008) *Immigrants at Work: Ethnicity and Nationality in the Irish Labour Market* Dublin: ESRI.

OECD (2007) *International Migration Outlook*, Paris: OECD.

O'Sullivan, Denis (2005) *Cultural Politics and Irish Education since the 1950's: Policies, Paradigms and Power*, Dublin: Institute of Public Administration.

Rhodes, Martin (1997) 'Globalization, Labour Markets and Welfare States: A Future of "Competitive Corporatism"?' *EUO Working Papers, RSC 97/36*, Florence: European University Institute.

Rottman, David and O'Connell, Phillip (2003) 'The Changing Social Structure' in Fanning, Bryan and McNamara, Tony (eds), *Ireland Develops: Administration and Social Policy 1953–2003*, Dublin: Institute of Public Administration, pp. 36–59.

Sen, Amartya (1993) 'Capability and Well-being', in Nussbaum, Martha and Sen, Amartya (eds), *The Quality of Life*, Oxford: Clarendon Press, pp. 30–53.

9

'What rough beast'? Monsters of post-Celtic Tiger Ireland

Kieran Keohane and Carmen Kuhling

What rough beast is coming in the wake of the death of the Celtic Tiger? Our hypothesis, formulated in the spirit of Yeats and Joyce, sees repetition and reiteration: that what will appear to us in the guise of the new is better understood in terms of recurrence.[1] For Joyce and for Yeats, recurrence represents a philosophy of history, taken from the Greeks through Vico (1999) and Nietzsche (1995), attuned and oriented to the politics of the present. For Yeats (1920a), recurrence is represented in 'The Second Coming' by the figure of the spiral gyre: recurring cycles of history marked by moments of dissolution of order, liminality and the imposition of a new order. Modernity sees the acceleration, intensification and apotheosis of cycles of historical recurrence. 'What rough beast', Yeats asks, emerges from this civilization at the moment of its apotheosis and simultaneous decadence (Yeats 1920a, pp. 10–11)? 'We

---

[1] The voyage of Ulysses in Homer is re lived in the mundane everyday world of his modern hero Leopold Bloom, and in *Finnegans Wake* the history of the world is enfolded in the recurring themes of his protagonist's dreamwork. The Finnegans, Humphrey Chimpden Earwicker ('Here Comes Everybody'), Anna Livia Plurabelle, Shem and Shaun, metempsychotically assume the forms of figures from myth, religion and 'real' history, as well as anthropomorphically personifying rivers and landscape, time, space and number, and they reiterate and play out the great themes of human history – conflict, the Fall, redemption all the while retaining their mundane identities as ordinary people. In the portmanteau words of *Finnegans Wake* 'the signifier "stuffs" [garnishes, overdetermines] the signified' (Lacan 1998, p. 37): the spirit of one word enters another, as does the spirit of one situation, or of one being. The doubling, punning movement of lives, histories, thoughts, actions, overlapping, intersecting, crossing over into one another, reflect the recursive movement of history – history as recurrence, repetition, rather than linear progress. For Joyce 'All forms proceed by incessant doublings and undoublings in which they remain enantiomorphous – that is, resembling each other but not superposable. This gives the world a wholeness that is not characterized by unity, but by adhesiveness' (Ellmann 1977, p. 95).

are legion' is the demon's answer. The rough beast has many different countenances: cold, egotistical calculation; the conduct of business without regard for persons; an 'iron cage' of rationalized acquisitiveness are faces that Max Weber sees (Weber 1958, p. 181); Karl Marx and Friedrich Engels describe it as 'naked, shameless, direct, brutal exploitation' (Marx and Engels 1985, p. 16); Emile Durkheim calls it a cult of egotistical individualism, amoral and self-destructive (Durkheim 1966, p. 209); while in the words of Adorno and Horkheimer further aspects of the beast involve stupefied 'mass consumers' deceived and manipulated by the 'culture industry'; and 'authoritarian personalities' looking to the strong master (Adorno and Horkheimer 1992 p. 120). The purportedly 'objective and self-regulating laws of the market', and the 'value-neutral' 'science' of economics; the 'fact' that 'there is no alternative' to a society organized on neo-liberal market principles are the beast's countenance in the current post-national, post-political, seemingly leaderless era.

Plutonomy and precariat

On the eve of the global financial crisis, researchers at the global banking giant Citigroup published an investment strategy report exploring opportunities associated with what they identified as the emerging 'plutonomy (Kapur, Macleod and Singh 2005). Plutonomy refers to the sector of the economy that produces goods and services for the super-wealthy – off-shore banking and wealth management services, luxury yachts, jets, private islands and similar real estate, supercars, bespoke jewellery and the like, consumer goods for a new caste of global billionaires. As the world divides more and more into the super-wealthy and the very poor, Citigroup identifies stock in the businesses servicing the plutonomy as an investment opportunity which would be relatively safe even in the event of recession in the wider economy. The USA and Canada, Australia, the UK and Italy are already plutonomies, according to the Citigroup report, and the trend has been accelerating. Until recently some Irish were – or imagined themselves to be – amongst the number of the global plutonomy, and some still are, even as the present crisis continues. National economies are thrown into deep recession, businesses go under, millions of people are unemployed, lose their homes, fall into poverty, but the plutonomy is still doing very well. Forbes 'Rich List' 2011 lists a 10 per cent rise in the number of billionaires since 2008, with their net worth rising quickly and steadily.

The etymology of the term 'plutonomy' is significant. Pluto (Hades) is the original Dark Lord: god of the underworld and god of wealth (from jewels and precious metals buried in the earth), prior to that wealth stored underground, and prior to that again Pluto represents the chthonic power of dark soil. He is also the god of the interior of the body, the bowels and the viscera, and thereby of consumption, of devouring, digesting and defecation. Pluto's voracious economy of consumption frequently gives him gas – bubbles, gaseous emissions that issued from caves and crevases that the Greeks identified as the gates of hell, and Pluto's breath has the sulphurous stench of flatus and corruption (Jones 1974).

Pluto abducts Persephone (Prosperina, from *prosperene* –'to emerge'), daughter of Demeter/Ceres. When she learns that Zeus was complicit in the rape of Persephone, Demeter (goddess of agriculture, bread, i.e. human food and life – sustaining resources – goddess of marriage, laws (stability) and the afterlife – continuity) leaves Olympus and refuses to enable growth. The world falls into darkness and Zeus becomes fearful that the world will be destroyed. He intervenes with Demeter, but she refuses to co-operate until Persephone is restored. Zeus sends Hermes to intercede with Pluto, but Prosperina has already tasted the fruit of Hades and she will die if she leaves. So a compromise is reached: Proserpina's time is divided between Pluto in the underworld and life with Demeter in the world, giving the corresponding seasons and cycles of autumn (scarcity and recession), winter (poverty and darkness), spring (recovery and growth), summer (prosperity and happiness). This is a mythic formula for a balanced and sustainable cosmopoiesis, but in a plutonomy, Pluto takes possession of Proserpina, holds her captive and the world becomes conflicted and falls towards darkness and death.

Plutonomy is a fusion of wealth and power and property wherein Pluto has an unfair share of Prosperina, as is the case in the concentrations of wealth and power in the emerging form of the neo-liberal post-democratic, re-privatized 'corporate republic'. While retaining some semblance of national democratic republican government, a corporate republic would be run primarily like a business, involving a board of directors and executives, as Greece, Italy and Ireland are currently managed and overseen by financial technocrats and former executives of Goldman-Sachs and similar banks. Utilities, including hospitals, schools, the army, the police force would be privatized, and the social welfare functions carried out by the State are instead carried out by corporations in the form of benefits to employees and 'stakeholders'. These patterns are now well established in the Anglo-American plutonomy especially and in other Western societies, including Ireland.

Recurrence of a dark age

The second coming of the rough beast means a recurrence of a social form resembling feudalism in terms of the eclipse of the sovereign democratic republican nation State by transnational institutions such as multinational corporations, banks and private hedge funds, the IMF, and technocratic bureaucratic matrices of power/knowledge and regimes of governmentality. These are the new sovereign powers that command and dictate; panoptic disciplinary surveillance mechanisms, managerial and auditing practices permeating the capillaries of social relations; powers that are subjectivized, internalized, that 'we bring to bear on ourselves as we have become part of its mechanism' (Foucault 1991, p. 217). We have come again to resemble, in many important respects, the serfs of the feudal dark ages, fully 'possessed' in the literal as well as figurative sense by the powers of the plutocracy. We are a new precariat, on our knees (precarious – from *pre care* 'to pray'), knuckling down, paying up, rendering ourselves to the Dark Lord of the markets. Like the bondsmen of earlier epochs the precariat are praying in two senses: 'on our knees', begging, powerless and pleading; 'without a prayer'; but also in awe, dumbstruck, humble, worshipping in the cult of the market and the celebrity entrepreneur.

Monsters of the Irish political unconscious

'He who fights with monsters should take care lest he become a monster', Nietzsche (Nietzsche 1989, p. 89) cautions us, and the history of Ireland is one of fighting with monsters and, in the process, becoming monsters ourselves. The name Bram Stoker gave to his vampire, 'Dracula', is an Irish name: '*droch fholla*' which translates as 'bad' (*droch*) 'blood' (*fholla*) – as in the usage *tá drochfholla idir a chéile* 'there is bad blood between them', meaning a grudge, ill-feeling, a poisoned relationship. *Drochfholla* – Dracula – is a condensed metaphor for Anglo-Irish relations in the nineteenth century; bad blood that courses through the veins and capillaries of a corrupt and corrupting Irish body politic. In this interminable stasis the collective Irish social body is preyed on by new generations of bloodsucking parasites in a never-ending repetition of the past.

The Count, the embodiment of this morbid condition, is the un-dead vestige of a remote past, descended from a once noble landed feudal lineage, but now decadent and corrupted. And not only do the un-dead aristocracy linger on, especially in the colonies, in places like nineteenth-century Ireland, but those who fight them, the modern bourgeoisie and bearers of Enlightenment, reason and reform, become in turn blood-sucking monsters themselves. Count Dracula's estate is in Transylvania, at the edge of Enlightened Europe and the traditional orient, Christianity and Islam. This is an analogue of Ireland's place in the symbolic order and imaginative structure of the British imperium: backward, dark, Catholic, still ruled by a landed gentry that the peasants hold in awe and in dread. Castle Dracula is not an eastern outpost of European civilization in Transylvania, but on its western frontier, in the wilds of Ireland. During the land-wars of the latter half of the nineteenth century, English landlords in Ireland moved from their Georgian country houses to neo-gothic medieval castles, built for security, complete with moat and bailey, defensive towers and battlements.

Count Dracula, and the Anglo-Irish lords of the nineteenth century (and most recently non-residential cosmopolitan tax exiles, international bondholders of Anglo-Irish debts to global banks and hedge-funds), are absentee landlords, who have moved to London, or to the Cayman Islands, but to sustain themselves there, they need the earth of the old estates, the bonded labour and the life-blood of their serfs. In the context of modern urban democratic society, the hereditary landed gentry are a dark and ambiguous presence, provoking ambivalent feelings of respect and repugnance. The Anglo-Irish gentry in London are like the Count; ambiguously civil and bestial. A shapeshifter, Count Dracula morphs from a powerful nobleman to an effeminate dandy, from a cultured cosmopolitan gentleman to a wolf, a rat, a lizard, a bat, a leech. Harker, the young English lawyer, perceives the Count with a mixture of awe and disgust:

> There he lay looking as if youth had been half-renewed, for the white hair and moustache were changed to dark iron grey; the cheeks were fuller, and the white skin seemed ruby red underneath; the mouth was redder than ever, for on the lips were gouts of fresh blood, which trickled from the corners of the mouth and ran over the chin and neck. Even the deep, burning eyes seemed set amongst swollen flesh, for the lids and pouches underneath were bloated. It seemed as if the whole awful creature were simply gorged with blood; he lay like a filthy leech, exhausted with his repletion. (Stoker 1993, p. 44)

The heroic lawyers of the Home Rule movement had fought this monster, but just as it seemed exhausted and about to pass away, like Count Dracula the Anglo-Irish landlords kept rejuvenating and coming back to life. To kill the monster, just as with Dracula, Enlightened reason would have to become alloyed with mysticism, passion and violence, and the vampire slayers would risk becoming monsters themselves.

Paddy the vampire slayer

The most fateful vampire slayer awakened during this period of cultural renaissance is Patrick Pearse, leader of the 1916 Rising and author of the Proclamation of the Irish Republic; the urbane and somewhat effeminate schoolteacher who, like Mina, a victim of the vampire as well as a vampire slayer, becomes a bloodthirsty monster. Pearse knows that to kill the monster he has to enlist the forces of the underworld, he has to raise the dead. In his necromantic oration at the graveside of O'Donovan-Rossa he says that while it seems as though the Imperial monster has won 'Life springs from death; and from the graves of patriot men and women spring living nations' (Pearse 1916, pp. 136–137). Thus Pearse calls back to life an Irish un-dead, bathed in blood, indestructible, through an unholy, violent revolutionary power, ritually sanctified by Pearse's articulation of the Easter Rising with Christ's Resurrection. But though these men of death and resurrection have the power to kill the vampire, Pearse has repeated the curse. 'A terrible beauty is born', Yeats (1920b) observes of Easter 1916, predicting that his own caste would be slain by this new generation. Pearse's un-dead men carry on, even when their work is done, and twentieth-century Ireland lived in the shadow of the gunman. And 'they haven't gone away you know!'

Metempsychosis of the gombeen man

But the gunman is not the only shadowy figure haunting modern Ireland. A much more insidious fiend is the 'gombeen man':

> A gombeen man is a man that linds you a few shillin's or a few pounds whin ye want it bad and then nivir laves ye till he has tuk all ye've got – yer land an' yer shanty an' yer holdin' an' yer money an' yer craps; an' he would take the blood out of yer body if he could sell it or use it anyhow. (Joyce 1994, p. 344)

These bloodsuckers are the members of a new native Irish class of 'strong farmers', shopkeepers and publicans: land-grabbers and opportunists who fattened on evictions and emigration, paying tenants' rents over their heads and appropriating their holdings; profiteers who made their fortunes as middle men, hoarding food and grain during famine; publicans who set up shop adjacent to Public Works and Relief projects, as payment stations *cum* shebeens and taverns, to relieve the destitute of their relief. The gombeen man – from *gambín* (Ir.) interest on a loan, from Middle English *cambie* – exchange, barter, from Latin *cambium* – is a village usurer, a native Irish petty bourgeois publican, merchant or estate agent: who, during the course of the nineteenth century these became the main supporters of the Home Rule movement. The Irish Labour organizer James Connolly participated in Pearse's 1916 Rising, though he was aware that the vampire was no longer British but had already assumed new forms:

> those leeches who, as gombeen men, middlemen and dealers of one kind or another in the small country town, sucked the life-blood of the agricultural population around them. Anyone acquainted with rural Ireland knows that, next to the merciless grinding by the landlord the tenantry suffers most from the ruthless exploitation of the classes just mentioned, and that, indeed, the buying out of the landlords in many cases served only to gorge still further the ever rapacious maw of those parasites upon rural life. But whereas the landlords were ever regarded in Ireland as alien to Irish life, the gombeen men and their kind, from their position in the country towns, their ostentatious parade of religion and their loud-mouthed assertions of patriotism, were usually the dominant influences in the councils of the local Home Rule or other constitutional nationalist organization. (Connolly, in Metscher 2002, pp. 256–257)

Stoker's character Renfield is representative of this incarnation of the rough beast. Renfield is diagnosed by Dr Seward as a 'zoophagous [life-eating] maniac'. He is in the service of the Count, his representative, as the estate agent – the forerunner of the modern Irish gombeen politician – businessman or accountant is in the service of the landlord. Renfield collects flies, which he feeds to spiders, which in turn he feeds to birds, which he then devours. He would like to have a cat to eat. What he really aspires to, of course, is to become a vampire himself! Renfield represents the avaricious desire of the new Irish indicted by Yeats, who 'fumble in a greasy till / and add the ha'pence to the pence / and prayer to shivering prayer / 'til you have dried the marrow from the bone' (Yeats 1916, pp. 33–34).

The gombeen man is the obscene body of the post colonial, post-Catholic, post-Nationalist, post-democratic-republican Irish who have ruled for the twentieth century; a swarming horde of native, local vampires; they are un-dead and they continue to feed. Corruption of the body politic is their symptom. Exposed to sunlight after lengthy court tribunals, and caught momentarily in the glare of grave crisis when the social body on which they have been gorging collapses into terminal debt, they slink away from public life, withdrawing to their crypts and vaults, only to re-emerge as 'independent candidates', 'special advisers' 'financial consultants' and 'board members' of new bodies politic. There they fasten their fangs again. Absentee proprietors, developers and speculators, they live an extra-corporal existence; disembodied, de-territorialized, transnational, they avoid what is otherwise unavoidable for mortals – death and taxes. Like Renfield they serve mysterious foreign masters – the shareholders of multinational corporations that use Ireland as a tax-minimizing profit siphon, sucking the fiscal life blood from the European social body; 'senior bondholders' of Ireland's private banking and sovereign debts; the IMF and ECB, and similar incarnations of the Dark Lord of the markets.

Ireland's night of the living dead

Marx famously described capital as 'dead labour which, vampire-like, lives only by sucking living labour, and lives the more, the more labour it sucks' (Marx 1992, p. 342). As Shaviro says, 'The nineteenth century, with its classic régime of industrial capitalism, was the age of the vampire, but the network society of the late twentieth and twenty-first centuries is rather characterised by a plague of zombies' (Shaviro 2002, p. 281). But vampires and zombies are mutually interdependent, for, as Shivaro notes, no predator or parasite can survive in the absence of prey, so vampire-capital can extract its surplus only by organizing its legions of zombie-labour. The zombie is the proletarian subject of the dawn of the dead as the age of global total capitalism. As Deleuze and Guattari put it, 'the only modern myth is the myth of zombies – mortified schizos, good for work' (Deleuze and Guittari 1983, p. 335).

It is now a common view that post-Celtic Tiger Ireland is a haunted landscape of ghost estates and zombie banks cannibalizing the State (Kirby 2010), but to see the full horror as Ireland's night of the living dead unfolds it is important to understand the cultural slippage around the figure of the zombie. In anthropology and in medicine, the zombie is both 'real' and 'imaginary'. The zombie is a liminal figure, suspended between life and death, between Western popular culture and non-Western lore and magic.

The zombie is a figure from the belief system of Haitian voudou, the blend of spiritualisms and rituals of the many different peoples who were uprooted from Africa and imported to Hispaniola during the slave trade. Under slavery, African culture and religion was suppressed, religious beliefs and practices were fragmented and recombined and Roman Catholicism was mixed into the rituals to disguise their 'pagan' religion from their masters who had forbidden them to practise it. From this complex mixture of African tribal and Christian religious ideas and practices emerged the creolized symbolic and imaginative structure that is Haitian voudou (Inglis 2011, p. 354). Medical practitioners in Haiti regard zombification as the consequence of poisoning, Christian clergy see it as the product of sorcery, while voudou sorcerors (*boku*) tend not to share their esoteric knowledge with anthropologists, or indeed with anyone. According to the folklore, a person becomes ill, then appears to be dead and is placed in a tomb, and is then 'stolen' by a *boku* 'and secretly returned to life and activity but not to full awareness and agency' (Littlewood and Douyon 1997, p. 1094). In zombification the victim's agency is extracted by the *boku* who retains this life force in a bottle or jar. The animated body remains without will or consciousness and becomes the slave of the *boku*, subdued by chaining, beating, poisoning and sorcery, and works secretly on his land or is sold to another *boko* (Littlewood and Douyon 1997, p. 1094). Thus, the figure of the dehumanized zombie whose will or agency has been stolen by a sorcerer is a Haitian collective representation of former slaves' fears of a return to the horrors of slavery. The Haitian fear is not of zombies, it is of *zombification*, of being turned into a zombie, a fearful nightmare the imaginative structure of which is rooted in the real experience of the brutal conditions of the lives of plantation slaves during the colonial period. The Haitian fear of zombies then is rather about "the body-snatcher" – the zombie master – who takes the living person and destroys their soul, making a living but mentally and emotionally dead being who obeys his will' (Inglis 2011, p. 354). Thus, the figure of the zombie represents the fear of history repeating itself, of a return to enslavement by an imperial master.

At the same time as the Young Irelanders were plotting their rebellion in 1798, and perhaps in part inspired by it, Haiti was already the first colony to become a republic, thanks to the revolution of former slaves who overthrew their French masters. Leaders of the Haitain revolts in 1791 were Boukman Dutty, a voudou priest, and Cecile Fatiman, a mulatto *mambo*, a voudou priestess. Their voudou ceremony that inaugurated the revolution combined animal sacrifice, a pact of blood brotherhood amongst the rebels, invocation of various divinities, all articulated with the Enlightenment principles of the American and French Revolutions.

Haiti was very much a social political anomaly and an object of wonder to nineteenth-century Europe (Inglis 2011, p. 356). But as the early idealism of the revolution degenerated into rivalry amongst the revolutionary leaders mirroring the Terror in France, combined with the machinations of global powers of France, England and Spain as they vied for hegemony, Western observers began to look at Haiti not with admiration but with disgust, and with deep ambivalence, for Haiti was a mirror for the failure of Western modernity to fulfil its own promises of

Enlightenment: reason and democracy; liberty, equality and fraternity. At the heart of the degeneration of Haiti however, was not the 'pact with the Devil' as the French plantation owners liked to portray the origins of the Revolution in voudou and the mysterious 'blood ceremony' held in the *Bois Caiman*, but a 'pact with the devil' in the form of French banks. Under threat of political and economic isolation, backed up by the sanction of massive military intervention, Haiti was forced to pay reparations of 150 million francs (equivalent to €100 billion today) to absentee former plantation and slave owners in France. This burden of debt purportedly owed by Haitians to senior bondholders in France bankrupted the nascent republic and effectively mortgaged the future generations of Haiti in perpetuity. Anyone who wishes to imagine what state the former Republic of Ireland will be in one hundred years from now may have much to learn from the state of Haiti today.

Zombie precarity and vampire plutonomy

In 2010, the Irish government negotiated the IMF–EU bail-out and rec- ommended a four-year National Recovery plan and a programmes of 'austerity budgets' which make huge cuts in social welfare rather than taxing the richest 1 per cent of the population who own 34 per cent of the national wealth, or the wealthiest 7 per cent of the Irish population whose combined wealth is more than €121 billion (Cronin 2010). The current (2012) budget disproportionately affects the worst off in Irish society: cuts to fuel allowance for the elderly; cuts to child benefits for large families; cuts in disability payments; cuts in community employ- ment schemes (virtually wiped out); cuts in back-to-school clothing and footwear allowance; cuts in provision for job seekers; and cuts to rent supplements. At the same time there was a VAT increase, another regressive, indirect form of stealth taxation: the Household Charge, an increase in motor tax and planned reintroduction of third-level student fees. In total, €2.2 billion of cuts were announced as well as €1.6 billion in additional taxes. These cuts are occurring in a context where the gap between rich and poor is widening.

According to the Central Statistics Office 'Survey on Income and Living Conditions', inequality in Ireland grew by more than 25 per cent in 2010. The average income of those in the top 20 per cent of the population was 5.5 times higher than the average of those in the poorest 20 per cent. A year earlier it had been just 4.3 times higher (Browne 2011). The concentration of wealth in Ireland is one of the highest in the EU-15. According to Taft (2011), who has been trying to calculate who the 99 per cent and 1 per cent in Ireland are, the top 1% in Ireland own approximately €130.2 billion. Austerity budgets looks to leave tax bands unchanged, with a rise in VAT, a flat rate property tax and the reduction of child benefit hitting those who can least afford it disproportionately while leaving our plutocracy relatively untouched – the rationale being that if plutocrats are taxed they will flee the country. In the words of Johnson (2011), 'We are all bondmaids now, the property of local chieftains themselves in thrall to feudal lords both domestic and overseas, and the state we are in is one that Cúchulainn would find not that unfamiliar at all'.

Irish monsters of the mythic age of globalization

'History is a nightmare from which I am trying to awake', Joyce says (Joyce 1998, p. 28). The recurrence of the nightmare in Irish history is a localized instantiation of the cycle of recurrence identified in Vico's *New Science* of the dark age of gods, the mythic age of heroes and the historical age of men. Modernity is an intensification of this cycle as a spiralling vortex wherein features of all three recurring ages can be seen at once in the accelerated culture of globalization: the recurrence of the age of the gods as the dark and obscure abstraction of forces and processes that are the markets; the recurrence of the age of heroes in the celebration of the entrepreneur as ideal type subject; and the recurrence of the historical age of men as the public, mass society. During dark ages, Vico says, the gods mingle with men, giving birth to a progeny of monstrous doubles, ambivalently and paradoxically god-like heroes and mere mortals; patricians and plebeians, masters and bondsmen, Joyce's terrible twins Shem and Shaun. Seeming opposites, as antitheses they are in fact intimately bound together in a spiral dialectical dance. Patrician heroes are bestial monsters, for 'next to their heroic deeds, we must place the intolerable pride, the insatiable greed, the merciless cruelty with which the Patricians treated the unfortunate plebeians' (Vico 1999, p. 26; p. 104; p. 272) and plebeians who become heroic by overthrowing the patrician tyrants turn out themselves to be monsters, for in the Roman period of imaginary popular liberty, when the tyrants had been replaced by the republic, the republic became a new tyranny in which the majority of plebeians in fact continued to serve those plebeians who had become patricians (Vico 1999, p. 68). And today, same as it ever was, '*precari unite, contra i padroni*' is the political graffiti on the streets of Rome.

Monster – from *monstrere/monter* – means to show, to put on display, as the monstrance ritually displays the sacred host, for example. Monsters de-monster-ate boundaries, the mysteries that lie beyond the limit of what can be known (as in the usage 'here be monsters' on explorers' maps) and not only the obscurities beyond external limits but internal darknesses too, for the Other turns out to be the Other in the interior. Mary Shelley's monster created by Dr Frankenstein represents the paradox and ambivalence in the dialectics of Enlightenment and the democratic revolution. The creature, the being created by the heroic modern Promethean enterprise of science, technology and industry remains nameless. The 'creature', that which we have created, the 'monster', is a metaphor for base humanity endowed with the power of reason and self-consciousness, a creature that demands recognition, demands rights, demands equality with its creator. As the creature's claims for equal recognition are not met it destroys those who brought it to life but who thought that they would circumscribe boundaries and limit its life, the Romantic aristocrats and modern progressive liberal democrats represented by Byron and Shelley and Wollstonecraft.

Frankenstein's monster is the plebeian, the proletariat, the new monstrous public, the social body politic made up of many base parts, the popular mob, the masses that overthrew a nobility that, like Dracula, had become decadent. But the plebeian creature that becomes heroic by fighting patrician monsters for its rights to recognition becomes a monster himself; terror follows every revolution in one form or another. The eternal conflict between heroes and men – patricians and plebeians, aristocratic masters and mass public bondsmen – is a motor driving history, the Italian philosopher Giambattista Vico tells us, one hundred years before Marx and Engels made it the central pivot of the *Communist Manifesto*. But whereas Marx was dazzled by a Hegelian Enlightenment vision of dialectical historical progress as linear, an upwards and always-improving unfolding of *Geist*, Vico (and Joyce and Yeats) saw in the dialectic an eternal recurrence whereby periods of Enlightenment inevitably become decadent, declining again into dark ages.

Conclusion: a first glimpse of the second coming

In the period of decadence into a recurring dark age there are 'two great maladies' according to Vico, namely, 'the perfect tyranny of anarchy [the anarchy of the free market] and the unbridled liberty of free peoples [mass society, the herd]' (Vico 1999, p. 487). In response to these two pathologies of civilization three patterns recur historically, Vico says. The first is the restoration of internal monarchy by a charismatic leader, a demagogue who restores order by powerful violence. A second pattern is that the decadent society becomes subject to conquest by superior nations, the ceding of republican sovereignty to the IMF, ECB and EU 'Troika' being an initial form of the broader historical eclipse of a decadent occident by an ascendant orient, to ownership and rule by a global dynasty of despotic plutocrats. And the third pattern is that we become bestial again – solitary, competitive, uncooperative, 'living like beasts, crowded together but divided amongst ourselves' (Vico 1999, p. 487). Tendencies towards all three are the clear and unambiguous signs of our times.

The Queen's 2011 visit to Ireland in this context gives us one of our first glimpses of the second coming. Simultaneously an anachronistic and a prophetic event – the sovereign of the former imperial power and amongst the world's wealthiest individuals lays a wreath at the Garden of Remembrance for Republican national sovereignty in the former colony at precisely the moment at which national sovereignty is eclipsed and Ireland becomes a neo-feudal fiefdom, a neo-colony of bonded taxserfs paying tribute to a global elite of senior bondholders, a new absentee aristocracy of bankers and multinational corporations.

Works cited

Adorno, Theodor and Horkheimer, Max (1992) *Dialectic of Enlightenment*, London: Verso.

Browne, Vincent (2011) 'Growing Inequality Met with General Indifference', available: http://politico.ie/social-issues/8138-our-indifference-to-inequality.html [accessed 12 October 2012].

Cronin, Michael (2010) 'We Are All in This Together?', available: http://politico.ie/country-is-broke/6944-we-are-all-in-this-together.html [accessed 12 October 2012].

Deleuze, Gilles and Guattari, Félix (1983) *Anti-Oedipus: Capitalism and Schizophrenia*, Minneapolis: University of Minnesota Press.

Durkheim, Emile (1966) [1897] *Suicide*, New York: Free Press.

Ellmann, Richard (1977) *The Consciousness of Joyce*, Oxford: Oxford University Press.

Foucault, Michel (1991) *Discipline and Punish: The Birth of the Prison*, London: Penguin.

Hegel, Georg Wilhelm Friedrich (1977) [1807] *The Phenomenology of Spirit*, Oxford: Oxford University Press.

Inglis, David (2011) 'Putting the Undead to Work: Wade Davis, Haitain Voudou, and the Social Uses of the Zombie', in edited by Moreman, C. M. and Rushton C. J., *Race, Oppression and the Zombie*, Jefferson, NC: McFarland, pp. 42–60.

Johnson, David (2011) 'A Chariot Worth 4.58 Million Bondsmaids', available: http://politico.ie/crisisjam/8141-a-chariot-worth-458-million-bondmaids.html [accessed 12 October 2012].

Jones, Ernest (1974) *Psycho Myth, Psycho History: Essays in Applied Psychoanalysis*, New York: Hillstone.

Joyce, James (1998) [1922] *Ulysses*, Oxford: Oxford University Press.

Joyce, James (1994) [1939] *Finnegans Wake*, London. Picador.

Kapur, Ajay, Macleod, Niall, and Singh, Narendra (2005), *The 'Plutonomy' Equity Strategy: part I 'Plutonomy: Buying Luxury, Explaining Global Imbalance'; part II 'Revisiting Plutonomy: The Rich Getting Richer'* New York: Citigroup Global Markets Inc.

Kaufmann, Walter (1968) *Nietzsche: Philosopher, Psychologist, Antichrist*, New York: Vintage.

Kirby, Peadar (2010) *Celtic Tiger in Collapse: Explaining the Weaknesses of the Irish Model*, London: Palgrave Macmillan.

Lacan, Jacques (1994) *Speech and Language in Psychoanalysis*, Baltimore: Johns Hopkins University Press.

Lacan, Jacques (1998) *Seminar 20: On Feminine Sexuality, the Limits of Love and Knowledge Encore*, translated by Bruce Fink, New York: Norton.

Littlewood, R. and Douyon, C. (1997) 'Clinical Findings in Three Cases of Zombification', *The Lancet* 350:9084, 1094–1096.

Marx, Karl (1992) [1867] *Capital: Volume 1: A Critique of Political Economy*, London: Penguin.

Marx, Karl and Engels Friedrich (1985) [1848] *The Communist Manifesto*, London: Penguin.

Metscher, Priscilla (2002) *James Connolly and the Reconquest of Ireland*, London: MEP Publications.

Nietzsche, Friedrich (1995) [1887] *Thus Spoke Zarathustra*, London: Penguin.

Nietzsche, Friedrich (1989) [1986] *Beyond Good and Evil: Prelude to a Philosophy of the Future*, New York: Vintage.

Pearse, P.H. (1916) *Collected Works of Padraic H. Pearse*, Dublin: Phoenix Publishing Co. Ltd.

Shaviro, Steven (2002) 'Capitalist Monsters: Children of Production', *Historical Materialism*, 10, pp. 281–290.

Shelley, Mary (1987) [1823] *Frankenstein, or the Modern Prometheus*, London: Marshall Cavendish.

Stoker, Bram (1993) [1897] *Dracula*, Ware: Wordsworth Classics.

Taft, Michael (2011) 'Notes from the Front: Commentary on Irish Political Economy', available: http://notesonthefront.typepad.com/politicaleconomy/2011/11/the-dublin-council-of-trades-unions-march-against-austerity-tomorrow-12-noon-from-the-garden-of-remembrance-is-taking-pl.html [accessed 12 October 2012].

Vico, Giambattista (1999) [1744] *New Science*, London: Penguin.

Weber, Max (1958) *The Protestant Ethic and the Spirit of Capitalism*, New York: Charles Scribner's Sons.

Yeats, William Butler (1916) 'September 1913', in *Responsibilities and Other Poems*, New York: Macmillan.

Yeats, William Butler (1920a) 'The Second Coming', in *Michael Robartes and the Dancer*, Dublin: The Cuala Press.

Yeats, William Butler (1920b) 'Easter 1916', in *Michael Robartes and the Dancer*, Dublin: The Cuala Press.

10

Women, fictional messages and a crucial decade

Mary Pierse

During the traumatic period of strife in Northern Ireland, Irish poets and artists were frequently exhorted to make their art relevant, to comment or perhaps to take sides. Despite the marked lack of public clamour for artistic involvement in cogitation, diagnosis or prescription regarding two decades of rollercoaster-ride from embryonic prosperity to economic austerity, much recent fiction by notable Irish women novelists has determinedly featured numerous depictions of experiences, actions and reactions during that time. Such fictional engagement evidences authorial concern with the shifting sands of cultural values, and a perceptive sensitivity to readers' preoccupations and situations. With no area of life neglected, the novels and short stories furnish important images of societal change; they paint portraits that interpret past failings, chronicle social history and supply ample material for productive reflection. Any post-prosperity lamentation about the lack of earlier contemporaneous societal critique appears to indicate that such novelistic voices and their important messages were unseen, unheard or perhaps disdainfully disregarded.[1] Revisiting examples from the pens of some authors (including Anne Enright, Éilís Ní Dhuibhne, Edna O'Brien, Cláir Ní Aonghusa, Belinda McKeon and Ríona Ní Chongáil) shows that they were not, and are not, Cassandras. A combination of their disparate fictional delineations provides a rich picture that allows some insight into mindsets, trends and calamities of recent years.

Negotiation of economic, religious, educational and social environments, attitudes to family and children, perceived constraints, relationship difficulties – they all emerge in novels and short stories written by women in this millennium and, almost universally, the ongoing changes of recent decades are clearly indicated. Those same subjects are also the

---

[1] The latter point was made succinctly by Éilís Ní Dhuibhne in a letter to the *Irish Times* (10 March 2010): 'Not enough men – famous men – have written fiction dealing with contemporary Ireland? Well then. But of course. Good fiction about contemporary Ireland does not exist. QED.'

basic fodder of Irish (and other) television dramas like *Fair City* and *Ros na Rún* and at least one novel might be said to share the ambitions of an Irish 'soap' in its embrace of a legion of dramatic situations. The playwright Frank McGuinness identifies Cláir Ní Aonghusa as a writer whose prose combines qualities of Maeve Binchy and John McGahern (Ní Aonghusa 2008, cover) and her *Civil and Strange* is encyclopaedic in its careful inclusion and articulation of practically every social phenomenon, incorporating what could be seen as likely reactions, whether apposite or unfortunate, and various survival techniques, Rather pedantically, the first chapter informs the reader that 'Rural Ireland isn't the place it was' (Ní Aonghusa 2008, p. 9), even if illustration of the point is initially confined to remarking the closure of village shops and the resultant shopping trips to supermarkets in the nearest town. However, as the central character adapts to village life, to teaching in a local school, to being single after leaving her husband and to an entanglement with a local man, the recounting of those experiences is set against a backdrop that has at least three notable features: punctuation of the narrative by the deaths of four young men, the prevalence of unhappy marriages and an apparently unremitting circulation of malicious gossip. Treatment of each element offers snatches of context and conflicting opinions and, while the main protagonists may be seen to escape the worst ills of community tribulations, their positive endeavours are not guaranteed to proof them against disaster or to deliver their ultimate happiness.

To introduce the separate deaths of four secondary characters in the novel, whether by suicide or by dangerous driving, undoubtedly echoes and underscores recent extreme anxiety in the real world concerning such phenomena and their apparent linkage to the trauma of boom and bust years, even though the extent of the tragic scene is not accepted statistically (Walsh and Walsh 2011, pp. 27–47).[2] Ní Aonghusa engages with putative causation in each case and possible underlying reasons appear to be lack of self-esteem (John), fear of impending redundancy (Dan), prejudice against gay men (unnamed twenty-two year-old) and alcohol-fuelled, reckless car racing (Denis). But the further suggestion is that each of the four shared an inability to voice worries, to disclose problems or to admit to vulnerability, and this incapacity is depicted as

[2] The paper provides a factual assessment: although increased alcohol consumption is significant for suicide in all men between fifteen and fifty-four, unemployment is significant for males in the age groups twenty-five to fourty-four. Yet the influence of alcohol is stronger than unemployment for suicide. Male suicides increased fourfold between 1960 and 1990 but, according to 2010 data, the overall suicide rate in Ireland is actually low at 1 in 800 (p. 44).

more general amongst other males in the story also. In every example, there are further complicating factors, from repressive parenting and money worries to spiteful chitchat, but alcohol is an ever-present ingredient in the events. Men are not the only victims, nor are they alone in perpetrating physical or psychological violence; the novel catalogues incidences of viciousness in a previous generation of rural matriarchs who, intent on gaining and preserving land and status, connived and manoeuvred and coerced family members into intolerable misery. At least two characters see improvement over the decades: '"Make the best of it!" screeched Paula. "Can you imagine!" "That sounds so sad, Mam," Niamh says. "Who'd want to do that!"' (Ní Aonghusa 2008, p. 52). Yet, it is clear that any real gains from that newfound freedom are not abundant in the rural environment from which a pregnant schoolgirl will still flee to have her baby in England (Ní Aonghusa 2008, p.169), and where a farm worker marries only for land (Ní Aonghusa 2008, pp. 212–215; 248–249).

The harshness of country life in previous years is confirmed by the characters of Edna O'Brien's story 'Old Wounds' (O'Brien 2011b) and the legacy of adversity and affliction is so ingrained that tentacles of memory and snapshots of incidents completely overshadow the present. No glimpse of today's modern life is afforded in this tale, other than passing references to Interflora, hoovers, fridges and telephone calls, all of which could belong to any of the past five decades. The links of blood, and the difficulty of shedding ancient hurts and prejudices, intermesh and cast a very dark shadow that threatens to continue for generations. While Cláir Ní Aonghusa permits her characters to elaborate on rural hatreds in their conversations, the paucity of dialogue in 'Old Wounds' can convey the same message and magnify its atmospherics and impact. And yet, there is a temporal chasm between that fictional world and O'Brien's public criticism of the 'ethos of envy' that she perceives in recent developments in Ireland: 'Ireland is more secular, but it went to their heads: a kind of hedonism. They're free, yes, but questions come with freedom.' Her diagnosis is that 'when you remove spirituality, or the quest for it, from people's lives, you remove something very precious'. When she asks 'What about conscience?' (O'Brien 2011c), it is a line that is repeated by a local priest in 'Inner Cowboy' (O'Brien 2011a), a story in which the barrenness and wasteland that O'Brien discerns in today's living is very much to the fore. In fact, the ruthlessness of small-town 'developers' like the McSorleys parallels and then outstrips the bleak cruelty of pastoral history, with the hint that brutality derives from their rural heritage. In her representation of the McSorley brothers and their foreman Seamus, O'Brien clearly identifies the greed and posturing of such latter-day entrepreneurs, their aesthetic ambitions and their easy resort to murder when threatened or thwarted. Water pollution must be covered up, hot money hidden, along with their 'crooked deeds and their crooked deals' (O'Brien 2011a, p. 98); the façade is one of 'topiary, sculptures the size of cannon, a fragrant wife … priceless paintings, a library of first editions, a yacht named after his daughter' (O'Brien 2011a, p. 95). The trappings are instantly recognizable as the consumer flauntables of very recent years, so often envied and coveted but now frequently repossessed and sometimes seized as criminal assets.

They may be treated very differently but the tropes of unwanted teenage pregnancy and murder are also present in Éilís Ní Dhuibhne's stories. The backdrop to 'The Moon Shines Clear, the Horseman's Here' (Ní Dhuibhne 2012b) is made up of a recollected rural childhood in the late 1960s, the subsequent life in Denmark and then home revisited twenty years later. The contrasting attitudes of time and in place are obvious in pregnant Polly's flight from home when faced with the uncontrolled rage of her parents whose stance Ní Dhuibhne links to their romantic ideas of a pure Gaelic Ireland. When she gets a job abroad three years later, Polly is relieved that 'nobody cared whether or not you were a single mother in Denmark'. More than that 'All the talk was of feminism and women's rights and the country was packed with creches and kindergartens where children were looked after free' (Ní Dhuibhne 2012b, p. 183). By the time she returns to her home valley two decades later, 'Nobody cares about what used to be called unmarried mothers now, either. There are heaps of them, even in the Gaeltacht' (Ní Dhuibhne 2012b, p. 184). Christmas lights have evolved from a single candle in the window to multiple and multicoloured strings of lamps (Ní Dhuibhne 2012b, p. 186). Her widowed mother's deafness and poor sight are emblematic, as is the embrace between Polly and Muriel, grandmother of Polly's child although the relationship was unknown to her up to that present moment. If Ní Aonghusa's pregnant teenager ultimately seems to have a better future within her own village (Ní Aonghusa 2008, pp. 263 and 268), Polly has already successfully achieved that objective, and reared Conor, the son who is now a marine biologist. The profession is significant because it establishes him as son of his father, a dead fisherman. The murder of Conor's father is attributed by his mother to a row at sea, but the *omertà* of the local fishermen ensured that the incident was always promulgated locally as a drowning accident. Ní Dhuibhne's weaving together of nature, genetic inheritance and societal change, is a reminder of more unforgiving times and the degree of transformation; simultaneously, it suggests the fragility and potential volatility of community structure. Reversal is not impossible.

In Ní Dhuibhne's fiction, there are identifiable strands that bind, preserve and foster a good social order in the face of attack. For Polly, there was the ongoing support of her friend Eileen. The title of a different tale, 'The Shelter of Neighbours' (Ní Dhuibhne 2012a), conveys belief in such aid and collaboration while the detail of the story shows that although its benefits are valuable, its existence is dependent on individual decision and so cannot be guaranteed. The setting in a Dublin suburb encompasses two decades of neighbourly encounters, shifting outlooks, career patterns, property speculation, immigration and class prejudice. When Mitzy Moriarty's property investments begin to fail, her allegations about feather-bedded public servants sour the friendship between her and Martha, who resents that slur on herself and her teacher husband (Ní Dhuibhne 2012a, pp. 123–124). But their previous history had seen close contact with Mitzy and her children, particularly when they helped at the time around the death of Martha's baby son from leukaemia (Ní Dhuibhne 2012a, p. 127); the links had later continued with weekly lunches. Martha may be convinced that Mitzy's daughter Siobhán has murdered a Polish woman who 'stole' her boyfriend, but will she give incriminating evidence to the Gardaí? Ní Dhuibhne's sophisticated structuring will not deliver a definite answer to that question but one might possibly be inferred. The hints arise in the story title, in Mitzy's rural roots, and in her more recently acquired custom of bestowing freshly baked bread on a new neighbour; they are also evident in Mitzy's own discernment of closeness within the farming community by comparison with the isolation and detachment of suburbia, and in her evocation of the old Irish saying about neighbours depending on one another: 'Ar scáth a chéile a mhaireann na daoine' (Ní Dhuibhne 2012a, p. 120). There is further such intimation in Martha's construal of birdsong ('*Help you me, help you me, help you me*') as the Gardaí look for her evidence (Ní Dhuibhne 2012a, p. 126). Whether or not Martha will withhold the vital clue, the tale reveals much of present urban actuality, work stresses and prevailing economic realities. Ní Dhuibhne's recording of constructive qualities in urban and rural environments is, interestingly, set against the grain or in spite of the expected: it is noted approvingly in 'The Moon Shines Clear, the Horseman's Here' that Conor's Dublin-born grandmother has 'an underlying toughness, an urban edge that is different from anything you get around here' (Ní Dhuibhne 2012b, p. 187); similarly, Mitzy's country origins are seen to contribute positively to urban living. However, suburban neighbourliness in this case does not mean suffocating closeness or squinting windows: Mitzy confides Siobhán's psychiatric confinement to Martha only some months after it happened (Ní Dhuibhne 2012a, p. 121).

Ní Dhuibhne has a keen eye for class distinction, a phenomenon once denied in Ireland Her portrayal of its characteristics can embody subtlety, hilarity and illustrations of the changing scene: Polly's family prayed for those 'who had power and prestige' and Polly thus felt connected to those people; despite the objective description of her mother as old-fashioned in dress and appearance, as well as in her shunning of bingo in favour of lace embroidery, her mother 'still considered herself and her family a wide cut above most of her neighbours' (Ní Dhuibhne 2012b, pp. 158–159). In Dunroon, the fictional Dublin suburb where Mitzy and Martha live, they avoid sending their children to the local school since the ones who had been 'democratic and tried it – it was in the middle of Lourdes Gardens – got beaten up' (Ní Dhuibhne 2012a, p. 113). Dunroon immediately 'assumed that somebody from Lourdes Gardens murdered the Polish woman. Those thugs were bound to murder someone, sooner or later' (Ní Dhuibhne 2012a, p. 125). The mutual reinforcement of economic advantage by educational opportunity facilitates lifestyles that bolster convictions of superiority in the holders and defeat in the beholder: in *Dordán*, schoolgirl Natasha observes richer fellow pupils Dáibhí and Melissa and recognizes a certain irony: 'na daoine órga áille a bhuaigh trí mhíle euro ar aiste a scríobh faoi ghanntanas airgid' (those golden beautiful people who won three thousand euros for writing an essay on the scarcity of money) (Ní Dhuibhne 2011, p. 62). In Dunroon, 'A year and a half into the downturn and their lunches hadn't changed. Or their clothes or their holidays. As yet nothing in their lives had changed' (Ní Dhuibhne 2012a, p. 123). They are neat reports on the uneven impact of austerity and the growing divisions of Irish society.

The outlook of somewhat younger writers endorses much of what is reflected in the prose of O'Brien, Ní Aonghusa and Ní Dhuibhne but with their own distinctive colour and slant. It is Christmas time in Belinda McKeon's story 'From Now On' (McKeon 2011) and, as four family members are set to spend the festival at the parental home in the country, the consequences of recession are evident and none is spared. Elaine is a single mother on half-time work; Eamon and James are unemployed and suffering from depression; looking at James, Eamon's father Brendan sees 'the glint of something wild and panicky in his eyes', just as he had previously perceived it in Eamon; stress is cracking the marriage between Claire and James, as it may have wrecked Elaine's partnership; the parents are on edge and Margaret's lies are intended to spare Brendan worry. However, Brendan recognizes his wife's reasons and 'he knows when it is best just to let the other person lie, and to hope and hope, along with them, that the lie will come true'. Maeve's joke that Eamon may be driving into the Shannon is not funny in the tense circumstances. Breaking the news that he intends to emigrate to Australia is sad for Eamon's sisters, and Elaine may wish that she too could go, but the juxtaposition of family warmth with the hopelessness of a down-and-out in the snow suggest the new start and the possibly better tomorrow that is intimated by the title 'From Now On'.

The decade between Éilís Ní Dhuibhne's 2001 short story 'Wuff Wuff Wuff for de Valera!' (Ní Dhuibhne 2003) and Anne Enright's 2011 novel *The Forgotten Waltz* is generally agreed to be a key period of waxing and waning on economic and cultural fronts in Irish society. Could those ten years effect any notable difference in scenario or message? Strangely, there are some similarities between the narrative voices (of Bernie and Gina) in each tale and a degree of coincidence in their purposely inconclusive endings. Moreover, each main character supplies highly selective retrospective accounts, with varying degrees of believability attaching to opinion and memory. In 'Wuff Wuff Wuff for de Valera!', Bernie is married, while her twin Pauline is a single mother with a handicapped son. Bernie's description of Pauline's job, 'something in the corporation, one of those 1950s sort of jobs nobody has nowadays' (Ní Dhuibhne 2003, p.1), establishes how she really sees the hierarchy of their relationship despite descriptions of Pauline's leadership in their youth. As she denigrates Pauline's appearance and independent lifestyle, Bernie's brittle, narcissistic commentary implicitly divulges her own climb up the social ladder, her embrace of money and position, and a rhetoric that barely clothes the smugness of 'I'm alright Jack', or perhaps 'the devil take the hindmost'. In wilful blindness to financial realities, Bernie chooses to assert that all could holiday abroad, 'anyone can afford Ryanair, and there's all those Superquinn breaks and so on' (Ní Dhuibhne 2003, p.1). In contrast to the depiction of their relatively impoverished upbringing, Bernie's intended purchase of a cottage in Umbria and her upcoming safari in Zimbabwe are markers of a luxurious lifestyle, an ostentatious display of belonging to a certain club. It is Pauline's rejoinder with a skipping rhyme ('Wuff wuff wuff for de Valera!') which succinctly explains unfinished business and decisively exposes falseness and betrayal by her twin.

The story is littered with symbols of a recent past, as well as with some familiar hypocritical attitudes. The working single mother cares for a handicapped child while the woman who will spend time refurbishing an Umbrian villa tosses off references to her son at Cambridge and her daughter's love of 'animals and ecology and all that crap' (Ní Dhuibhne 2003, p.1); if Pauline is, allegedly, 'too forthright about her atheism' (Ní Dhuibhne 2003, p.7), Bernie and her husband know 'that it's better for the kids to be Catholic and of course it's essential for your career' (Ní Dhuibhne 2003, p. 8); Pauline may not know the way to the airport departure gates but Bernie is there 'forty times a year, at least' (Ní Dhuibhne 2003, p. 2). The divided worlds were well established by 2001 and, in the case of the twins from Crumlin, disparities were between independent single and comfortably married: 'marriage can be a safety net, let's face facts'; inequalities were also between working in 'the sewerage section' and residing in Palmerston Park; most noticeably, there are differences between those who say 'it's wiser to be discreet' about being a single mother, and the single mother who trumpets her status. *Au fond*, it is one twin's dishonest conformity to fashionable expectation as opposed to the other's frank acknowledgement of the factual position that is presented.

Since no economic downturn overshadows Bernie's account, it could be assumed from the picture painted of the twins that their present will also be their future; hindsight indicates a contrary likelihood, however. With its initial events set in 2002, Gina in *The Forgotten Waltz* lived in a similar bubble of unreality at that time. As the years go by however, the intervention of deaths, separation, uncertainty, the housing crash and a thousand 'ifs' enter into her musings, and daily existence both defies and punctuates her unreliable narrative. Assisted by the burden of an over-large mortgage, Gina manages to lose her husband, get entangled with Seán who moves in with her after he has been thrown out by his wife, and she ends up in a romance-free ménage dominated by Seán's relationship with his adolescent daughter Evie. Dream and life diverge and still Gina seems not quite to grasp the situation. For all her self-delusion, she can ultimately say 'whether her father stays with me or goes, I will lose this girl' but does it really matter to Gina when she sees the relationship only as a link to Seán, and her opinion of Evie is merely 'I think I love her myself, a little'. In reply to Gina, Evie is brief in her summary of who broke up her parents' marriage: 'It was you' (Enright 2011, pp. 229–230). The multiple and wonderful descriptions of behaviour, the insightful throw away remarks, the myriad pen pictures of houses and their denizens and the attachment of popular song titles to chapters all work to flesh out an urban scene that is galloping way out of the control of the players. Aside from its excellence as a literary novel – or perhaps because of that quality – *The Forgotten Waltz* is a route map through a decade, plotting a recognizable course, and peopling its pages with the flotsam and jetsam of excess. Its final pages do not accord the protagonist anything other than half-anaesthetized acceptance of the barely tolerable.

In total contradistinction to Enright's cool eye and scalpel-like paring away of urban pretence is the message delivered by a young writer, Ríona Ní Chongáil, who is still in her twenties. There is special significance attaching to her novelistic approach because she chooses to explain and to fight the downturn in a book for children. Rather than resigned acceptance of hardship, Ní Chongáil's text projects a refusal to be totally cast down in the face of acknowledged difficulty, and in fact suggests a resolve and a method to recover from adversity. Thus her own understanding, as well as her intention, can be understood as determination to communicate a philosophy of life that says 'Is féidir linn' (Yes we can). The target audience necessitates that the cultural backdrop is in evidence, simply sketched, and is successfully negotiated. The accomplishment of those aims maps a mindset within Irish society and while it may be a minority trend, or just a less visible inclination, recording its existence adds to the gallery of depictions. There is ambiguity in the book's title which underlines the diverse understandings of adults and children: while the literal translation of *Saol an Mhadra Bháin* (Ní Chongáil 2011) is the life of the white dog, adults would understand the phrase as the high life or the life of Reilly. And that high life is what vanishes in the story. First of all, Ciara (probably aged eight or nine) is told that the planned visit to New York, one that would make her the envy of all her friends, has to be postponed because the family will have less money in future. Ciara's loneliness is eased by playing with a little white dog owned by the people who live in a nearby huge mansion. On one dramatic morning, her father does not get up for work and on the same day men are seen removing all the furniture from the mansion. The bank has taken that house. The assembled media circus (Ciara goes looking for elephants and clowns when she hears what is down the street!) comments that the life of the white dog is over. Construing that message literally, Ciara is distraught. However, her father brings the dog to live with them, Ciara accepts the strange clothes that her father puts on as the new local postman, and she is relieved and content that the life of the white dog has been secured. In keeping with the tradition of more modern children's stories, the hardships of contemporary life enter into the mix while the complexities of economic and social conditions can still go over the heads of the intended readers, and no space is given to the fate of the unpleasant denizens of the big house. An economic cycle has been condensed into a short tale and there is light of some kind at the end of the tunnel. Both the textual message and its accompanying artistic illustrations convey the warmth of close family ties and their power in times of adversity, just as can be perceived in McKeon's short story. As befits a book for children, *Saol an Mhadra Bháin* is simple; however, its importance lies in its young author's choice of children's literature for her purposeful intervention recording current ills and fore-grounding one course of positive action.

It might be surmised that authors who provide vivid portraits of individuals and society could well be dilettante artists whose next canvases will feature different subjects and whose talent is more photographic than engaged. In the case of the novels and stories dipped into here, the additional public pronouncements of their authors provide definite evidence of underlying purpose and they add weight to its subsequent translation into fiction. In the light of their diverse presentations of society at macro and micro level, consideration of voiced authorial opinion confirms that the goal is to make their art relevant and meaningful. On the subject of marriage and romance, Éilís Ní Dhuibhne notes that the tradition of romantic novels ending with marriage has gone and now 'they usually end with surviving. Going on is a more typical ending' (Moloney and Thompson 2003, p. 112). That chimes perfectly with the central relationship in Cláir Ní Aonghusa's *Civil and Strange* and even more completely with Gina's path in *The Forgotten Waltz*. Bernie's marriage is not the end of the story in 'Wuff Wuff Wuff for de Valera!' and what seeps out from between the lines is the commercial nature of the contract – Conor pays, Bernie plays. Even Ciara's parents in *Saol an Mhadra Bháin* are more taken up with coping than with claiming a 'happy ever after'. Anne Enright's opinion on the matter is a gem of ironic understatement: 'I am interested by the happy ending, something particularly hard to achieve in life or fiction' (Moloney and Thompson 2003, p. 59).

Cláir Ní Aonghusa has expressed concern about a consumer society: 'When people define themselves in terms of their spending power and lose sight of their values, I see huge dangers for society, in particular for the less well-off sectors'. She identifies a countervailing power in 'a sense of social and communal responsibility' (Moloney and Thompson 2003, p. 89). It is no accident that strands of that responsibility contribute positively, if only spasmodically, to brighter moments in *Civil and Strange*. Ní Aonghusa is far from alone in identification of the male vulnerability that is particularly evident in that novel in the suicides and in inability to express feelings. Quite empathetically, Ní Aonghusa has a character opine: 'all these men end up in a lonely place – desolate and forlorn' (Ní Aonghusa 2008, p. 254). Another Irish writer, Miriam Dunne (author of *Blessed Art Thou a Monk Swimming*, 1997), sympathizes with the plight of a generation of men who 'are not encouraged to express their feelings … They are made redundant both at work and within the family.' Dunne also says boys underachieve at school relative to girls and she implicitly links that to the suicide rate for boys which she calls 'an epidemic' (Moloney and Thompson 2003, p.47). Enright remarks another and possibly related factor: 'when we look back at the literature of the late twentieth century we will be amazed at the pure weight of unpleasantness in male fiction – so guilt driven and excessive' (Moloney and Thompson 2003, p.59).

In comparing fiction in recent decades with that of half a century before, the increased freedoms for women are strikingly apparent and so taken for granted that they are frequently not remarked upon within novel and story. The female protagonists of *Civil and Strange* and *The Forgotten Waltz* see nothing strange in their liberty to have career and financial independence, to choose sexual activity and relationships outside of marriage, to take off for celebratory nights or weekends. Those dramatic advances in autonomy constitute one of the remarkable cultural and societal shifts of latter years and the fact that they are often part of novelistic scenery, so to speak, emphasizes the degree to which expectations have evolved and patterns become accepted. Bernie and Pauline (in 'Wuff Wuff Wuff for de Valera!') knew another time: visiting a family-planning clinic, they 'sneaked off to it, looking over our shoulders in case anyone we knew would spot us'; as for keeping an 'illegitimate' child, 'You'd be a leper' (Ní Dhuibhne 2003, p.5).

In fictional treatment and in public comment, women writers have contributed enormously to recording change, decline and upset in recent times. They have noted calamity, resistance, doubt and divergent attitudes and brought situations to life with almost uncanny accuracy and clarity. In many instances, the artistry is optimal. How could it be claimed that the storms and misfortunes and remarkable developments were insufficiently broadcast or considered? It seems even more perverse to then disparage some treatment of those themes because it features in what is arbitrarily decried as 'chick lit'. Is wilful blindness induced by humankind clinging to the vague hope that civilization is ever-evolving and improving, that we cannot face the reality of an unchanging human nature that merely evinces different manifestations in each generation? Or could it possibly relate to a gender bias so forcefully diagnosed by Anne Enright: 'if Joyce was a woman she would have been locked up for writing psychotic, scatological gibberish; for sleeping with the serving classes and getting herself pregnant; for fleeing her native place in a state of hysteria' (Moloney and Thompson 2003, p.57).

Whatever may be the various questions to those questions, there are some distinctive qualities apparent in the examples of fiction referred to here. This chapter has refrained from using the term 'Celtic Tiger', mirroring its avoidance by the authors considered. It is undoubtedly significant that the words 'Celtic Tiger' do not appear at all in *The Forgotten Waltz*, in 'The Moon Shines Clear, the Horseman's Here' or in Edna O'Brien's stories 'Inner Cowboy' and 'Old Wounds'. Neither is the phrase employed in Belinda McKeon's 'From Now On' or in Cláir Ní Aonghusa's *Civil and Strange*. In fact, the only time the appellation is used is a single brief reference in 'The Shelter of Neighbours' (Ní Dhuibhne 2012a, p. 118). The firm rejection of that terminology epitomizes its superficial glibness and its distance from Irish reality. Instead, the fiction of a crucial decade reflects an affirmation of change, and a realistic acceptance of uncharted evolution with multiple manifestations of life and lifestyle, all with distinctly Irish backdrops. It neither romanticizes nor idealizes the past and it queries orthodoxy in sect and politics. In many places, it depicts coping classes in diverse environments, faced with moral choice; the decisions are often required of young people rather than taken for them by their elders. Place emerges as a critical element and rootedness as a potentially saving factor. With a *dinnseanchas*[3] flavour to some featured place-names (Dunroon, Ballindoon), it may be somewhat ironic that French is the language in which one strong, underlying dynamic is expressed: a chapter heading from *Dordán* reads: 'Reculer pour mieux sauter' (Ní Dhuibhne 2011, p. 57). Amongst all the fictional messages delivered, that is a recurring trope: failure to embrace it leaves no tomorrow.

Works cited

Dunne, Miriam (1997) *Blessed Art Thou a Monk Swimming*, London: Routledge.

Enright, Anne (2011) *The Forgotten Waltz*, London: Jonathan Cape.

McKeon, Belinda (2011) 'From Now On', *Irish Times Magazine*, 24 December, pp. 13–15.

Moloney, Caitriona and Thompson, Helen (2003) *Irish Women Writers Speak Out*, Syracuse, NY: Syracuse University Press.

Ní Aonghusa, Cláir (2008) *Civil and Strange*, Dublin: Penguin.

Ní Chongáil, Ríona (2011) *Saol an Mhadra Bháin*, Baile Átha Cliath: Comhar.

Ní Dhuibhne, Éilís (2003) 'Wuff Wuff Wuff for de Valera!', in *Midwife to the Fairies*, Cork: Attic Press, pp. 1–8.

Ní Dhuibhne, Éilís (2011) *Dordán*, Baile Átha Cliath: Cois Life.

Ní Dhuibhne, Éilís (2012a) 'The Shelter of Neighbours', in *The Shelter of Neighbours*, Belfast: Blackstaff Press, pp. 107–128.

[3] Dinnseanchas is a genre of writing in early Irish literature, recounting the origins of place-names and traditions through associated events and characters.

Ní Dhuibhne, Éilís (2012b) 'The Moon Shines Clear, the Horseman's Here', in *The Shelter of Neighbours*, Belfast: Blackstaff Press, pp. 157–188.

O'Brien, Edna (2011a) 'Inner Cowboy', in *Saints and Sinners*, London: Faber & Faber, pp. 85–109.

O'Brien, Edna (2011b) 'Old Wounds', in *Saints and Sinners*, London: Faber & Faber, pp. 183–208.

O'Brien, Edna (2011c) 'A Writer's Imaginative Life Commences in Childhood' (interviewed by Rachel Cooke), *The Observer*, 6 February, available: www.guardian.co.uk/books/2011/feb/06/edna-obrine-ireland-interview [accessed 22 June 2012].

Walsh, Brendan and Walsh, Dermot (2011) 'Suicide in Ireland: The Influence of Alcohol and Unemployment', *Economic & Social Review*, 42:1, pp. 27–47.

11

'A hundred thousand welcomes': food and wine as cultural signifiers

Brian Murphy

Food and drink have always played an important role in Irish society. Memories of famine and all its associated deprivation still exist in the national psyche. Ireland has a worldwide reputation for the quality of our meat and dairy produce and the country is synonymous with a wide range of iconic products such as whiskey and smoked salmon. Indeed, Eugene O'Brien argues that a commodity such as Guinness acts 'as a synecdoche of Ireland and has taken on a fetishistic association with the country' (O'Brien 2009). In conjunction with these strong links to food and drink is a historic association with hospitality. This art of hospitality held such esteem in early medieval times that the title of 'Hospitaller' or 'Briugu' was bestowed on wealthy men who had the ability to provide generous hospitality to their guests. According to Molloy: 'A chief briugu had similar status to a minor king or a chief poet' (Molloy 2002, p. 14). In more recent decades, visitors from abroad have always associated Ireland as a 'place' where the Irish welcome could be guaranteed. So successful was this reputation that we exported the culture of that 'Céad Míle Fáilte' (a hundred thousand welcomes) across the world. People from Ireland were commonly believed to possess an inherent aptitude for hospitality and service. Because of this, the Irish have become prominent in all aspects of the hospitality and tourism industry on the international stage.

During the Celtic Tiger years, both Ireland's gastronomic culture and the story of Irish hospitality changed dramatically. Our distinctive service culture began to decline and Ireland was no longer the land of a hundred thousand welcomes. Over the same period attitudes to food and wine have changed. This chapter argues that Ireland has been revolutionized in culinary terms during the Celtic Tiger years, and has, in fact, developed its own version of a gastronomic cultural field. However, these dramatic culinary changes have also contributed to the departure and denigration of Ireland's once strong reputation for offering visitors 'one hundred thousand welcomes'.

In the 1970s and early 1980s, for the majority of Irish people, eating outside the home in a formal dining environment was reserved for very special occasions. Many of these occasions revolved around religious ceremonies such as Communions, weddings, funerals, anniversaries or birthdays. Independent fine dining restaurants were relatively rare and often the preserve of the more wealthy in society. Research by Máirtín Mac Con Iomaire (2009) confirms this view in an interview with Patrick Guilbaud, when he suggests that in 1980s Ireland eating out involved two extremes, fast food and fine dining, depending on whether one belonged to the wealthy minority or the poorer, and more widespread, majority:

> In Ireland in the 80s going out to eat was very expensive, so the concept of going out to eat cheap food in a restaurant, people didn't know. Either you had a bit of money and you went anywhere, or you had no money and didn't go anywhere. It was either McDonald's or Guilbaud's. (Mac Con Iomaire 2009, p. 599)

People in the main were almost fearful of very high end hotels and haute cuisine restaurants, being scared off in particular by the air of overt superiority they sensed among the clientele and staff. Many of these restaurants were often considered as being out of the reach of the majority of Irish people and as the preserve of the well-to-do, perhaps a throwback to much earlier decades when a servile attitude prevailed among Ireland's working classes when it came to their aristocratic landlords of the past. Dishes and food items now common in the modern middle-class lexicon were absent. For the majority, it was a time when coffee came from a jar or, if you were lucky, from a cafetière pot. Plates of food were considered satisfactory if piled high. Service was considered good if extra portions were offered. The desire for a 'good feed' often surpassed the yearning for a high-quality dining experience. Terms such as 'nouvelle cuisine' and 'gastropub' had not yet arrived on our shores. In that same 2008 interview with the well-known restaurateur Patrick Guilbaud, it was suggested that even the range of foods available in the main Dublin food markets was very limited at that time and consisted of only the most basic of ingredients (Mac Con Iomaire 2009, p. 598). As an Island nation, with little access to expensive air transport, foreign travel was relatively rare among the masses, and exposure to the food and drink of foreign cultures even rarer. The image of the pre-celebrity-era chef was for the most part rooted in working-class Ireland, a career associated with unsocial hours and difficult hot conditions working a range of early morning, late and split shifts. As a society, our perceptions of food were based more on physiological requirements rather than the social needs that would later become more prominent.

It was not until the mid-1980s that things began to change and we had the emergence of more modern purpose-built restaurants targeting the masses. Restaurants appeared on the Dublin scene such as Flanagan's, Gallagher's, Blake's of Stillorgan, and, later, Roly's Bistro in 1992. These restaurants offered a more casual dining experience, one that greatly appealed to the clientele at the time. According to staff who worked in Blake's during this period, popular dishes of the day included Corn on the Cob, Egg Mayonnaise, Mixed Grills and Steaks with Banana Splits or Black Forest Gateaux for dessert, all washed down with copious amounts of wines such as Black Tower, Piat d'Or or Mateus Rosé (Fanthom 2012). Eating out for purely social enjoyment was becoming more commonplace among middle-class Ireland, and attitudes to hospitality generally were changing. Ireland's food and drink culture was emerging, and a conversation was developing around food and wine both at home and in the media that would reflect the economic progress that was about to occur as Ireland moved from recession into the early Celtic Tiger years.

It is difficult to imagine now but there was a time when the common lexicon did not include terms such as 'Cappuccino', 'Americano' and 'Espresso'. Restaurant terms such as 'early bird' and 'pre-theatre menus', 'first and second sittings', 'tasting menus', 'amuse bouche' and 'pre-starters' all became part of common parlance during the Celtic Tiger period. Complex culinary terms and cooking methods that used to be the preserve of the professional chef or the elite diner who frequented our few well-known fine dining restaurants became commonplace. Depending on one's point of view, knowledge of this lexicon could be perceived as a sign either of pomposity or of superior social status afforded only to those who were privy to the typically French menu descriptors that adorned the à la carte menus of the time. The development of a gastronomic cultural field during this period changed all that. For the first time through the media, and in particular television, language and cultural barriers between professional chefs and the public were being torn down. Pseudo-reality TV introduced us to the language of the professional where terms such as 'sous-chef', 'covers', 'chef de partie', 'sommelier', 'the pass', 'Barista' and others came into common usage. Frequent violent outbursts from celebrity chefs such as Gordon Ramsay on reality TV using foul language caught the public's imagination and encouraged further knowledge of things culinary. Up until now such language had been kept 'back of house'.

At the other end of the spectrum we have had the popularity of media cooks like Nigella Lawson who are chastised regularly for their choice of food language and accusations of the near-sexualization of the food world abound with new terms such as 'gastroporn' coming to the fore in recent years. We have had the emergence of openly visible kitchens where diners could watch and listen to staff interaction. A number of high-end restaurants have taken this concept to a new level by placing a private customer table in the actual kitchen so that willing diners can now experience the sounds, smells and techniques of the professional kitchen up close while enjoying their meal experience. Michelin-starred restaurant Chapter One in Dublin introduced such a 'Chef's Table' in 2009. Its chef/owner Ross Lewis said in a recent radio interview that customers who booked the 'Chef's Table' often expressed surprise that the language and communication evident in the kitchen during service did not reflect the angry confrontational environment they were expecting (Lewis 2012).

As Ireland's food and wine culture evolved, dramatic changes also took place right across the hospitality industry. The number of hotel rooms in Ireland rocketed from 26,400 in 1996 to 45,700 in 2005 (Bacon 2009, p.11). There were commensurate increases in employment opportunities in the hospitality and tourism sector. According to the *CERT Employment Survey 2000*, in 1996 there were 144,143 people employed in Ireland across the hotel, guesthouse, restaurant and licensed premises sector: this rose to 184,140 in 2000 (CHL Consulting 2000, p.6). A later, more comprehensive, Fáilte Ireland survey in 2005 concluded that when the entire sector was taken into account by 2005 245,959 people were employed (Fáilte Ireland 2005, p.1). As the sector burgeoned, Ireland was rapidly coming of age in gastronomic terms. As we became more affluent, eating and drinking outside the home became more customary and we developed a new-found gastronomic confidence. We believed ourselves to be more sophisticated in our attitudes to hospitality and service. Along with our desire to accumulate economic capital during this period, a similar desire to accumulate social capital began to emerge and attitudes to those involved in the hospitality service sector changed. Our authentic Irish welcome started to come under serious threat.

Pierre Bourdieu emphasizes the importance of different types of capital in his 1986 essay *The Forms of Capital*. He believed that along with the more obvious desire for economic capital we should note that other forms of capital are every bit as vital to the structure and functioning of society (Bourdieu 1986, p.242). It is in particular these Bourdieusian concepts of cultural and social capital that should be explored when we examine how food and drink can be viewed as cultural signifiers during the Celtic Tiger era. Of course we cannot ignore economic capital and it is important to observe that our food and drink culture has been, and always will be, inextricably linked to economics in that it operates in the public sphere exclusively as a business. Restaurants, hotels, bars and wine stores all exist with profit as their ultimate motivator. In fact, Peillon discusses the tensions that exist between culture and economic capital in Ireland and suggests that the inimical relationship between the two is not something new in this country (Peillon 2002, pp. 40–41). He cites Hutchinson and Kane, both of whom intimate that, in various spheres of 1970s Ireland, culture was seen to impede economic progress in some way. But it is Bourdieu who explains that both cultural and social capital also have the potential to be converted into money, even though this conversion is not as immediate as it is with economic capital. It could be argued that the gastronomic field is one most suited to analysis through this Bourdieusian lens of cultural and social capital.

Take a business lunch in a Michelin-starred restaurant as a typical example. Exposure to fine dining etiquette and using appropriate social interaction while eating out is one of the key skills necessary to advance or progress in such a situation. These required cultural skills can be achieved in a number of ways. For particular groups within society, such skills are acquired at home, while growing up, where a certain etiquette is observed. Alternatively, assuming appropriate access to resources, such cultural etiquette can be learned as adults with exposure to fine dining restaurant situations. In some instances, it may even be necessary for employers to train their staff formally in such skills, if such upskilling is appropriate to their role. These skills are a form of Bourdieu's cultural capital in that they have the capacity to cement a business relationship or close a financial deal. During Ireland's Celtic Tiger years a gastronomic transformation took place among a broad range of the middle class. In a relatively short period of time, they went from the toasted special in the local pub to brunches, lunches and dinners in upmarket restaurants, wine bars and hotels. A gastronomic cultural field developed and with it emerged the necessity for the accumulation of cultural capital.

A variety of factors encouraged the development of this field and the consequent requirement for people involved in that field to enhance their cultural capital. Improved financial stability played a part, but there were other things such as an increased exposure to gastronomy through cheaper travel with the arrival of carriers such as Ryanair. The huge influx of a returning diaspora during the period was also a contributory factor. However, the most important component revolved around the relatively new exposure to things culinary in all areas of the media. Television programmes emerged initially in the UK and then on terrestrial channels in Ireland which extolled the skills and personalities of 'celebrity chefs'. A range of magazines such as *Food and Wine* and *Wine Ireland* became popular. Newspapers began including extensive weekend supplements on food and wine, which provided a raft of information on current happenings in the gastronomic world. Farmers' markets, slow food and organic movements started to take hold. The number of restaurants awarded the prestigious Michelin star increased from just two in the early 1990s to a high of nine in 1998, with Ireland achieving two two-star restaurants for the first time between 2001 and 2005. All of these elements point to the emergence of an Irish gastronomic cultural field and a new-found emphasis on cultural, and indeed social, capital.

Priscilla Parkhurst Ferguson (2001) uses Bourdieusian field theory to argue that gastronomy first became a cultural field in nineteenth-century France. Although Parkhurst Ferguson later argues the uniqueness of France in this regard, it can be posited that Celtic Tiger Ireland, in at least some ways, mirrored this development between the early 1990s and the present day. Parkhurst Ferguson introduces five key structural factors in this process and I would suggest that Celtic Tiger Ireland mirrors many of them and therefore constitutes its own, admittedly limited, version of a gastronomic cultural field. Firstly, she suggests that in France at the time 'new social and cultural conditions stimulated production, sustained broad social participation and encouraged a general cultural enthusiasm for the product in question'. In Ireland, the increase in personal disposable income, along with the returning diaspora and increased foreign travel from the mid-1990s until the end of the Celtic Tiger period, led to the new social and cultural conditions necessary for our version of a gastronomic field to emerge. Parkhust Ferguson goes on to note that 'specific sites become dedicated to cultural production and consumption'. By comparison, Ireland had the increased popularity of various Irish institutions that became the focus of gastronomic production and consumption. Examples included destination dining restaurants, private cookery schools such as Ballymaloe House and even new high-level culinary courses up to and including Master's degree levels in third-level colleges. Thirdly, Parkhurst Ferguson suggests that 'the institution of standards and models of authority ensure an acute critical consciousness that focused and checked, yet also legitimated the expression of cultural excitement'. Ireland experienced the introduction and enforcement of various rules and regulations governing how our restaurants operate as well as awarding bodies and guides that have allowed the food and drink industry to become legitimized and standardized. At the same time, particularly in the case of Michelin, a fervour has been created around the awarding of particular accolades. The author also suggested that 'subfields generated by the continued expansion of the field assured the simultaneous concord and conflict of the parties involved'. One could argue that gastronomic subfields in the form of things like the previously mentioned farmers' markets, artisan producers, organic and slow food movements have developed in Ireland and contributed to the continuing expansion of the field and the on-going debate with regard to their legitimacy or otherwise. Finally, Parkhurst Ferguson observes that in nineteenth-century France, 'networks of individuals and institutions forged links with adjacent fields and it is these links that are largely responsible for the social prestige of gastronomy' (Parkhurst-Ferguson 2001, p. 9). This final factor is particularly evident in the Ireland of recent years with the developing links between gastronomy and other legitimate fields such as history, literature, health and even art, through the popularity of disciplines such as food photography, food and wine journalism, and gastronomy-themed theatre.

If we accept that Celtic Tiger Ireland did in fact develop its own version of a gastronomic cultural field, how can this relate to our original premise that along with the arrival of such a gastronomic culture our reputation for hospitality declined? Did we become so involved in our desire to become gastronomically superior that our attitudes to service changed? Kathy Sheridan wrote an article in 1999 entitled 'Frosty Fáilte' that underlined the cultural shift that was in motion with regard to our attitudes to hospitality and service. She explains how the hospitable attitudes that prevailed among the Irish for so long had begun to disappear during the Celtic Tiger period. She offers the example of the Belgian tourists who found the Irish rude and off-hand. She discusses the American couple who discovered a 'very real lack of warmth and hospitality' and the German and Danish visitors to a well-known Clare pub 'who were asked to leave because they were lingering too long over the drinks that they had ordered and paid for' (Sheridan 1999). Such a shift in our collective attitude may well have been inevitable given the economic growth that was experienced in Ireland over the Celtic Tiger years and the accompanying greed that resulted. Sheridan suggests reasons why this situation has come about:

It's not that we hadn't been warned. The chat, the craic, the curiosity, were always what made us different. They even made us 'cool'. So cool in fact that we began to fancy ourselves as being above all that aul' stuff. Like an aging starlet, we fell for our own publicity: world conquerors of the music, film, (River) dance and literature stakes, churning out one bestseller after another, renowned every last one of us for spouting Heaney, Yeats and bits of *Ulysses* at the drop of a hat, dreamily indifferent to the international stars fetching up at the airport, falling in love with us and craving a bit of property at Paris prices ... Sure what had we to learn from blow-ins? And why should we bother with them at all? (Sheridan 1999)

Bourdieu's concept of social capital would suggest that a mentality developed among some groups in Celtic Tiger Ireland that allowed them to believe they were superior because of their perceived association with 'cool Ireland'. And as Sheridan's article indicates, this group felt that this collectively owned social capital enhanced and reaffirmed their status to such a degree that they no longer needed to bother with our long-standing national reputation for hospitality and friendliness. The emerging gastronomic class composed mainly of younger prosperous Irish men and women had begun forming themselves into a social group who now looked upon gastronomic experiences or interactions at all levels as being part of their lives in a way that they had not been for previous generations. In tandem with this cultural entitlement came a negative attitude to our traditional service culture and a view that this group of young Irish Celtic Tiger cubs no longer had regard for jobs within the hospitality sector. Irish attitudes to welcome and service changed perceptibly. This new social grouping was eating and drinking out more. Social expectation was often governed by what people experienced abroad, or picked up through the media and, indeed, through interaction with their own social groups. As a nation of gastronomes emerged, accompanying attitudes towards hospitality and service deteriorated. Social capital was being accumulated through gastronomic experiences such as eating in the latest Michelin-starred restaurant, or drinking in the trendiest of bars.

At the end of 1998 Henry O Neill, then Chief Executive of the Restaurant Association of Ireland, suggested the emergence of:

a new generation of restaurant owner catering to a demand born of a Celtic Tiger whose cubs have a greater disposable income, have travelled more widely and have watched more eccentric cookery programmes than their parents ever did. Into the stew pot add the concentration of people now living in the city, and returned emigrants, and you have a melting pot of spend happy eaters. (Holland 1998)

There was a lot of discussion in the media during this period of the role that immigration played, and references were regularly made to immigrants taking on roles in the service industry. Demands for

reductions in the minimum wage were made time and again by representatives of the business community, and commentary regarding the
hospitality industry becoming a 'race to the bottom' in terms of pay and
conditions was common. Frequent reference was also made to the fact
that the indigenous Irish no longer wanted to work in restaurants and
hotels and that vacancies were being taken up by unskilled immigrants.
As this new gastronomic social group was emerging, the same article
suggested that staffing was becoming the greatest source of pressure
in the hospitality industry. In a country that was nearing full employment, many restaurateurs were looking abroad to recruit staff. The
CERT Employment Survey of the Tourism Sector at the end of 1998
recorded a 16 per cent increase in the number of restaurants in Ireland
in the space of just two years with a commensurate employee shortfall
estimated at 5,632 (CHL Consulting 2000). 'This acute skills shortage
is put down variously to anti-social hours, low wages and burn out – all
of which, in turn, contribute to the increasingly prevalent perception of
the industry as a short term, transitory career option' (O'Neill 1998).
One must qualify this with the fact that there was an abundance of
available employment in industries outside the hospitality sector during
this period also.

In March 2000 a restaurant proprietor whose restaurant had just
closed owing to an inability to attract suitable staff claimed 'that
getting even untrained staff to serve lunch and dinner was proving
difficult despite wages of £200 per week with the same in tips' (Keena
2000). The service sector was now competing with other more attractive industries in the search for good employees and the service sector
was losing. A year after Sheridan's 'Frosty Fáilte' article, the same
journalist once more brought up the topic of hospitality and service in
an article entitled 'Is Smugness Going to Do for Us in the End?' In it,
she echoes the sentiments above in suggesting that Dublin in the new
millennium had become vastly overpriced with an underperforming
service staff:

> In the real world, a Dublin restaurateur can charge £14 (per head) for a few
> slivers of cheese after lunch. His peers in the hotel and restaurant business
> grow steadily more contemptuous of their patrons as they charge Paris
> prices for uninspiring food served by untrained students and offensively
> casual (and probably underpaid) staff. A confident professional at this level
> is a rare sight. (Sheridan 2000)

She goes on to question where these attitudes regarding hospitality and
service will ultimately lead Celtic Tiger Ireland. Later in the piece she
quite rightly asks:

Is this hubris going to do for us in the end? As we rear our children to perceive university-based education as our success standard and continue to confuse service with servility, where are the front-line workers capable of providing a Cipriani-type service going to come from? (Sheridan 2000)

The answer to Sheridan's question became very clear throughout the early 2000s and the vacuum that existed in the space once occupied by our world-renowned service mentality was to be filled using frequently imported and often untrained labour from a variety of Eastern European countries such as Poland and Lithuania. Though many of these employees competently filled the service roles that the Irish were no longer willing to fill, it led to further inevitable claims that the Irish welcome could not be authentically offered by non-Irish personnel and thus to a perception that such a welcome was again in decline.

Conclusion

It seems that towards the end of the Celtic Tiger period things had almost come full circle. A new type of gastronomic field had emerged in an Ireland populated by cuisine-savvy Celtic Tiger gastronomes who now knew their Pinot Noir from their Pinot Grigio and who could converse in a language previously the preserve of the professional restaurateur. Not for them the career that we associated with, as Sheridan rightly observed, servility rather than service. We could leave those particular jobs in hospitality and tourism to a new wave of immigrants, while we basked in the idea of ourselves as fully fledged gastronomes. And perhaps the small price worth paying would have to be a denigration of Ireland's world-renowned reputation for hospitality. But no matter, because we would never again need to trade on our reputation for hospitality and service owing to the wealth of opportunity that existed elsewhere in Ireland's Tiger economy. And this is perhaps how our culinary story might have ended except that the Celtic Tiger that carried us so gloriously forward into gastronomic accomplishment unfortunately keeled over suddenly and died in 2007!

But for the Irish watching the Tiger's demise, the culinary genie was out of the bottle and could not be put back. We could not return to pre-Celtic Tiger Ireland to consume our Corn on the Cob starter and our Black Tower wine. Our Celtic cubs could not unlearn the art of the gastronome. After an initial decline with the demise of the Celtic Tiger, it is interesting to note that wine sales in Ireland have recently increased from 8.7 million cases at the height of the boom to 9 million cases in

2011 (Irish Wine Association, 2011). Sales of gourmet coffee machines for use in the home have also increased. There has been an explosion in retail offers of 'Dine-In Meals for Two' in stores such as Tesco's and Marks and Spencer's. The Irish gastronome has not gone away. He/she has merely retreated into the lavish kitchen of their negatively leveraged home. They can be found sitting at their 'kitchen island' on a Friday night matching wines from German discount stores to Tesco's 'Dine-In' meal range while verbally admonishing the men and women who killed our Celtic Tiger.

And what then of the decline in our reputation for hospitality? Just as economic boom appeared to focus the Irish mind on how to acquire economic, cultural and social capital, perhaps the subsequent decline in Ireland's economic fortunes is leading our population to return once again to sectors such as food, agriculture and, of course, hospitality and tourism. At the 2011 global economic forum in Farmleigh, former US president Bill Clinton was keen to highlight the potential for tourism development in Ireland and future employment in the area. At the very heart of plans for future growth in tourism has to be our attitudes to hospitality and service and, with a new focus on tourism, perhaps a new era of hospitality is beginning to emerge. Every day we hear of success stories in our food and agricultural sectors and hospitality and tourism was one of the few areas reporting growth in employment in 2011–2012. In 2009, ten years after her 'Frosty Fáilte' article, Kathy Sheridan wrote one entitled 'It's All Smiles as "Ireland of the Welcomes" Reopens for Business'. In this piece, she quotes Jim Deegan of Railtours Ireland: 'The Celtic Tiger was no friend to tourism, we became too busy ... tourists were only getting in the way of ourselves ... We started losing the welcome ... now you see people going out of their way because they're appreciative again' (Sheridan 2009).

It seems that our worldwide reputation for hospitality was not wholly devoured by the Celtic Tiger and a new revived culture of service is emerging, less driven by economic greed and more closely related to that long association with the 'Céad Míle Fáilte' so ingrained in the Irish psyche down through the years. Ireland can now compete on the world stage in terms of our food quality and restaurant offering and it appears that a renewed post-Celtic Tiger focus on hospitality and service is continuing to have benefits for a sector that has gone through so much change recently. Influential Chief Editor of *Le Guide du Routard*, Pierre Josse, recently observed:

> Thirty years ago, when we first started the Irish edition, the food here was a disaster. It was very poor and there was no imagination. Now the level

of food in Ireland is nothing short of tremendous. The food is gorgeous, it's now very reasonably priced and there is a very high level of service. All in all, I would say the Irish dining experience is now as good, if not better, than anywhere else in the world. (Bramhill 2011)

Josse's comments emphasize one of the few positive outcomes to emerge from the economic trauma of recent years and signify that as a society we have perhaps begun to grow up in terms of our food and drink culture. Hopefully our new-found gastronomic appreciation can thrive and go hand-in-hand with a more mature and enlightened attitude to our traditional reputation for hospitality and service. It is to be hoped that our 'Frosty Fáilte' attitude is now in terminal decline and that Ireland may once again become renowned for its 'hundred thousand welcomes'.

Works cited

Bacon, Peter (2009) *Over-Capacity in the Irish Hotel Industry and Required Elements of a Recovery Programme*, Peter Bacon and Associates, Wexford.

Bourdieu, Pierre (1986) 'The Forms of Capital', in Richardson, J. (ed.), *Handbook of Theory and Research for the Sociology of Education*, New York: Greenwood Press, pp. 241–258.

Bramhill, Nick (2011) 'Irish Chefs Best in World', *Sunday Independent*, 9 January, available: www.independent.ie/national-news/irish-chefs-best-in-world 2489465.html?service=Print [accessed 6 October 2012].

Chapteronerestaurant.com (2012), available: www.chapteronerestaurant.com/chefstable.html [accessed 26 July 2012].

CHL Consulting (2000) Dublin: CERT Employment Survey of the Tourism Industry in Ireland 2000, CERT Limited.

Fáilte Ireland (2005) *Tourism Facts 2005*, available: www.failteireland.ie/Failte Ireland/media/WebsiteStructure/Documents/3_Research_Insight/3_General_ SurveysReports/TourismIreland2005.pdf?ext=.pdf [accessed 28 September 2012].

Fanthom, Orla (2012) Phone Interview carried out by author with former employee of Blake's Restaurant (1982–1985).

Holland, Kitty (1998) 'The Waiting Game' *The Irish Times*, 29 December, available: 0-www.irishtimes.com.millennium.itallaght.ie/newspaper/features/1998/1229/98122900077.html [accessed 25 June 2012].

Keena, Colm (2000) 'Shortage of Staff Closes Successful Dublin Restaurant', *The Irish Times*, 23 March, available: 0-www.irishtimes.com.millennium. ittallaght.ie/newspaper/finance/2000/0323/00032300136.html [accessed 25 June 2012].

Lewis, Ross (2012) *CountryWide* RTE Radio interview, available: www.rte.ie/radio1/podcast/podcast_countrywide.xml [accessed 4 October 2012].

Mac Con Iomaire, Máirtin (2009) 'The Emergence, Development and Influence of French Haute Cuisine on Public Dining in Dublin Restaurants 1900–2000: An Oral History', unpublished PhD thesis, Dublin Institute of Technology.

Molloy, Cian (2002) *The Story of the Irish Pub*, Dublin: Liffey Press.

O'Brien, Eugene (2009) *'Kicking Bishop Brennan Up the Arse': Negotiating Text and Contexts in Contemporary Irish Studies*, Oxford: Peter Lang.

Parkhurst Ferguson, Priscilla (2001) 'A Cultural Field in the Making: Gastronomy in 19th Century France', in Schehr, L. and Weiss, A. (eds), *French Food on the Table, on the Page and in French Culture*, New York: Routledge, pp. 5–45.

Peillon, Michel (2002) 'Culture and State in Ireland's New Economy', in Kirby, P., Gibbons, L. and Cronin, M. (eds), *Reinventing Ireland: Culture, Society and the Global Economy*, London: Pluto Press.

Sheridan, Kathy (1999) 'Frosty Fáilte', *The Irish Times*, 23 January, available: 0-www.irishtimes.com.millennium.ittallaght.ie/newspaper/weekend/1999/0123/99012300184.html [accessed 29 June 2012].

Sheridan, Kathy (2000) 'Is Smugness Going to Do for Us in the End?', *The Irish Times*, 30 March, available: 0-www.irishtimes.com.millennium.ittallaght.ie/newspaper/opinion/2000/0330/00033000098.html [accessed 27 June 2012].

Sheridan, Kathy (2009) 'It's All smiles as Ireland of the Welcomes Reopens for Business', *The Irish Times*, 2 May, available: 0-www.irishtimes.com.millennium.it-tallaght.ie/newspaper/weekend/2009/0502/1224245821629.html [accessed 29 September 2012].

The Irish Wine Association (2011) *The Irish Wine Market 2011*, available: www.abfi.ie/Sectors/ABFI/ABFI.nsf/vPages/Sector_Association__Irish_Wine_Association~industry-profile/$file/ABFI_Wine%20Facts%20Brochure-WEB%202011.pdf [accessed 15 September 2012].

12

Contemporary Irish fiction and the indirect gaze

Neil Murphy

As one of the most dramatic socio-economic transformative periods in modern Irish history, the Celtic Tiger years offer us a provocative opportunity to consider the relationship between Irish literary fiction and its contexts. Since 1995, Irish society has experienced a plethora of complex adjustments to the economy, to the demographic distribution of people living in Ireland and to the religious landscape, and Ireland has become both an international brand name in the arts and a poster-girl for twenty-first century capitalist success (and, ultimately, excess). The emergence of Ireland as a viable European financial power would itself have represented a major transformation, but the subsequent collapse of that retrospectively dubious status created an inverted doubling of the earlier years of untrammelled enthusiasm. This extraordinary reconstitution of Irish society offers a context as disruptive as any in modern times and would appear to offer an inviting range of imaginative possibilities to its writers. In fact, throughout these years Irish writers were achieving levels of commercial success utterly disproportionate to the size of the population, and global validation of their work reached significantly new levels. Irish writers won the Nobel prize, the Pulitzer prize twice, the Booker prize twice, the James Tait Black Memorial Prize, the Whitbread/Costa award thrice, the IMPAC Dublin Literary Award twice, the Los Angeles Times Novel of the Year, and the David Cohen prize twice.

But, of course, prizes represent contentious measures of value; more crucial for the present discussion is that deeper levels of engagement with the transformation of the nation by Ireland's major authors are not as immediately apparent as one might assume. In reality, several younger Irish writers have bemoaned an apparent indifference to 'modern' Ireland by the major fiction-writers over the past few decades. Julian Gough, for example, has criticized the refusal, or inability, of both the major figures (he specifically mentions Banville and Barry) and their younger counterparts to write about Irish experience: 'The role of

the Irish writer is not really to win prizes in Ireland; their role historically has been to get kicked out of the country for telling the truth. And
there's not quite enough of that going on. Just when we need a furious
army of novelists, we are getting fairly polite stuff published by Faber &
Faber that fits into the grand tradition' (cited in Flood 2010). Whether
or not Irish writers have ever fitted Gough's description is, of course,
questionable, but the sense of dismay at a perceived lack of awareness
of contemporary life is clear. Similarly, Paul Murray admits to a sense
of frustration with younger Irish writers: 'It is disappointing when you
read a young novelist who seems to make no effort at all to engage with
modernity', although he concedes that writers should write as they wish
(cited in Flood 2010).

Revealing an awareness of modernity in one's fiction is not quite the
same as writing Celtic Tiger fiction that focuses on the housing boom
and/or ghosts estates, irregular banking practices or political corruption. Gough, after all, admires both Mike McCormack and Kevin Barry,
two of the more technically innovative younger Irish writers, neither of
whom writes explicitly of such matters. However, discussing what she
calls 'boom-bust fiction', Arminta Wallace points out that contrary to
general opinion several younger Irish writers have written very successful novels of this kind, particularly Peter Cunningham, Anne Haverty,
Gerard Donovan, Éilis Ní Dhuibhne and Claire Kilroy (Wallace 2012).
Nevertheless, many works by major Irish writers published since 1995
offer scant attention to the momentous social transformations that shook
the country during these years. While more cosmopolitan plot elements
are certainly evident, the fundamental artistic processes and the primary
concerns of the authors rarely reflect a primary fascination with the
socio-economic revolution that more fully characterizes the landscape.

The relationship between society and the novel has always been
complex in Ireland. For example, Joyce's legendary declared disengage-
ment with politics in general, his largely unconcerned response to the
revolutionary upheavals in Ireland between 1916 and 1923, and the
absence of any direct impact on his work by the First World War, despite
the fact that *Ulysses*'s composition timeframe coincides with these historically cataclysmic years, is artistically revealing. Of course, this is not
quite the same as suggesting that one cannot read Joyce's work politically, as Derek Attridge, Emer Nolan and Declan Kiberd among others
have convincingly demonstrated. But Joyce's commitment to style as a
central emblem of his primary artistic intent is also well documented
both in terms of his admonishing of those who privileged politics above
style ('For God's sake don't talk politics. I'm not interested in politics.
The only thing that interests me is style') (Ellmann 1983, p. 697), and his

apparent downright refusal to entangle himself in the politics of the new Irish State, as noted by Ellmann: 'Joyce declined to attend as guest of honor a St. Patrick's Day party in 1932 for fear that the presence of the Irish Ambassador, Count O'Kelly, would imply his endorsement of the new state. "I do not mind 'larking' with Dulanty in London but I care nothing about politics"' (Ellmann 1983, p. 643). Of course, contemporary critically acceptable materialist norms insist that such a disavowal nevertheless reveals a political disposition but one cannot simply ignore the centrality of the technical experiment to Joyce's achievement.

More emphatically perhaps, Beckett asks, 'Is there any reason why that terrible arbitrary materiality of the word's surface should not be permitted to dissolve …?' (Beckett 1984, p. 172), in a direct, antagonistic gesture both towards referential writing in general, and to any simplistic here-and-now conception of the complex public and private realities that define much of human discourse, particularly in sophisticated literary narratives. Similarly, Flann O'Brien's experimental *At Swim-Two-Birds* and *The Third Policeman* were both written immediately before, and during, the first throes of the Second World War, although it is not at all apparent from the subject matter of either. In fact, as I have argued elsewhere (Murphy 2011), neither of O'Brien's two early masterpieces lends itself particularly well to materialist readings because of their deep engagement with metafictional concerns and their obvious allegiance to an anti-realist tradition in European literature, stretching from Cervantes and Rabelais to Swift and Sterne, while Borges includes Joyce's work in the Irish branch of this family when claiming that '[t]he Irish have always been the iconoclasts of the British Isles' (Borges 1999, p. 14). Richard Kearney too has written extensively about what he has named an Irish 'counter' tradition that transforms the 'traditional narrative of quest into a critical narrative of self-questioning' (Kearney 1988, p. 83), with an emphasis on the novels of Joyce, Beckett, Flann O'Brien, John Banville and Aidan Higgins.

While I will later offer more detailed consideration of Banville's *The Sea* (2005), it is clear that Banville's fiction has never been what one might describe as socially engaged, or overtly Irish in subject matter. In fact, Banville's declared resistance to 'social' literature has always remained consistent, as when he observes to Derek Hand, 'I'm not interested in politics, I'm not interested in society, I'm not interested in Man. I seem to be just interested in this voice that goes on and on and on in my head' (Hand 2006, p. 201). As we shall see, the concerns in Banville's work instead revolve around the troubled relationship between the world and our capacity to know and speak of it, and the significance of art. Similarly, Sebastian Barry's sequence of novels, *The*

Whereabouts of Eneas McNulty (1998), *Annie Dunne* (2002), *A Long Long Way* (2005) *The Secret Scripture* (2008) and *On Canaan's Side* (2011), repeatedly circle around the difficulty of locating acceptable models of truth, particularly historical truth, as they excavate the fictionalized histories of forgotten members of Barry's own family. For example, in *The Whereabouts of Eneas McNulty* the narratorial voice claims of the protagonist, Eneas: 'He can tell nothing from anything any more, there are no signs, no means to nose your way along the roads' (Barry 1998, p. 103). McNulty thus becomes a fictional incarnation of the idea that the world may be unknowable. This central characteristic is always apparent in Barry's work, as in Lily Bere's quiet, desperate musing on her life in *On Canaan's Side*: 'And be thinking, remembering. Trying to. All difficult dark stuff, stories stuffed away, like old socks into old pillowcases' (Barry 2011, p. 27). Similarly, although Anne Enright's haunted tale of familial damage and sexual abuse, *The Gathering*, is set during the Celtic Tiger years, a similar resistance to fixed meanings characterizes Veronica's deeply troubled voice as she tries to reconstruct the lost traumatic memories of her youth: 'And even though I know it is *true* that this happened, I do not know if I have the true picture in my mind's eye' (Enright 2007, p. 144). Still, *The Gathering*'s complex engagement with its social context is extremely nuanced, particularly in terms of its implicit suggestion that context might afford the opportunity for change, and reminding us of the interconnected relationships between inner struggles and the pressures of one's society.

The multi-textured fictive landscapes that we find in Dermot Healy's work often struggle to contain the extraordinary central figures who dominate his major novels, *A Goat's Song* (1995) and *Long Time No See* (2011). In *A Goat's Song*, Jack Ferris's imaginative possession of the world is infused with longing and loss and ruled by his alcoholism and fragile consciousness, while the intensity of Jonathan Adams's religious and political beliefs offer useful indications of the way context can be radically reconstructed by perspective. During one of Jack's particularly fraught alcohol-fuelled sequences, the very materiality of things is challenged:

> Objects took on other presences. For a certain amount of time the objects remained what they were – chairs, stones, shadows, a holy picture, a bend in the bed, a bottle – then there would be a slight alien encroachment, a vague déjà-vu, but before they could entirely become something else, the hint of change receded. (Healy 1995, p. 405)

Healy's work frequently features such pivotal moments of puzzlement at the world, moments in which the fixity of things is as indistinct as the fluidity of memory, or his character's capacity to grasp material reality.

Of course, the question of how a work of literary fiction responds to any given epoch is central to a discussion on the relationship between text and context. Kevin Myers, writing approvingly of Peter Cunningham's novel *Capital Sins* (2010), argues that '[t]he accusation often levelled at Irish novelists is that they write about the past: the safe, secure, easy-to-capture historical episodes that have an ending we all know about' (Myers 2010), and proceeds to suggest that many of the major authors of the Celtic Tiger years had evaded their responsibility as social critics. This kind of position, not uncommon among social-materialist-minded commentators, represents a significant narrowing of comprehension of how literary art works, and raises the question of whether writers are even required to be socially responsive. Even a relatively politicized author like Gabriel García Márquez argues against what he calls 'committed' literature, or the literature of 'social protest', in order to avoid rendering his work polemical (cited in Oberhelman 1991, p. 71). Myers's position also assumes that the relationship between text and context is a simplistic representational one, the kind one might discover in a political commentary, or a newspaper opinion piece, for example. In fact, one of the central threads of fascination in post-Joycean Irish writing is the troubled relationship between text and context, between artistic image and the world from which, in some fashion, it was derived. Far from offering neat realist versions of 'safe, secure, easy-to-capture historical episodes', works by Banville, Barry, Enright, Healy, McCabe, McCormack, Keegan, McNamee, McLiam Wilson, Jordan and many others repeatedly revolve around the problems of historical reconstruction, the vagrancy of memory, the indistinct nature of human perception and the inevitable transformative effect of linguistic expression. Related to this is a sense among many modern writers everywhere that a necessary distance is in fact essential for artistic endeavour, and the struggle to find this necessary distance, between subject and work of art, is deeply embedded in much of contemporary Irish fiction.

On its most obvious level, in Banville's work, each fictional image contains the DNA of its own transformative zeal. So when Morden (also known as Max), in *The Sea*, offers one of the many glimpses of his world, he imbues it with an artistic zeal that far outstrips descriptive reportage: 'It was a sumptuous, oh, truly a sumptuous day, all Byzantine coppers and golds under a Tiepolo sky of enamelled blue, the countryside all fixed and glassy, seeming not so much itself as its own reflection in the still surface of a lake' (Banville 2005, p. 45). Framed against an intertextual reference to Tiepolo's richly textured frescos, Morden's scene-setting contains an acknowledgement of its own invented, or reflective, mirroring. The world, he admits, is both itself and imaginary other. This gap is also evident throughout Enright's *The Gathering*, in which Veronica, for reasons very different from those of Morden, continually alerts us to the unpredictability of the images rescued from time: 'history is such a romantic place, with its jarveys and urchins and side-buttoned boots. If it would just stay still, I think, and settle down. If it would just stop sliding around in my head' (Enright 2007, p. 13). Deep-rooted, human issues of loss, love and recovery are Enright's central concerns but she knows too that the world is reasserted in the frames of art. The versions of events that Veronica offers are frequently accompanied by an acceptance of their tenuous nature and also by a simultaneous expression of the necessary transformation of actual event into narrated subject: 'And though common sense says that these two events should not have happened on the same day, I say that they did' (Enright 2007, p. 50), and by an understanding that events plucked from the past are partly approximate guesses: 'After that, there must have been the sea. Ada bringing us for red lemonade into a pub ... We must have caught the bus back to the station at the hospital gates' (Enright 2007, p. 116).

The fluidity of historical reconstruction is also centrally engaged, as a subject in itself, in the various accounts of the death of Roseanne Clear's (née McNulty) father in Barry's *The Secret Scripture*. The reader is first offered Roseanne's own testimony via her private diary, refracted through her mottled hundred-year-old memory and the trauma of the initial event, followed by Dr Grene's summary of Fr Gaunt's account (via old mental institution records), followed by Dr Grene's admission of his inaccurate summary. The actual truth remains embedded in the vanished world of the past and we, like Dr Grene, must embrace a multiplicity of splinters of story or, as he rhetorically asks, are not 'all our histories tangled and almost foreign to ourselves, I mean to our imaginations?' (Barry 2008, p. 181). Our capacity to reconstruct past experiences is but part of the issue; Grene suggests an essential rupture between our imaginations and the actual events that we have lived through, and it is that fissure, that sense of dislocation, that lies at the centre of the artistic task.

Yeats's insistence that 'all imaginative art remains at a distance and this distance, once chosen, must be firmly held against a pushing world' (Yeats 1961, p. 224) resonates with the various kinds of imaginative distancing that inform the work of many major Irish authors. Banville's fictional worlds both contain a persistent sense of that distance and remind us of the essential complacency of things. As Morden, of *The Sea*, informs us, 'I marvelled, not for the first time, at the cruel complacency of ordinary things. But no, not cruel, not complacent, only indifferent, as how could they be otherwise?' (Banville 2005, p. 20). This indifference is also embodied in the characters or, as Rüdiger Imhof argues, with reference to Morden's childhood sweetheart, Chloe: 'her willful vagueness tormented and infuriated him, and he had to put up with her caprices, her high-handedness. But it was she who gave him his first experience of the absolute otherness of people' (Imhof 2006, p. 175). Banville's work has always been concerned with the sense of otherness that the indifferent world generates. The indifference or 'disinterestedness' is reciprocal in that while the world stands aloof from us, the artist too must locate a correct sense of distance.

The sense of distance between the imaginative mind and the world upon which it muses is, according to Denis Donoghue, a quality that resides at the centre of artistic activity: 'Autonomy, disinterestedness, and impersonality are the values to be recognized' (Donoghue 2003, p. 81). The indifference in art is a mirror of the world's essential indifference. So, when Morden, near the close of his account, again reminds us of the 'great world's shrugs of indifference', Banville is alerting us to both the peculiar sense of dislocation that one feels in the face of the world and the odd, mirrored, otherness that works of art possess, a point emphasized by Susanne Langer in her discussion of the arts in general: 'Every real work of art has a tendency to appear thus dissociated from its mundane environment. The most immediate impression it creates is one of "otherness" from reality – the impression of an illusion enfolding the thing, action, statement, or flow of sound that constitutes the work.' This otherness, she argues, has been variously described as 'strangeness', 'semblance', 'illusion', 'transparency', 'autonomy' or 'self-sufficiency' (Langer 1953, pp. 45–46). Banville has frequently voiced his conviction that the world's strangeness, and his characters' puzzlement in the face of it, best define his work (Hand 2006, p. 206). Thus, the very texture of the fictional context, almost as an unavoidable characteristic, lies in true relation to the world from which it was originally derived. The connection is relational rather than representational. Furthermore, it may also be the case, especially with an author like Banville or Beckett, that the fictional world doesn't have a natural counterpoint in social reality beyond limited surface signposting. Linda Hutcheon raises this very point in an effort to acknowledge the possible autonomous nature of fictional worlds: 'In literature words create worlds; they are not necessarily counters, however adequate, to any extraordinary reality. In that very fact lies their aesthetic validity and their ontological status' (Hutcheon 1980, pp. 102–103).

One of the ways in which literary texts establish a non-realist 'onto-logical status', or as Thomas Pavel describes it, 'a theoretical description of a universe' (Pavel in McHale 2001, p. 27), is by framing their fictional worlds against a carefully textured intertextual universe. Banville's fictions are multi-dimensional spaces in which several levels of intertextual density are evident. Not only do allusive patterns and echoes offer aesthetic pleasure in a formal sense but one perpetually has a sense of a densely textured mode of existence in which the formal patterned arrangements echo the textured nature of reality. *The Sea* exemplifies the way that Banville typically constructs a secondary allusive ontology, beneath, or beside, the primary surface reality of plot. So, while Morden ostensibly recounts a series of events from his youth, populated by feasible characters and a landscape that resembles many seaside towns in 1950s Ireland, a simultaneous intertextual world hums with significance. Carlo Grace is both man and God, the 'Poseidon of our Summer' and 'the one who appeared to be in command over us all, a laughing deity' (Banville 2005, p. 123), a 'grinning goat god' (Banville 2005, p. 125) and a satyr (Banville 2005, p. 233). His family, the Graces, are simultaneously flesh-and-blood children *and* the graces of Greek myth, while Myles, Carlo's son, is both a boy and a 'malignant sprite' with webbed toes. His sister, Chloe, blows 'an archaic pipe-note on a blade of grass', echoing Pan, while Rose is 'Ariadne on the Naxos Shore' (Banville 2005, pp. 245–246) and our narrator is a 'lyreless Orpheus' (Banville 2005, p. 24) lost and broken after the death of his wife. Banville is not simply borrowing the allusive significance of these mythic figures; the secondary ontological intertextual frame is so pervasive that the primary ontological frame is actually punctured by it in a number of ways, as when Constance Grace at one point transforms, in Max's delirium, from woman to daemon and back to woman, in 'an instant of divinity' (Banville 2005, p. 118), and Rose appears and disappears in a way that continually puzzles Morden. In fact, the texture of the primary ontological level is so frequently destabilized that one loses a fixed sense of its primacy. Even the characters that ostensibly inhabit the plot are not quite real, with many of them (Chloe, Charlie, Weiss, Anna, Rose, Max/Morden) returning from Banville's previous novels.

Furthermore, the artistic texture of this primary reality is also partially constructed via a series of allusions to paintings by Tenniel, Tiepolo, Whistler, Vermeer, Van Gogh and Bonnard. Morden's fascination with Bonnard alerts us to the intertwined relation between Bonnard's paintings of his wife, Marthe, both during and after her life, and Morden's remembered reconstruction of Anna. The correspondences with Morden's Anna are frequently made, as when Bonnard's Marthe's hand resting on her thigh reminds him of 'Anna's hands on the table that first day we came back from Mr Todd, her helpless hands with palms upturned' (Banville 2005, p.153). The effect of the persistent artistic, mythic and literary references, and the blending of ontological levels is to render the surface of the plotted storyworld deeply unstable, and all of Morden's musings ultimately lead to the following question: 'Who, if not ourselves, were we? All right, leave Anna out of it. Who, if not myself, was I?' (Banville 2005, p.217), followed by 'Anyway, where are the paragons of authenticity against whom my concocted self might be measured?' (Banville 2005, p.218). In many ways, this is what Banville's protagonists have always been asking in different voices and varied stories, without ever being able to provide an answer, like Bonnard trying to find his Marthe by painting her over and over.

As mentioned already, the prospect of direct social representation or commentary in Banville's work is remote. The philosophical and artistic rationale cannot accommodate the realist mode because reality itself is viewed to be unstable and unknowable. But even with literary fictions more clearly derived than Banville's from a recognizable social context, Linda Hutcheon's point about the essential autonomy of story worlds holds good. Anne Enright's *The Gathering* offers a discernible backdrop of comfortable, middle-class Ireland of the Celtic Tiger years, and the incessant work-culture that pays for it, but this is not central to the primary haunting fascinations that breach multiple time-zones and imaginative lives in order to engage deep-rooted, fundamental, human issues. As a reading experience, what is foregrounded in *The Gathering* are the constant time-shifts, frequently without narratorial signposting, and a sense that the characters are being constructed as we read ('He must be reassembled; click clack') (Enright 2007, p.14). The constructed nature of the projected world is everywhere evident, and the containment of an increasingly erratic consciousness, continually drifting free of any single ontological centre, is the primary source of the novel's *artistic* success. Enright's context, to echo those of Langer and Banville, also projects Veronica's persistent sense of dislocation. In a particularly unsettling scene, she loses a concrete sense of herself: 'I can not feel the weight of my body on the bed. I can not feel the line of my skin along the sheet. I am swinging an inch or so off the mattress, and I do not believe in myself – in the way I breathe or turn – and I do not believe in Tom beside me' (Enright 2007, p.133). While such moments are a demonstration of the narrator's increasingly uncertain grasp on her surroundings, they also point to a subjectivization of reality, and an overtly internalized and aestheticized universe.

Dermot Healy's work too is marked by a recurring fascination with the ways in which objective reality is subsumed into an often haunted subjectivity, and 'reality' itself comes to us only as a result of a troubled negotiation within the consciousnesses of the characters. Both *A Goat's Song* (1994) and *Long Time No See* (2011) feature fictional ontologies that are framed against a deep sense of unease at the insubstantiality of the world. Healy's major novel, *A Goat's Song*, repeatedly circles around its major characters' difficulties with assigning precise distinction to their experiences, as when Jack Ferris experiences a pre-linguistic moment that prevents him from imposing an ordered narrative shape on his surroundings: 'He was thinking in another language. The eerie language of the half-formed and the unsayable' (Healy 1995, p. 380). The prospect of locating adequate linguistic shape with which the world might be named is daunting for all the major characters at different points and, to emphasize this, the novel repeats the following line (or slight variants of it) three times: 'to give form to that which cannot be uttered' (Healy 1995, p. 5; p. 99; p. 202). In fact, the novel's primary emphasis might be described as an attempt to find ways to know and speak of a world that never remains fixed. In Healy's most recent novel, *Long Time No See*, the world again remains stubbornly resistant to the forms of our knowledge and evasive of our attempt to fix it in words. Mr Psyche (Philip), for example, frequently experiences moments in which the solidity of the world recedes and gives way to near-hallucinatory events that are infused with something beyond materiality:

> The night was not over yet. I got up and dressed and took the lantern and started walking. It was eerie. I was holding the lantern in my right hand by my thigh, and as I walked the shadows of my two legs grew huge to my left. I was taller than the hedge of tall olearia. Another huge black version of me was walking the beach like a mad colossus. (Healy 2011, p. 46)

Mr Psyche also experiences some extremely odd moments of dislocation as he builds a stone wall, imagining a former builder, long since vanished in time, building beside him, and many of the other characters appear both to participate in the action and to exist simultaneously as creatures separate, aloof in their own consciousnesses, like Psyche's mother who at one point pauses on the stairs lost in a moment only to, a second later, look 'to where she had been standing on the stairs and gave this quaint satisfied nod to herself' (Healy 2011, p. 28). Characters exist in a curious relationship to any material sense of reality throughout the novel which, nevertheless, is, nominally at least, based in Sligo during the Celtic Tiger years. The contemporary social context is purring in the background but its felt significance is apparent only in terms of how it impinges on the oddly mythic small-town lives of these characters. The extraordinary fluid form of the novel, which Healy claims was generated from his desire not to impose fixed meanings – 'In a way, I was trying to stay out of it and let the reader take over and run with it. So I would often put the meaning of a passage in, then take it out again' – accommodates far more dialogue than is usual for prose fiction, the result of which is that the story world is largely constructed in and through direct dialogue, replete with the inevitable misunderstandings (cited in O'Hagan 2011). Without a persistent anchoring narrative voice, the fictional landscape doesn't have an obvious, overt, fixed shape, a feature that accommodates a more fluid sense of how one might aesthetically reflect reality in fiction.

Contemporary Irish writers assert their aestheticizing agendas in diverse ways but a declared awareness of the transformative process that governs the process of narrated experience remains constant. When Joyce places 'style' at the heart of his endeavour he doesn't abandon the terrestrial claims of reality, but he knows that reality is reconstituted through the forms of art. For style, one may substitute, form, or narrative process, or what Donoghue refers to as the 'wrenching of language from the propriety of its normal reference' (Donoghue 2008, p. 135) that one finds in works of literary art. Similarly, Kim Worthington argues that language 'loses its pragmatic representational functions, and becomes the very medium for the interpretative conceptualization of one's self' in her efforts to rationalize the relationship between self and narrative (Worthington 2001, pp 102–103). In a variation of this position, Nabokov offers a crucial distinction between what he calls 'average reality' and a higher order of reality when he suggests that '[a]verage reality begins to rot and stink as soon as the act of individual creation ceases to animate a subjectively perceived texture' (Nabokov 1990, p. 118). The attainment of 'true reality', as projected in literary fiction, alternatively involves a formal reconceiving of reality and allows one to re-envision the constituent parts of the reflected reality. Several of the novels mentioned above project overtly constructed worlds, corresponding to Nabokov's 'true reality', which is reflected in fiction only by the construction of 'real, authentic worlds' (Nabokov 1990, p. 118). Fiction of the kind demanded by Myers reflects only a journalistic reality, or what Nabokov terms the reality of 'general ideas, conventional forms of humdrummery, current editorials' (Nabokov 1990, p. 118).

One should not mistake the absence of a direct social-representational mode for an absence of authentic artistic and philosophical engagement. If there is a distinct pattern that emerges during these years it is a deep, persistent acknowledgement of the essential challenge that accompanies one's efforts to know the world, and one's self in that world, and these are not negligible concerns. In fact, they may well condition our capacity to respond to any social environment. The social-economic transformations that define Ireland during these years may in fact find powerful expression not by holding up a realist mirror but by sustained imaginative engagement with how we internalize the vastness of change, or by locating an artistic mode that is adequate to contain what Wallace Stevens called 'the transposition of an objective reality to a subjective reality' (Stevens 1989, p. 229). Furthermore, as Calvino argues, the most potent and successful art works to stand in relation to the world with 'indirect vision' rather than in mimicry, to seek far-reaching insight without being anchored to the everyday or Nabokov's 'average reality' (Calvino 1993, p. 7). In fact, a desire to see social reality directly reflected in novels may be a retrograde desire. As Jeanette Winterson points out, the future of the novel depends on diversity of imaginative approach rather than the production of replicas of the real: 'If prose fiction is to survive it will have to do more than to tell a story. Fiction that is printed television is redundant fiction. Fiction that is a copy of a nineteenth century novel is no better than any other kind of reproduction furniture' (Winterson 1997, p. 176). There are many ways that a work of fiction can position itself in relation to the world, one of which Adorno claims is directly connected to formal expression as opposed to realist description: 'The unresolved antagonisms of reality reappear in art in the guise of immanent problems of artistic form. This, and not the deliberate injection of objective moments or social content, defines art's relationship to society' (Adorno 1984, p. 8).

As we have seen, many contemporary Irish writers engage with 'the unresolved antagonisms of reality' and with the deeply felt epistemological and artistic challenges that define much of contemporary writing everywhere. In Irish writing, this asserts itself as a persistent acknowledgement of the mutability of human experience and a self-reflexive awareness of the artistic challenge associated with mapping that mutability. And while authors like Enright, Banville, Barry and Healy appear to gaze backwards in time, or into the depths of highly personalized ontological questions, or at the conundrums of artistic form, if one tilts the glass just a little it may be that the reflected image offers us a few useful glimpses of the Celtic Tiger years after all, but by potent, indirect vision.

Works cited

Adorno, Theodor (1984) [1970] *Aesthetic Theory*, London: Routledge and Kegan Paul.

Banville, John (2005) *The Sea*, London: Picador.

Banville, John (2012) *Ancient Light*, London: Viking.

Barry, Sebastian (1998) *The Whereabouts of Eneas McNulty*, Harmondsworth: Penguin.

Barry, Sebastian (2008) *The Secret Scripture*, London: Faber & Faber.

Barry, Sebastian (2011) *On Canaan's Side*, London: Faber & Faber.

Beckett, Samuel (1984) *Disjecta: Miscellaneous Writings and a Dramatic Fragment*, edited by, Ruby Cohn, New York: Grove Press.

Borges, Jorge Luis (1999) *Selected Non-Fictions*, edited by, E. Weinberger, New York: Penguin.

Calvino, Italo (1993) *Six Memos for the New Millennium*, New York: Vintage.

Donoghue, Denis (2003) *Speaking of Beauty*, New Haven: Yale University Press.

Donoghue, Denis (2008) *On Eloquence*, New Haven: Yale University Press.

Ellmann, Richard (1983) *James Joyce*, Oxford: Oxford University Press.

Enright, Anne (2007) *The Gathering*, New York: Black Cat.

Flood, Alison (2010) 'Julian Gough Slams Fellow Irish Novelists as Priestly Caste Cut Off from the Culture', *The Guardian*, 11 February, available: www.guardian.co.uk/books/2010/feb/11/julian-gough-irish-novlists-priestly-caste [accessed 30 September 2012].

Hand, Derek (2006) 'John Banville and Derek Hand in Conversation', *Irish University Review*, 36:1, pp. 200–215.

Healy, Dermot (1995) *A Goat's Song*, London: Harvill.

Healy, Dermot (2011) *Long Time No See*, London: Faber and Faber.

Hutcheon, Linda (1980) *Narcissistic Narrative: The Metafictional Paradox*, Waterloo, Ontario: Wilfrid Laurier University Press.

Imhof, Rüdiger (2006) 'The Sea: Was't Well Done?', *Irish University Review*, 36:1, pp. 165–181.

Kearney, Richard (1988) *Transitions: Narratives in Irish Culture*, Dublin: Wolfhound Press.

Langer, Susanne Katherina Knauth (1953) *Feeling and Form: A Theory of Art*, New York: Scribner.

McHale, Brian (2001) *Postmodernist Fiction*, London: Routledge.

Murphy, Neil (2011) 'Flann O'Brien's *The Hard Life* & the Gaze of the Medusa', *Review of Contemporary Fiction*, 31:3, pp. 148–161.

Myers, Kevin (2010) 'If There Is To Be a Genre of Celtic Tiger Fiction, "Capital Sins" Will Be the Foundation Stone', *The Irish Independent*, 1 July, available: www.independent.ie/opinion/columnists/kevin-myers/kevin-myers-if-there-is-to-be-a-genre-of-celtic-tiger-fiction-capital-sins-will-be-the-foundation-stone-2241241.html [accessed 30 September 2012].

Nabokov, Vladimir (1990) *Strong Opinions*, New York: Vintage.

Oberhelman, Harley D. (1991) 'Excerpts from *The Fragrance of Guava*', in *Gabriel Garcia Marquez: A Study of the Short Fiction*, Boston: Twayne Publishers.

O'Brien, Flann (1993) [1939] *At Swim-Two-Birds*, Normal, IL: Dalkey Archive Press.

O'Brien, Flann (1999) [1968] *The Third Policeman*, Normal, IL: Dalkey Archive Press.

O'Hagan, Sean (2011) 'Dermot Healy: "I try to stay out of it and let the reader take over": Interview with Sean O'Hagan', *The Observer*, 3 April 2011, available: http://www.guardian.co.uk/books/2011/apr/03/dermot-healy-interview-long-time [accessed 30 September 2012].

Stevens, Wallace (1989) [1957] *Opus Posthumous*, New York: Knopf.

Wallace, Arminta (2012) 'I Wondered How on Earth We Ended up Where We Did', *The Irish Times*, 18 September, available: www.irishtimes.com/newspaper/features/2012/0918/1224324117646.html [accessed 30 September 2012].

Winterson, Jeanette (1997) *Art Objects: Essays on Ecstasy and Effrontery*, New York: Vintage Books.

Worthington, Kim (2001) *Self as Narrative: Subjectivity and Community in Contemporary Fiction*, Oxford: Clarendon Press.

Yeats, William Butler (1961) *Essays and Introductions*, New York: Macmillan.

13

'Holes in the ground': theatre as critic and conscience of Celtic Tiger Ireland

Vic Merriman

> Article 43.1 The State acknowledges that man, in virtue of his rational being, has the natural right, antecedent to positive law, to the private ownership of external goods.
> Article 43.2 The State accordingly guarantees to pass no law attempting to abolish the right of private ownership or the general right to transfer, bequeath, and inherit property. (*Bunreacht na h-Éireann / The Constitution of Ireland*, 2002, p. 166)

> Every productivist society probably counts intellectual laziness, the loathing of thought, as its dominant passion. (Badiou 2008, p. 195)

> The dominant appetite is the appetite for prey of one kind or another. (Hibbard 1977, p. xx)

During the years of economic boom, a tone of smug self-regard achieved cultural, social and political hegemony in Celtic Tiger Ireland. 'Holes in the ground' explores how acts of performance cast light on the social logic of that hegemony, and how its influence was contested. Both at work and at play, the driver of the Celtic Tiger phenomenon was the turbo-charge given to a small number of key persons and companies in the building industry by influential members of successive Fianna Fáil governments, including successive *taoisigh*. As others have shown (O'Toole 2009; Clancy, Connor and Dillon 2010), technical arrangements, legal instruments and felicitous opportunities combined with relationships which were close, personal and interdependent, to produce what might variously be described as a 'climate for', or a 'culture of' individualistic wealth accumulation. While the economic effectiveness of business relationships sailing close to the wind of conflicts of interest depended on circumspection, if not secrecy, their cultural efficacy relied on their being conducted in plain sight. The closeness of 'developers', legislators, banking and media which underpinned the hegemonic tone of Celtic Tiger Ireland was not only not concealed, it was performed aggressively in elaborate displays of affluence, leisure and bonhomie. During the years of 'Spend! Spend! Spend!' those who sated themselves from the country's holdings gathered annually to 'party' in a tent in Galway, during Race Week. The mutation of the word 'party' from noun to verb is an apt signifier for Tiger Ireland, and this was a party where all present partied for the Party – Fianna Fáil. The people in the tent formed what amounted to a national caucus for private wealth accumulation. Those who were not there were literally not 'at the races' when it came to involvement in that caucus and its accompanying national circus of affluent display. As ever in Ireland, the appearance of the word 'national' prompts vigilance; all will not be as it seems. In fact, all will not be all, but a rhetorical substitution of elite concerns and practices for those more widely shared, understood and struggled over in the mass of the population.

No person living in Ireland was unaware of the relationships and dynamics underpinning the boom in conspicuous consumption. The *Sunday Independent*, house magazine of Ireland Successful, lionized moneyed people, their children and their hangers-on. Lawyers, bankers, restaurateurs and media figures – providing they were ideologically aligned with a cult of individualism – became celebrities, and qualified for an endless round of public appearances, from write-ups of nights out among the beautiful people to celebrity chef programmes on television. Neither was the national broadcaster found wanting as a cheerleader. Not even news bulletins were safe: league tables of helicopter ownership or ratios of golf courses to population were the subjects of breathless propagandizing; in short, anything which buttressed the narrative 'Aren't We Great!' was draped in faux evidential robes and sent parading down the national catwalk of self-regard. The disinterested endorsement of the broadcaster itself[1] was crucial to the authentication of contributions to that narrative, and this was achieved by means of enthusiastic commentaries solicited on-air from self-styled 'Corporates', 'Wealth Creators', Think Tanks, and other Journalists (capitalization intended). Indeed, the roar of the Celtic Tiger was, in effect, a cacophony of such endorsements with all the cultural impact of a wall of white noise. Dissent from, let alone opposition to, this 'national' consensus was so marginalized that, by 2007, Bartholomew (Bertie) Ahern TD, third-term Taoiseach[2] and leader of Fianna Fáil, would say of those who questioned the health or sustainability of the Tiger economy, 'Sitting on

[1] 'Ryan Tubridy is one of Ireland's most recognised and respected opinion formers and media personalities.' Statement on back flap of Ryan Tubridy, *JFK in Ireland: Four Days that Changed a President* (Tubridy 2010).
[2] Ahern formed a government with the support of the Green Party on 14 June 2007, following the General Election held on Thursday 24 May 2007.

the sidelines, cribbing and moaning is a lost opportunity. I don't know how people who engage in that don't commit suicide' (Ahern 2007).

Here, in broad strokes, are the cultural contours of Celtic Tiger Ireland; a public space constitutionally hostile to critical scrutiny. Throughout the economic boom, critical warnings of the consequences of indenturing a generation to the banks by means of grossly inflated housing costs were dismissed as the concerns of academics (Ruddock 2009),[3] and those travestied as beneficiaries of 'the poverty industry'. The State, in its new guise as Competition State that 'prioritises goals of economic competitiveness over those of social cohesion and welfare' (Kirby 2010, p. 141), was doing little or nothing to address the needs of the majority of people, and this inertia greatly facilitated elites. It is instructive here that when a second edition of Peadar Kirby's *Celtic Tiger in Distress: Growth with Inequality in Ireland* (2002) was published, it was retitled *Celtic Tiger in Collapse: Explaining the Weaknesses of the Irish Model* (2010). Some sociologists were critically engaged, then, as were cultural historians, especially Joe Lee (1999):

> This is an entity – it can hardly be called a society – based in exclusion. It is defined in terms of the exclusion of those who fail to conform to the model of the geographically mobile, who have no need of a sense of place. People exist only as producers and consumers. There is only one generation involved, there being no place for the uneconomic. It is a one-generational Ireland, it is an economy, not a society. (cited in Kirby 2002, p. 145)

Avowedly oppositional drama has always had a difficult reception in Ireland, but to oppose the accumulating consensus articulated so aggressively by Ahern required not only a sharp sense of what had to be opposed but an ethical commitment to theatre's capacity to do so. Most importantly, as will be argued, it required the judicious selection of performative forms.

The year 2002 was an election year, and it began and ended at the Abbey Theatre with plays confronting the topical matter of political corruption: *Hinterland*, by Sebastian Barry (January–February 2002), and *Ariel*, by Marina Carr (September–November 2002). Both plays locate

---

[3] *The Irish Times*, I suspect, would call it balance. After running a series of articles by some of Ireland's more successful businessmen, each offering his advice to Brian Cowen on how he could reinvigorate the Irish economy, the paper of record followed with a piece of unmitigated gloom from Morgan Kelly, the economics professor at University College Dublin. House prices will halve, he said, so buyers should just stay away from the market. And if that wasn't bad enough, he added that we were entering a ten-year recession. (Ruddock 2008).

corruption as a function of an individual bent on power at all costs, and both deploy classical dramatic models to explore this premise. Harvey O'Brien (2002) offers an insightful account of problems besetting both works:

[*Ariel*] attempts to explore the anxieties of a modern Ireland with recourse to premodern theatrical forms, stopping along the way to touch on the themes of family, religion, and politics which have traditionally occupied Irish dramatists. This has been attempted before, even as recently as Sebastian Barry's *Hinterland*. Barry used Shakespeare as a reference point and failed to find the required level of high drama in the life of former Taoiseach Charles Haughey. Carr is not necessarily any more successful. Her evident care with language and at least some successful attempts to blend the narrative spaces of naturalistic drama with monumental villainy of the Greek tragedy do make it interesting. Unfortunately, by the time the play reaches its multiple climaxes complete with ghostly apparitions, wailing from the wings, and on-stage bloodletting, some of the audience had given over to inappropriate laughter, suggesting that true balance between elements has not been achieved. (O'Brien 2002)

Hinterland found itself embroiled in controversy to such an extent that, at a press conference called to defend the theatre's decision to programme the work, Ben Barnes (artistic director of the Abbey Theatre) remarked on the irony of Irish journalists weeping crocodile tears for the sensitivities of members of the Haughey family. *Ariel* was not regarded as one of Marina Carr's finer achievements, and it may be that the perceived unsatisfactoriness of such high-profile works led to the emergence of a view that theatre failed the test of this historical moment. O'Toole's television documentary *Power Plays* (2011) confined his concern to a perceived dearth of large, main stage productions confronting the venality of Tiger Ireland. Lamenting the fact that Julian Gough's *The Great Goat Bubble* (Galway Arts Festival, 2012) hadn't been staged in 2003, Fintan O'Toole put this point with considerable force:

As a play, and therefore a public act, it would have said two things at the same time. One is that our bubble is inflated by insanity and is bound to burst. The other is that we can't even talk about it because we have a consensus that is almost as coercive as if we were living in a police state. But of course, neither of these things was actually said in the Irish theatre at the time. Of course, this is not the fault of Gough or of Fishamble [Dublin-based theatre company] and the play is certainly better late than never. It more than earns its place in the present tense. But it is thinner than it would have been a decade ago, missing that whole layer of insinuating subversion ... Nonetheless, it deserves to tour widely and to be seen both for entertainment and instruction. It might be slightly depressing in reminding us of what Irish theatre failed to do but it shows that there is no big subject that can't be done now, with courage and imagination and without the benefit of hindsight. (O'Toole 2012)

The charge specifically levelled in this review goes further than the argument in *Power Plays*, but it can be sustained only if a number of direct challenges to Tiger hegemony, and to its 'appetite for prey', are deliberately ignored. Such plays include Páraic Breathnach and others, *Site: A Builder's Tale* (Fir Clis, Galway, 1999); Brian Desmond and Máirtín de Cógáin, *Thailand: What's Love Got to Do with It?* (Be Your own Banana Theatre Company, various venues in Cork, 2007); Tom Hall, *Boss* (Meridian Theatre Company, Cork, 2008); Pom Boyd, Declan Lynch, Arthur Riordan, *Boomtown!* (Rough Magic Theatre Company, Dublin, 1999 and 2009); David McWilliams, *Outsiders* (Peacock Theatre, Dublin, 2010). The time spanned by these works includes the statistical highpoint of Tiger 'success' (1999–2002), through to 2008, when the banks collapsed the economy, and on to 2010, as the public demand for answers and culprits resulted in a 'riot at the ballot box'.[4]

All these plays – *Outsiders* included, but excluding *Thailand*, which merits thorough consideration in its own right – are about building, and about the public culture produced by profits made from holes in the ground. Each is haunted by the spectre of collapse, a kind of premonitory shiver at the dereliction encoded in the very framework of the edifices erected to mark the progress of the Celtic Tiger. They are very clearly about systems of corruption, and dramatize a series of relationships and exchanges, rather than the actions of uniquely venal individuals, as in *Hinterland* or *Ariel*. *Site: A Builder's Tale* was staged in the open air at Fisheries Field in Galway, in 1999, twelve years before *The Great Goat Bubble*. It thematized the circumstances of a young couple contemplating house-purchase in Ireland and the fact that, in pursuit of affordability, many were coming to accept long commuter journeys to Dublin and other population centres as an inevitable consequence of 'getting into the market'. Fittingly – Ahern's Finance Minister, and successor as Taoiseach, Brian Cowen, represented County Offaly in Dáil Éireann – the remote housing estate which they visit as prospective purchasers is called 'Offaly Close'. During the course of the play, which stages the couple's buffeting by a cabal of rapacious local politicians and builders, including Páidí Mé Féin and Buff Murphy, a house in

---

[4] A remark attributed to 'a senior Fianna Fáil politician', following his party's decimation in the election of 25 February 2011. The incoming Taoiseach, Enda Kenny, described the result as 'a democratic revolution' (*Irish Times*, 28 February 2011).

Offaly Close inflates in price from IR£100,000 to IR£260,000. In *Site*, the implied threat of dereliction is fulfilled literally, in the levelling of a house constructed in front of the audience, by workers cheated of their wages.

Tom Hall's play for solo performer, *Boss* (Meridian Theatre Company, Granary Theatre, Cork, 2008) stages the vicissitudes of Jim Kielty, during a dark night of the soul, at his villa in Spain. Kielty has been named in a long-running tribunal of inquiry into planning corruption, and has been tracked to his bolt-hole by the ubiquitous Charlie Bird, political reporter with RTÉ television. His angry confessional narrative takes the audience into the underbelly of the Tiger economy, and exposes the genesis of its aggressive individualism in power relations embedded in Independent Ireland since the 1920s. O'Toole's summary of *The Great Goat Bubble* could have been written with *Boss* in mind: 'The point is not that it is in itself a theatrical masterpiece, but rather that it shows how a large political subject can be handled on stage with very modest resources'. O'Toole's charge, in 2012, that 'it is uncomfortable to reflect that it has taken almost a decade for such a story to become fit matter for the stage' (O'Toole 2012), is somewhat compromised in light of the explicit concerns of the plays mentioned (1999; 2008). The real difficulties attending *Site* and *Boss*, according to the writers and producers of both plays, had to do with the obstacles to producing oppositional work – including funding, the experience of playing critical work into 'a consensus that is almost as coercive as if we were living in a police state' (O'Toole 2012) and a more general problem of having risky, underfunded work acknowledged in mainstream media. For his part, Breathnach went into print to excoriate a creeping managerialism in arts funding policy (Siggins 2000), which denied *Site* a modest touring grant, in the face of its outstanding success. Even though Meridian Theatre Company was prepared to stage Hall's work, there were tense exchanges in the rehearsal room over how those who were pulling the levers of 'Ireland Successful' might be represented. Hall's dramaturgical battle with the director, Johnny Hanrahan, concentrated particularly on the use of images of actual events and people. Hanrahan seems to have known his audience, as such references as survived the engagement greatly irritated reviewer Rachel Andrews:

> So present is it – it makes pointed reference to people such as Tony O'Reilly, Michael Smurfit and Charles Haughey – that one senses, at times, that the work could be transposed to the back pages of a newspaper, where Hall (or indeed Kielty) could take his place as an enraged columnist. If, in some

respects, this appears unfair – after all, Hall is a lyrical writer, and there is more substance to this work than exists in many newspaper columns – it is the tone of the monologue that forces the comparison. Kielty is angry and hectoring, and his accusations confrontational; the more he hectors and accuses, the more we, as an audience, reach for our defences. There is a difference between being encouraged to consider a particular point of view and being beaten over the head to do so. The biggest difficulty with Hall's narrative is that, clever and illusory though it is, it lacks a fundamental subtlety, necessary for theatre to impose itself upon the mind. (Andrews 2008, p. 96)

Boss's shortcomings are presented as an affront to a view of theatre as an 'innocent and prosperous ritual' (Badiou 2008, p. 187). Rather than engage with the critical content of the play – systemic corruption in Ireland – the review charges the playwright with tone-crimes. When theatre takes on the venality and blindness of a smug society, it is dismissed for not confining itself to safe and predictable material couched in subtleties to be appreciated in a kind of stupor of detachment from lived experience. Without overdoing the significance either of *Boss* or of the position of its reviewer, Andrews offers an example of the stifling consensus towards the status quo which was excoriated by Fintan O'Toole. Even if agreement could be reached on what subtlety means, it would be a very poor tone to adopt in response to conditions in Ireland in the decade under discussion.

Two incidents attending the production of *Site* give a sense of the impact of what amounted to a gold rush on everyday living. When Footsbarn's Rod Goodall returned to Galway to direct the revival of the play, after an absence of a few years, he 'asked for a native Galwegian guide to help familiarise him with the new city that has grown up in his absence' (*City Tribune* 2000). On the opening night of the 1999 Festival, the actor Pauline McLynn drove almost ninety miles from Kilkenny to Galway in two hours, but had to finish her journey to the opening ceremony at which she was guest speaker on foot. She had spent one hour attempting to travel some five miles or so through roads clogged with traffic generated by the concentration of new houses around the city's perimeter, 'That led her to suggest that Galway's traffic chaos should become a theme for a festival show next year, similar to the way that the building industry has been highlighted this year by Fir Clis's show, *Site*' (*City Tribune* 16 April 1999). It goes without saying that traffic congestion was not a separate issue, but a function of poorly planned suburban 'development'. In *Site* and, as will be seen, Rough Magic's *Boomtown!* (1999), artists are confronted with the ecstatic veneration of capital acquisition and a feeding frenzy for property, and they turn to the least subtle of dramatic forms, satire, as a counterblast.

In David McWilliams's *Outsiders* (directed by Conall Morrison, Peacock Theatre, Dublin, June 2010), dramatic form all but disappears, and McWilliams delivers a compelling presentation, precisely akin to that which might be given by a well-informed newspaper columnist, whether enraged or not. *Outsiders* followed a season in which the National Theatre turned to documentary drama to cope, firstly, with child abuse. In *Outsiders*, less a solo play than a public lecture with stage effects, McWilliams sustains a forensic examination of the structured cronyism that collapsed Ireland's economy from within. The show attracted capacity houses – including political and media figures – for its angry response and radical economic prescription: Ireland must not socialize private bank debt; there must be a managed default. McWilliams may write with the benefit of hindsight, but *Outsiders* is not at all 'a rueful retrospect, evoking sad laughter' (O'Toole 2012). On the contrary, it agitates for an end to 'Insider Culture' in Irish public affairs, and the applause it drew anticipates precisely the defenestration from office of Fianna Fáil and the Green Party some months later.

In considering critical dramaturgy produced during the boom period, it is essential to reflect not only on the perceived quality of the work as mediated by print and broadcast media but on the intention of each 'public act', the resources available to realize it, and the degree of distance between the dramatic action and the prevailing consensus. These tensions are nowhere more evident than in Rough Magic's *Boomtown!* (1999 and 2009). *Boomtown!*'s production history presents a unique opportunity to track the development of public attitudes to critical theatre practice over a period of extraordinary collapse from individual excess to public penury. It was critically lambasted in its original production in 1999, and the sharp contrast between that dismissal and enthusiastic public responses to its revival, in staged reading form in 2009, exposes a trajectory over ten years, from denial to angry recrimination. It also foregrounds questions of representation and interpretation which, at a time of economic collapse, are set to be very sharply posed as theatre struggles between historical responsibilities to critique the social order and aggressive imperatives not to rock a sinking ship.

In 1999, Lynne Parker, artistic director of Rough Magic Theatre Company, decided that 'after a couple of elegant comedies of manners, the company wanted to respond, viscerally and noisily, to the burgeoning Celtic Tiger, and to remind Ireland where we all came from' (Parker 2012). Parker described *Boomtown!* as 'a big graphic novel; a dark comedic cartoon' (Parker 2012). The company placed the 'grosser aspects of the dark underbelly of the Celtic Tiger onstage, and some people found it unpalatable as a result'. Rough Magic compounded the difficulties accompanying its dramaturgical ambition by constructing, from scratch, a wooden theatre modelled on Shakespeare's Globe to accommodate the performance; a project 'well beyond our capabilities in terms of production infrastructure and immediate resources' (Parker 2012). This contributed to what seems to have been an unsatisfactory theatrical experience, or, as Gerry Colgan wrote in *The Irish Times*:

> Occasionally, one has the sense of a production – usually of a new play – freewheeling downhill from its conception to its opening night. Over the edge it goes, to the dismay of its audience. How on earth did it happen that no-one shouted, 'Stop!'? (Colgan 1999)

Boomtown! opens in Temple Bar, in Dublin city centre, at 7.00 am on 29 September 1979. Traffic has been banned from the area between the canals, as this is the day that Pope John Paul II will celebrate Mass in front of a million people in the city's Phoenix Park. After a brief prologue which explains that a few knowledgeable persons have breached the police cordon, the action begins with a five-car pile-up, involving a ministerial Mercedes, a Jaguar, a Toyota Hi-ace van, a Citroën Dyane and a Fiat Bambino – all Irish life is here. The Jaguar is owned by developer Gerry Wall, the Mercedes is the official car used by Noel 'the Flank' Mongy TD, the modest Dyane contains Colmo and Carmo from the southern suburbs, the Bambino, Diarmaid and heavily pregnant Gráinne, and from the Hi-ace emerge Daddy and Mammy, a monstrous pair of muck-savages on the make. The crash scene is overlooked by a well-known landmark, The Rare Oul' Times public house. We learn that the pub is packed to capacity with priests awaiting delivery of ID cards to enable them access to the Pope's Mass; the country, it appears, is awash with fake priests. Wall and Mongy were on their way to a rendezvous with Fr Dermot Hole in the Furry Glen in the Phoenix Park, but Mongy reveals that Fr Hole actually owns The Rare Oul' Times, and is among the waiting priests within.

Wall's assistant, Regina Fingerty, draws out of Mongy the outlines of the deal he and Wall are to close with Fr Hole, a criminal scheme on which the dramatic action turns: Hole will transfer 660 acres of church land to Wall's company, Omnivore, and Omnivore will sign 49 per cent of the land over to Mongy's wife's company, Chieftain Holdings, for £1. Mongy will ensure no government action is taken on foot of rumours of child abuse at the Corrective Academy for the Sons of the Unruly run by Fr Hole and his brother, Fr Gabriel Hole. By the end of the act, however, Mammy and Daddy have avenged the sexual abuse of their friends' son by killing and eating Father Hole, and taking possession of his pub. Punk Alice, the mother of Mongy's child, has fallen to her death from the roof of the pub, during a conversation with Fingerty; this leaves Wall and Fingerty in possession of a document entitling Alice's son to a share of Chieftain Holdings. Mongy himself is set upon and apparently eaten by Mammy and Daddy, and various other *dramatis personae* are involved in set pieces around swapped babies, stolen money, theft and drug-dealing. The penultimate scene of Act I features three drunken priests at the topmost windows of The Rare Oul' Times, speaking an interwoven commentary on the Pope's progress through Dublin, and a horse race. In the former narrative, much is made of the Pope's ignoring of people assembled at a poor inner-city church, in honour of the ascetic Workman Saint, Matt Talbot; in the latter, the race is won by Aren't We Great, with Irish Image trailing far behind the field.

Act II opens in the same location, exactly twenty years later, in 1999. Broadcasting from The Rare Oul' Times, now known as the ROT, the unctuous chat show host Cora McCarthy interviews people for her show, *Let's Face It*, on the twentieth anniversary of the visit of Pope John Paul II. Her special guest is Oisín, former lead singer of Boyzarse. On his global travels with Boyzarse, Oisín has learned that 'everyone loves the Irish … We're Irish. Wow!' Fr Hole's shade wanders undetected through the action, bitterly cursing his fate and delivering jeremiads, unheard by those who are 'doing well'. An orgy of self-congratulation, *Let's Face It* shares the ROT with Margadh Mór, a massive property clearance sale upstairs in the Bualadh Bas Lounge. As Rachel Fingerty of Coolaboola Chieftain Omnivore Corporation asks, 'Why buy a house in Dublin when you could buy a whole street in Derry?' Finally, after disguises are abandoned and identities restored, Oisín performs his 'song for Ireland', *Aren't We Great?*

Reflecting on the play's reception, and on the impact of the reworked script's revival in rehearsed reading form in 2009, Parker concludes, '*Boomtown!* was a very important show, and I'd defend to the last our right to put it on' (Parker 2012). As she told the then Director of An Chomhairle Ealaíon / The Arts Council, Patricia Quinn, who 'carpeted' her for the perceived poor quality of the play, 'It was catastrophic, maybe, but not mediocre!' Neither Lynne Parker nor this analysis proposes that *Boomtown!* was a string of pearls cast before swine; it 'lacked coherence', and 'needed a decent dramaturge and a bit more time to make it into a decent piece of theatre' (Parker 2012). But, Parker concluded, in introducing the 2009 reading, 'There is actually great stuff here. It is about something. It had an intention, and its intention was to satirise in a really excoriating way what was going on in Irish society, and funnily enough it still has something to say' (Parker 2009). If the audience response to the 2009 reading is anything to go by, there may well be more than a grain of truth in Sara Keating's observation in *The Irish Times*: 'sordid, yes; "an extraordinary failure" – as Declan Hughes called it – perhaps; but maybe it was a play that just came before its time' (Keating 2009).

This is a reasonable starting point to ponder what this play's reception may reveal about the development and interpretation of critical dramaturgies in Ireland, during a period of extraordinary social, economic and cultural upheaval. In the first place, the 1979/1999 time span is significant, both economically and culturally. The visit of John Paul II in 1979 was an event in which a hegemonic Church whose step was faltering invested a great deal of resources and aspirations. A man widely touted as a charismatic and engaging figure would 'bring all the lapsed Catholics back to the Church'.[5] He would also insert religious steel in the spines of those who would emerge as a socially regressive right-wing force, during the fifteen years following his visit. Retrospectively, 1979 is seen as a great cultural watershed, to the extent that David McWilliams's 2005 state-of-the-nation bestseller was called *The Pope's Children: Ireland's New Elite*. It is not uncommon, though it is unfortunate, to hear people speak of that visit as the beginning of a new national self-confidence, fully manifest in the Tiger economy. The reality was that the 1980s reprised much of the social malaise of the 1950s, most notably in the re-emergence of the abiding scourge of Independent Ireland, emigration. None the less, the papal visit of 1979 is frequently referenced as a kind of nativity story for the Celtic Tiger. Casting a jaundiced eye on what the citizenry was actually preoccupied with on that day is a provocative choice, and signals the intention of *Boomtown!*, at least in part, as looking for trouble. The idea that *Boomtown!*'s venal Dublin in 1999 is not a travesty of this mythical moment but the fruition of forces already at work in Ireland in 1979 sets up the satirical impact of Act II.

If Fr Hole's property dealings are the stuff of secrets in Act I, Act II stages the centrality of the ostentatious performance of property ownership, social connections and conspicuous consumption which characterizes Tiger Ireland; in Ireland, rogues prosper, and rogues and cheats are everywhere. Oisín, for instance, is not Oisín, the son born to Diarmaid and Gráinne in Act I, but the son of Mongy and Punk Alice swapped for Gráinne's newborn child in the chaos of the papal visit. While Wall and Fingerty are in trouble, they are not before the courts, but traipse in and out of tribunals of inquiry; they're still 'in business'. The truly egregious Daddy and Mammy are sleek and prosperous, living well on

---

[5] A comment made to the author in 1979 by a parish priest serving in a large working-class area of west Dublin.

the proceeds of murder, cannibalism and unearned money. Daddy has mellowed in the role of proprietor, and has mastered pop psychology:

> Cora: Y'know, as a journalist, the biggest thrill is when I come in contact with real people like yourselves. And these days whenever I do I like to ask a straightforward, no-nonsense, hard journalism real person question ... What is it that makes Irish people so great; do you know what I mean?
> Mammy: Well, eh, that's a ten marker, and no mistake.
> Daddy: Well y'know, Cora I think I'd put it down to a charming paradox in the Irish psyche ... so none of us dare to think of ourselves as great, which, paradoxically, is what makes us ... so great. (Pom Boyd, Declan Lynch, Arthur Riordan, *Boomtown!* 2009 version)

From the mid-1980s on, the authority of empty self-congratulation over critical discourse was identified by Joseph Lee, Luke Gibbons, Joe Cleary, Peadar Kirby and others, as a core structural weakness in Irish public life. By staging the grubby proprietors of the ROT as they are lionized by the national broadcaster, *Boomtown!* exposes to plain view the means by which such authority is achieved and celebrated. It is worth pointing out that Bertie Ahern's persona, the 'Teflon Taoiseach', was itself created and sustained by print and broadcast media at a level of brazenness that is quite breathtaking. Act II of *Boomtown!* tracks the working through of a culture of self-promotion and dismissal which reached its zenith in Ahern's 2007 remarks, so it is hardly surprising that, in 1999, 'some people condemned [*Boomtown!*] as unpatriotic' (Parker 2012). While the connection between an empty media culture and the state of the country was not lost on *Boomtown!*'s audience in 2009, it was never even discussed in 1999.

With no shortage of critical content, formal choices become crucial. According to Harvey O'Brien and others, poor use of classical drama-turgical models disabled both *Hinterland* and *Ariel*. Rough Magic and its panel of writers turned deliberately to Jacobean city comedy as a model for 'a strong, immediate, satirical response to an emerging situation'. Tim Prentki, author of *The Fool in European Theatre: Stages of Folly*, defends the instinct that such a model was appropriate to the nature and scale of the task:

> Just as the boom years of the Irish economy gave rise to a complacent, 'get rich quick' attitude among the cronies of the politicians with access to the gravy trough, so the hangers-on at the court of King James and their nouveau riche accomplices in the newly prosperous mercantile class spawned a type of venture capitalism out of the risky but enormous profits in the wake of global, naval exploration/exploitation. (Prentki personal communication 2012)

As a critical cultural intervention, however, *Boomtown!*'s first iteration was unsuccessful, for reasons deeper than its success or failure as a night out in Theatre Festival season; they are the problems of satire itself. Prentki argues:

> Satire is the mode of outrage and its aim is to provoke reform of corruption within the system. It does not, however, encompass the possibility of reform to the deep structures of a society, still less of revolution. In both periods of 'we've never had it so good' the emphasis of the satirists was more on extending the social range of 'we' than questioning whether 'it' was morally, socially or politically defensible. (Prentki personal communication 2012).

Thanking the 2009 director, Darragh McKeown, for having 'corralled the beast for us' (Parker 2009), Lynne Parker acknowledges flaws in *Boomtown!* which suggest not only lack of time but – perhaps – a lack of developed playwriting capacity in what is a notoriously untameable dramatic form.

Neither *Hinterland*, *Ariel*, *Site*, *Boomtown!*, *Boss* nor *Outsiders* sits easily among critical narratives of great Irish theatre. The practical, critical and dramaturgical struggles involved in bringing them to the stage are none the less of considerable interest as the trajectories of the spectacular ascent of the few, and the catastrophic fall of the many, are analysed for what they reveal of what remains of civil society under advanced capitalism. In 2000, Joe Cleary argued that Ireland was 'a society with neither the resources nor the strategies required to meet the challenges of the future' (Cleary 2000). Current government policy is heavily vested in recapturing economic sovereignty from the neo-colonial clutches of the EU/IMF Troika, by 2014–15. The problem is that what is being protected in the face of a wholesale withdrawal of the State and its services is the failed economic infrastructure. Minimum social guarantees are disappearing in the face of a frenzied assault by new beasts, whose 'appetite for prey' is greater than any tiger – the voracious demons of the global market economy. Since Ireland's economic collapse, the social landscape is marked by abandoned homes, a collapse in living standards, closed-up shops and mass emigration. It should be a cause for deep concern that, since then, the aspect of life that ultimately shocks most is not these indicators of human misery – Irish people have seen them before – but the continuity of influence on public consciousness and public memory of those 'opinion formers' who were the cheerleaders of the Land of the Spree. Who will counter their clamour for more of the same, when the Troika departs, and the ship of state floats once again?

The clock ticks towards the centenaries of the proclamation of the Republic (2016), and the Democratic Programme of the First Dáil (2018). There is latent potential for progressive futures for an Irish Republic, in the formidable output of the *Think Tank for Action on Social Change* (TASC), the opportunity to review the State's constitution, and the public espousal by President Michael D. Higgins of the need to renew the republic. Joe Cleary's conclusion was grounded, not in an analysis of state formation and economic data alone, but in an engaged critical reading of cultural production. Its lucidity and prescience suggest that, in its present crisis, Ireland needs a cultural project, a mobilization of both critical and creative energy in the interests of the common good, and a shared goal of a decent, democratic, society.

Works cited

Ahern, Bertie (2007) 'Address to Irish Congress of Trades Unions, 3 July 2007', available: www.youtube.com/watch?v=hfjGSfuSQpA_[accessed 20 September 2012].

Andrews, Rachel (2008) 'Review: *Boss* by Thomas Hall', *Irish Theatre Magazine*, 8:35 (Summer), pp. 94–96.

Badiou, Alain (2008) 'Rhapsody for the Theatre: A Short Philosophical Treatise', *Theatre Survey*, American Society for Theatre Research, 49:2 (November), pp. 187–238.

Boyd, Pom, Lynch, Declan and Riordan, Arthur (2009) *Boomtown!*, Dublin: Rough Magic Theatre Company, DVD recording of rehearsed reading at Project Arts Centre, 2009. All script references are to this performance.

Bunreacht na h-Éireann / The Constitution of Ireland (2002) Dublin: Government Publications.

Clancy, Paula, O'Connor, Nat and Dillon, Kevin (2010) *Mapping the Golden Circle*, Dublin: TASC.

Cleary, Joseph (2000) 'Modernization and Aesthetic Ideology in Contemporary Irish Culture', in Ryan Ray, (ed.), *Writing in the Irish Republic: Literature, Culture, Politics 1949–1999*, Basingstoke: Macmillan, pp. 106–129.

Colgan, Gerry (1999) 'Review of *Boomtown!*', *Irish Times*, 10 October.

'From Footsbarn to Fir Clis' (2000) *City Tribune* (Galway, 7 April).

Hibbard, G. R. (1977) 'Introduction' to Ben Jonson, *Bartholmew Fair*, London: Ernest Benn Ltd.

Jonson, Ben (1977) [1631] *Bartholmew Fair*, London: Ernest Benn Ltd.

Keating, Sara (2009) 'The Rough Magic and Method in Its Madness', *Irish Times*, 8 April.

Kirby, Peadar (2002) *Celtic Tiger in Distress: Growth with Inequality in Ireland*, Basingstoke: Macmillan.

Kirby, Peadar (2010) *Celtic Tiger in Collapse: Explaining the Weaknesses of the Irish Model*, London: Palgrave Macmillan.

O'Brien, Harvey (2002) '*Ariel* by Marina Carr', available: www.culturevulture. net/Theater/Airtel.htm_[accessed 20 September 2012].

O'Toole, Fintan (2009) *Ship of Fools: How Stupidity and Corruption Sank the Celtic Tiger*, London: Faber.

O'Toole, Fintan (2011) *Power Plays*, Midas Productions for RTÉ1; broadcast 7 June.

O'Toole, Fintan (2012) 'Observe the Great Goat Circling the Rotting Remains of the Tiger', *Irish Times*, 4 August.

Parker, Lynne (2009) *Introductory Remarks* at Rehearsed Reading of *Boomtown!* (Project Arts Centre, 2009).

Parker, Lynne (2012) Interview with the author, February.

Prentki, Tim (2012) *The Fool in European Theatre: Stages of Folly*, Basingstoke: Palgrave Macmillan.

Ruddock, Alan (2008) 'Cowen Must Take the Advice of Wealth Creators', *Sunday Independent*, 17 August.

Siggins, Lorna (2000) 'Theatre Director Plans Protest at Arts Council', *Irish Times*, 17 April.

Tubridy, Ryan (2010) *JFK in Ireland: Four Days that Changed a President*, London: HarperCollins.

14

'Ship of fools': the Celtic Tiger and poetry as social critique

Eóin Flannery

> The public consists of all those who are affected by the indirect conse-
> quences of transactions to such an extent that it is deemed necessary to
> have these consequences systematically cared for. Officials are those who
> look out for and take care of the interests thus affected. Since those who
> are indirectly affected are not direct participants in the transactions in
> question, it is necessary that certain persons be set apart to represent them,
> and to see to it that their interests are conserved and protected. (Dewey
> 1927, pp. 15–16)

Politics, public art and poetry

We might justifiably ask: why should we pursue an examination of the
relationship between poetry and the Celtic Tiger? Are there lessons to
be learned from heeding the lyrical engagements with the ecological and
socio-economic fall-out of the country's recent prosperity? In another,
perhaps more universal, way we are concerned with the problematic
of where and how poetry can intervene or speak out in contemporary
'public' debates. And if we consider this last point urgent in the Irish
context, then one of Astrid Franke's arguments in her survey of public
poetry in the United States could serve as a productive point of departure for our critique. In Franke's view, and this appears entirely apposite
in reading Irish poetry under the recent and current conjuncture, what
poets who participate in public dialogues

> have in common is that they understand the public role of poetry not as
> a given but as a challenge; to think the public anew and to devise ways
> in which common concerns could be expressed demands innovation in
> language, in subject matter, and in social roles, not least that of the poet.
> Thus aesthetic innovation and public commitment, though there may be a
> tension between them, are yet intertwined. (Franke 2010, p. 5)

It would be presumptuous, and arguably misplaced, to advocate
here that any of the poets under scrutiny have *consciously* assumed

high-profile social roles. But what is certain is that their combined, but differentiated, stylistic innovations and thematic preoccupations are forceful and varied affirmations of the necessity for poetry to partake in the public reckonings with the legacies of the Celtic Tiger. As Franke highlights, poetry's role in the public sphere cannot be taken for granted. Poetry must itself be challenging as it confronts the challenge of registering as an effective and an affective medium in on-going public debates in Ireland.

This very contention is apparent in a recent piece in *The Irish Times* by Fintan O'Toole, where he moves away from his more sustained anatomizations of the iniquities of Ireland's erstwhile political and financial elites, to focus on the role of culture in the post-Celtic Tiger era. For O'Toole 'the boom was resolutely unpoetic', while 'its hard-faced greed' offered 'an impossible challenge to the lyricism that is the first resort of Irish writing' (O'Toole 2011). As we will detail below, Irish poetry did respond to the hypocrisies and the inequities of the 'boom' years in Ireland with frustration, irony and black humour. We can intuit from O'Toole's argument that art and culture became commoditized during the Celtic Tiger years and, in addition, that the idioms of Irish creative expression were too often warped by the imported and reifying codes of global capitalism. Where culture was not commoditized, it was alienated from Irish society, as the self-reflexive, often critical, function of public art was no longer relevant in a culture defined by consumption and self-congratulation. In O'Toole's estimation, since this triumphalist phase of recent Irish history is now past, 'there is now a need to somehow make up for that absence, to engage with the afterlife of a period that was hard to write about when it was unfolding' (O'Toole 2011). In what follows, we will see poetic reflections and critiques of the Celtic Tiger period in Ireland by Dennis O'Driscoll, Rita Ann Higgins, Alice Lyons and, by way of preface, John Updike. These works were written, variously, during the 'ascendancy' of the Celtic Tiger and after its decline, and represent a range of poetry that responds to social dislocation, moral hypocrisy, cultural inauthenticity and ecological 'ruination'.

Visiting the Celtic Tiger – John Updike

'Too many plugs and switches in the room', John Updike writes at the opening of his poem 'New Resort Hotel, Portmarnock', thus capturing, metonymically, the culture of wasteful excess that prevailed during much of the Celtic Tiger years (Updike 2009, p. 67). Updike's poem is part of a triptych of Petrarchan sonnets grouped under the title 'A Wee Irish

Suite', and appeared in his 2009 collection *Endpoint and Other Poems*. 'New Resort Hotel, Portmarnock' is the third sonnet in the sequence and the only one that deals with Updike's localized impressions of Ireland's, at that point, fading economic buoyancy. Yet it is Updike's ironic take on the Celtic Tiger that proves most effective in this short poem, concentrated, primarily, in the octet, where he writes: 'Too many outlets for the well- / connected businessman, too much Preferred / Lifestyle, here in formerly lovely Eire' (Updike 2009, p. 67). Notwithstanding the potentially grating nostalgia of the final clause, again it is the vision of excessive connectivity without actual connection that exercises Updike's poetic irony. He condenses this in his selection of phrases, 'Too many' and 'Too much', which repeat and echo, in turn, the opening enunciation of the poem. These, then, work in combination with his ironic reference to the frequently circulated jargon of consumerism – 'Preferred Lifestyle' – to depict a country that is not only remote from the financial poverty of its historical and recent past, but is just as remote from itself in the present. Accumulation, liquidity and consumerist impulses do not seem to be symptoms of historical progress in Updike's snapshot of Ireland, but, rather, they are those of cultural and social vertigo.

At the same time as Updike subjects the Celtic Tigerishness of Ireland to poetic scrutiny, he also identifies pitiable features of the fervent aspirationalism of its more materialistic citizens. In an image recalling Joyce's 'cracked looking glass', Updike writes: 'The Celtic Tiger still has crooked teeth, / the twinkle of the doomed-to-come-up-short' (Updike 2009, p. 67). Either there is something tragic about what Updike perceives in Ireland's Celtic Tiger condition, or we could suggest that there is a hint of dismissive condescension in his figuration. Regardless, the sense that Ireland's thriving economy was, in many ways, constructed upon temporary foundations and/or concealed deeper levels of ingrained material poverty lends legitimacy to Updike's lines.

Indeed, not only is there an echo of Joyce in the opening image of the sestet; Updike's idea of an impoverished anti-hero acquiring wealth, but who is tragically bound to failure or revelation as a fraud, casts the country as a species of Victorian literary character, not out of place in Dickens. For Updike, there is a dishonesty and a shallowness to Ireland's transient embrace of hyper-consumerism. While some of his rhetoric skirts perilously close to a lamentation for a more 'authentic' Irish culture, his cursory poetic intervention is an instructive *international* perspective on Celtic Tiger Ireland.

The Celtic Tiger years – Dennis O'Driscoll

Originally published in his 1999 collection *Weather Permitting*, and sharing a title with Paul Durcan's poem in *The Art of Life* (2004), Dennis O'Driscoll's 'The Celtic Tiger' offers a sequence of, by now, clichéd set pieces from that period. Made up of nine stanzas, the poem displays superficial accommodation with, even unselfconscious indulgence in, the bounties of economic affluence. But in crucial ways, in tone and form, the poem betrays a healthy disquiet with the material fortunes of the 'boom' times in Ireland. Apart from the interconnected yet discrete vignettes from Celtic Tiger Ireland, one of the more revealing formal, linguistic features of O'Driscoll's poem is the fact that the poetic voice never once speaks in the first person. Indeed, not only is the first-person singular absent, the first-person plural is also omitted, which, again, suggests physical, financial or ethical distance from these scenes of copious consumption. The poem's 'narrative' is relayed entirely in the second and third persons, intimating a degree of removal or separation from the depicted theatre of conspicuous wealth. In aggregation, these formal features of the poem, particularly given the historical context of the work, convey a sense that there may well be interaction and shared experiences of consumption, but these activities are devoid of authentic human relations and/or community. This simple tactic by O'Driscoll implies that the social sensibilities of the Irish have been altered under the sway of financial largesse – a trend that is further evidenced in the carnivalesque or baroque scenes depicted in the individual stanzas of the poem's first half.

The poem opens with a bald statement, immediately immersing the reader in, and preparing us for, the subsequent sights and sounds of the cityscape: 'Ireland's boom is in full swing' (O'Driscoll 1999, p. 15). But while this opening line clearly sites the poem in a specific location, it also hints at the impersonality characteristic of the narrative arc of the remainder of the poem. As if to make this point even more starkly, the following two lines revel in the abstract facticity of the country's economic ascendancy: 'Rows of numbers, set in a cloudless blue / computer background, prove the point' (O'Driscoll 1999, p. 15). Abundance in abstracted statistics proves abundance in material riches; O'Driscoll here ironizes the impersonality of wealth creation and evaluation, an ironic gesture that is made all the more effective by the concluding plosives of 'prove the point'. Both ironic and defensive, these plosives, then, are also intimations that statistics are inherently contestable. Indeed the initial emphatic tone of this opening stanza firmly establishes the ironic register of 'The Celtic Tiger', and, in its reference to the statistical verifiability of

Ireland's copious wealth, reminds us of the counter-arguments of critical voices in Irish society who have consistently highlighted the outrageous material disparities that accompanied the Celtic Tiger 'boom'.

The stanzas that succeed this abstract validation of the 'boom' portray a variety of performances of Irish Celtic Tiger identities, which are consonant with O'Toole's argument in *Enough Is Enough* that '[t]he Celtic Tiger wasn't just an economic ideology. It was also a substitute identity. It was a new way of being' (O'Toole 2010, p. 3). As we noted above, from a contemporary vantage point, they read as stereotypical, yet from O'Driscoll's perspective, at the cusp of the millennium, these are caustic and incisive descriptions. Formally these slices of Irish life are discrete within the poem, but, as we have suggested, their generic and anonymous qualities connote various levels of inauthenticity and vacuousness. Just as identity as performance changed during the Celtic Tiger, a significant fraction of this evolution manifested in linguistic forms and modes of verbal expression employed in the public and private spheres. As this poem displays, Irish citizens became adept at, even fluent in, new vocabularies of excess and consumerism. And it is in the third, fourth and fifth stanzas of 'The Celtic Tiger' that O'Driscoll dramatizes the most explicit theatrics of Celtic Tiger identity. With a microscopic attention to diction and syntax, the poem utilizes compounds, vague generic titles, alliteration and half-rhyme to establish its critique of un-ironic posturing and reinvention. While the three stanzas stand apart, they could well describe a single spatial location, as the poet once more reaches for the generic to undermine the authenticity of such individual and communal performances of *arriviste* identities. The third stanza ironizes a postmodernist and consumerist appetite for mediated 'culture' as the nouveau riche prostrate themselves 'Outside new antique pubs', the oxymoron suggesting a crude commodification of Irish history in the service of consumption. We are offered a picture of simulated authenticity as national identity is given as a hostage to new-found fortune. The third stanza also sees the greatest concentration of compound adjectives, as the poet describes: 'well-toned women, gel-slick men', who 'drain long-necked bottles of imported beer' (O'Driscoll 1999, p. 15).

There are erotic qualities to these lines, with a premium placed on physical appearance and on the sensuousness of physical consumption. The Celtic Tiger streetscapes possess a cosmopolitan feel, a globalized ambience, in which new identities can be shaped and explored. And this progression into the erotic and the sensual is further apparent in the following stanza, which, beginning with another compound adjective, takes on a specifically gendered form of sexualized performance: 'Lip-glossed cigarettes are poised / at coy angles, a black bra strap / slides strategically from a Rocha top' (O'Driscoll 1999, p. 15). Combining the generic with the specific – 'Rocha' – O'Driscoll suggests a level of liberated female sexual agency, and, at the same time, eroticizes, in contemporary form, a variant of national allegory. The coupling of the alliterated sequence, 'black bra strap / slides strategically', connotes sexual boldness, as well as a sensual performance. In these two stanzas, then, it is *action*, physical, bodily action, that counts and that is privileged. Yet in the next stanza, 'talk' enters, but is, firstly, centred on sterile property markets and, more significantly, is drowned out by another more insistent sound: 'Talk of tax-exempted town-house lettings / is muffled by rap music blasted / from a passing four-wheel drive' (O'Driscoll 1999, p. 15). Again we see a concentration of compound adjectives and impersonal nouns, as the poet details the commodities accumulated and traded by the affluent. What is more telling, though, is the content of the 'muffled' 'talk', as O'Driscoll points to the re-calibration of language, of conversation topics and of personal priorities during the 'boom' years.

Once more the ways in which language was employed and the contents of public and private discourse became conditioned by the props and potential accruals of economic success. Across 'The Celtic Tiger' language, together with the poetic form and content, are laced with both local and international indices of cultural and social change, and many of these are ironized as superficial features of depthless Irish identities during the period of the Celtic Tiger. O'Driscoll's poem ironizes the linguistic inventions and neologisms that accompanied the altered sociocultural sensibilities of the Celtic Tiger years. In the end, 'performance' seems to be a key issue for O'Driscoll in this poem, as new self-images are formed that are firmly wedded to what he perceives as transient and insubstantial brands of inauthentic consumerist identities.

Outside the 'boom' – Rita Ann Higgins

In his piece on poetry and the Celtic Tiger, cited above, O'Toole proposes the work and the career of the Galway-based poet Rita Ann Higgins as exemplary of the unwavering honesty and integrity required of art as the unseemly aftermath of the 'boom' unfolds. Her poetic landscapes have always been marginal to political and economic hegemony in Ireland, and she has consistently been, and remains, the poetic voice of what O'Toole terms 'the territory of abandonment' (O'Toole 2011). And while such 'territories' were rendered invisible during the 'boom' years, we are now confronted with much more substantial 'territories of abandonment' in the contemporary moment. In a series of poems across her most recent collection, *Ireland Is Changing Mother*, Higgins maintains her bleakly humorous and unsentimental exposure of the neglected and destitute recesses of modern Ireland. As we have said, such thematics dominate Higgins's oeuvre, but in this context we will draw her most recent work into on-going debates on poetic meditations on the excesses and the privations of the Celtic Tiger. Dealing with desire and frustration, often in acerbic and witty terms, Higgins's poetry is suitably pitched to engage with the deflated fantasies of Celtic Tiger Ireland.

The penultimate poem in *Ireland Is Changing Mother* reminds us that Ireland's 'boom' years were not just marked by relative experiences of material well-being and deprivation, but that the crises of the Celtic Tiger and its legacies are equally issues of ecological and social justice. 'The Brent Geese Chorus' narrates, in poetic form, the long-running tensions between a consortium of companies headed by Royal Dutch Shell and the activist-residents (and external supporters) in the north-west Mayo region of Erris. With a more protracted prehistory than the immediate Celtic Tiger period, the poem is consistent with many others in the collection that rail against the social injustices and the environmental wounds that the 'boom' occasioned. Indeed, in reading Higgins's work in the context of the Celtic Tiger, it is worth attending to her poetic aggregation of ecological and social justice. The battle, physical and legal, over access to and potential exploitation of the Corrib Gas Field is the most ecological contention in modern Irish history, and Higgins's work provides a poeticised 'brief history' of the corrupted procedures of those intent on securing a viable and profitable pipeline. Her poem details a corporate campaign of 'soft' and then 'hard' persuasion by Shell, until the State is revealed as comfortably complicit in the coercion of its own resistant citizens. And again, such alienation of peripheral citizens from and by the Irish State is symptomatic, not just of Higgins's body of work but, more recently, of how the fantasy-drama of the Celtic Tiger played out.

Parodying the Messianism of the most extreme advocates of progressive liberal capitalism, the poem's opening two stanzas express the contradictory relations that obtain between profit and environmental equilibrium: 'On the seventh day God rested, / [...] And on the eighth day along came Shell / at first with wheels and then with wings / and later dozers, a lot of dozers / two-legged and four legged' (Higgins 2011, p. 68). Not only are there echoes of Orwell's polemic on corrupted ideals in *Animal Farm* in the final lines here, but in the next line, which opens stanza two, we can visualize Wellsian intruders on a vulnerable world: 'They took long strides across your fields / measuring profit with every step. / Then they flew over, looking down, coveting. / A voice in wellingtons and a suit said, / People of North Mayo you will be rich / you will have jobs a plenty / the gravy train is coming / but we want your fields to park it in' (Higgins 2011, p. 68). Progress takes the form of scale in this stanza, and it outsizes as it processes towards prosperity. Equally, Higgins ironizes a common metaphor, one that coalesces easily with fantasies of easy and inevitable enrichment. The 'fields' repeated in the stanza localize the promises of the disembodied prophet of wealth and, also, localize the ecological crisis, which is central to the entire Corrib dispute. This ecological sensibility is developed still further as we move from the landscape to include non-human species: 'When we looked down on you, which was often, / we decided that you were the chosen ones / We saw a few geese, a whale or two, an old dolphin on his last legs / and all that unspoilt beauty / waiting to be spoiled, / and god knows we can spoil' (Higgins 2011, p. 69). The different resonances of 'spoil' resound beyond this stanza, even as they work to good effect within it to accent the brute transgressions of the solicitous corporation.

Yet Higgins alerts us to the agency of the local community in cultivating an efficacious campaign of resistance, and this appears to be metaphorized as the durable, migratory Brent Geese: 'And there as a chorus of Brent Geese / singing all over Erris / Shell to hell, to hell with Shell, / and that chorus ran in and out of the bog / and it was everywhere in North Mayo' (Higgins 2011, p. 70). Higgins's localization of the politics of ecological despoliation is suffused with ethical indignation. These activist-residents thoroughly engage with the corporate transvaluation of their physical environment, and, as we shall see below, parallel the more lateral indignation about the ecological, as well as financial, legacies of the country's property 'boom'.

Higgins addresses the property frenzy of the Celtic Tiger in 'Where Have All Our Scullions Gone', another relatively lengthy piece on the iniquities and inequalities of Irish casino economics. In an opening stanza that succinctly encapsulates the vanity and cynicism of those years, Higgins writes: 'It was hard hats and photo ops, / yella bellies and Gucci dresses / cutting ribbons on concrete schemes. / They were kissing babies / and talking roads, / they knew the bankers / would give them loads' (Higgins 2011, p. 54). Once more the poetic voice is distanced from the dynamic players of the central drama described in this stanza. In fact, the poem is book-ended by this stanza. But as the poem develops, we notice the poetic reades of this first, and also of the final, stanza is muted in favour of the voice(s) of the 'boom-time' economy. Again such a manoeuvre allows Higgins, firstly, and quite literally, to demonstrate the relative voicelessness of her familiar poetic constituency. In addition, giving over so much of the poem to the voice(s) of speculation and of development is a way for Higgins to ironize further these social groups, as their chattering exposes the venality of their attitudes and actions. We read: 'Why have one tunnel / when you could have two? Or as any fool knows / two expensive tunnels / are better than none / bend over, spend over / let's have some fun' (Higgins 2011, p. 54). Higgins is direct and playful in her evocation of this voice within the poem, yet the gross hyperbole does not blunt the incisiveness of the critical wit operative here. And this effective tone continues, as the speaker asks: 'Why have one motorway / when you could have four? Not in your constituency / but in mine, that's fine. / Bend over, spend over / and don't fucking whine' (Higgins 2011, p. 54). The most obvious formal linkage between the two preceding stanzas is the concluding refrain; while not identical, they do articulate equivalent sentiments of wanton greed and violent acquisition. And versions of this two-line refrain are repeated seven times across the poem, as Higgins's lyric response to economic misappropriation begins to resemble the technical codes of the 'protest' song.

In common with the poems of Alice Lyons below, 'Where Have All Our Scullions Gone' also addresses the workings of Ireland's commercial and residential property 'boom'. In short, terse lines the poet exposes the waste and the excess fed by, and that fed, the accelerated transvaluation of 'fields': 'Millions for half empty office / millions for fields / not a brick laid / not a thistle cleared' (Higgins 2011, p. 55). These private-sector follies are joined in Higgins's catalogue by ruinous misinvestments of the State during the same period: 'Let's buy Thornton Hall / for our gangsters galore. / At thirty million, it's a steal / not a dollar more. / The money was spent / not a brick was laid, / another twelve million / the legals were paid' (Higgins 2011, p. 55). Thornton Hall was a government-purchased site intended to house an upgraded prison to replace Mountjoy. The site itself cost €30 million, as Higgins details, with a further €15 million run up in associated legal and administrative costs on a site that remains unused. The later stanzas of the poem concern themselves with emptiness, with lavish waste and with incompleteness, and it is as if the disposal of money is an end in itself, rather than an act designed to realise a definite return. And it is the inequality associated with such lavish waste that not only animates Higgins in 'Where Have All Our Scullions Gone' but exercises her moral indignation across several of her poems in this recent collection.

'After the boom' – Alice Lyons

Working in both visual, site-specific formats and in textual forms, the artist Alice Lyons has produced a compact but compelling body of works on the imprints of Ireland's property developments in rural Ireland. Lyons is a resident of Cootehall in County Roscommon, and has used that locale's acute experience of deforming property construction as the basis for several recent works. Of particular significance in terms of the 'poetics of ruination' are two poems published in the periodical *Poetry* in 2011, 'Developers' and 'The Boom and After the Boom', both of which centre on the disfiguring presence of unfinished housing estates in the Cootehall area. Lyons is not native to this region, though she is a long-time resident, and her poems articulate, in often curt poetic expression, the palpable human absences of these stalled housing developments. In a way that is familiar to an erstwhile Cootehall denizen, John McGahern, these housing estates, local sites of ruination, bear more universal significance in relation to the nation's priorities and self-regulatory procedures during the peak years of the Celtic Tiger.

'Developers' opens with an unembellished statement, 'Greed got in the way', and, while the emphatic certainty of the culpability of material appetites is clear, what precisely it impeded or obscured remains open to speculation – though more egalitarian material and moral economies are surely parts of Lyons's alternative (Lyons 2011a, p. 218). The harsh plosives that initiate the poem, then, operate in alliterative conjunction as they signal the tonal pitch of the verse. But this is only one half of the first line, which is divided into two sentences; the first of five syllables, the second with six. The second sentence complements, in a highly suggestive manner, the similarly declarative opening clause with 'We built a fake estate' (Lyons 2011a, p. 218). Lyons compacts a great deal into this assertion, including authenticity, history and collective responsibility. From a technical standpoint the assonant 'a' of 'estate' completes an internal rhyme with the opening line, but it is the evocations of the word 'estate' itself that are most arresting in both historical and contemporary contexts.

Of course, the term is part of the contemporary moniker 'ghost estate', which haunts and defaces these landscapes, but the notion, and memory, of a landed estate is equally provocative in the longer-term histories of Ireland's scattered localities. Perhaps it was crude and simplistic to align the country's appetite for property and fetishization of home ownership – the highest in Europe – with Ireland's colonial history of territorial dispossession. Yet there is a sense that, through such heightened levels of acquisitiveness, we have, in fact, caused our own dispossession yet again. In another way, Lyons's diction brings to mind the rampant culture of absenteeism and irresponsible rack-renting practised across Ireland under the system of landlordism in the nineteenth century. Without constructing untenable facile historical analogies, Lyons does, however, gesture to the differential continuity of landed irresponsibility in Irish history. But from a figurative perspective, the 'fake estate', part of our propertied Ponzi scheme in Ireland, serves as a metaphor and metonym for Lyons. It is metaphoric of the country's dire economic condition; while at the same time metonymic of the larger overdeveloped whole of the country's geography.

The notion of collectivity, hinted at in the collective construction of and desire for these 'fake estates', and the use of the personal pronoun, first-person plural, is expanded in more empathetic ways in the ensuing couplets. Lyons remains with the idioms of hauntedness and ruination in the lines 'doorbells, rows of them, glow in the night village / a string of lit invitations no elbow has leaned into / (both arms embracing messages). Unanswered / the doors are rotting from the bottom up' (Lyons 2011a, p.218). Reminiscent of the 'candle in the window' attached to Irish emigrant history and popularized by the former President Mary Robinson, the fixtures and fittings are an index of absence on this estate; these houses have never been lived in and the development remains structurally incomplete. Deprived of ever having functioned in the ways they are designed to, these houses, with their fittings, stand adrift as reminders of lapsed possibilities, of bankrupted lives and unrealized relationships. At the same time, Lyons imagines interpersonal relations, she imagines the cultivation of community even as she regards the unfinished husks of these buildings that never became homes and never became part of a living human community. These houses and estates can be read, as Lyons suggests in her opening line here, in relation to the personal motivations that once energized their unfettered construction. Reflections of these Celtic Tiger 'ruins' and 'artefacts' are not just suggestive of contemporary national penury but must also be considered as revelatory of the compulsions and motivations so widespread in Ireland during the Celtic Tiger years. Public perceptions of 'ghost estates' across many localities in Ireland are conditioned by the absences that suffuse these locations. The sole remains of human presence are scattered detritus, once more suggestive of post-apocalyptic abandonment, if on a localized Irish scale in this case. In a pair of couplets Lyons later, and further, ironizes the country's destructive obsession with property and construction in a series of harsh consonantal clauses.

The basic materials on which the country's financial future was mortgaged, as well as that of tens of thousands of its citizens, are laid bare as little more than waste now by Lyons: 'a petered-out plot of Tayto / tumbleweeds, bin bags, rebar, roof slates, offcuts, / guttering, drain grilles, doodads, infill, gravel! / A not-as-yet nice establishment, possessing potential' (Lyons 2011a, p.218). Fashioning both alliteration and rhyme out of this inventory of waste, Lyons proceeds, almost breath-lessly, beyond the exclamation mark to another identification of incom-pleteness and absence. From these lines, we note a crucial difference between traditional historical ruins and the 'ruins' of 'ghost estates': the absences and the fractures of these latter-day Irish ruins are caused not by the gradual mouldering of the buildings but by the materials men-tioned here which were never adhered to or built into these houses in the first instance. Thus, contemporary 'ruination' is less about incremental decline and, with it, the assumption of 'damaged grandeur', but is linked with the legacies and the limits of unregulated material desire.

Lyons's 'The Boom and After the Boom' also deals with the aftermath of the Celtic Tiger building frenzy, but is equally concerned with the ecological imprints of the designer construction industry and with the migration patterns into Ireland occasioned by its era of economic sol-vency. Indeed, Lyons gestures to the notions of temporality and legacy in her title, which, tellingly, refers to 'After the Boom', rather than the more frequently employed and sharp-edged 'Bust' (Lyons 2011b, p. 222). The poem consists of four eight-line stanzas: the first three centre on the period during which luxurious riverside properties were built along the banks of the river Shannon. According to Lyons there is a deliber-ate cinematic form to 'The Boom and After the Boom' (Lyons 2011c, p. 224), but just as prominent as the visual structuration of the stanzas is Lyons's attentiveness to aurality across the first three stanzas. While the visual set pieces provided by Lyons allow us to witness the insistent pro-gression of construction along the course of the river Shannon, the aural register is just as effective in establishing a form of ecocritical response to the building culture of the Celtic Tiger. The poem opens with an anonymous, even generic, boat cruising the river – a further index of the commercialization of the Irish landscape to initiate this poetic critique of Celtic Tiger Ireland: 'The Shannon when it washes / the shoreline in the wake / of a cruiser susurruses / exactly like the Polish / language you hear in LIDL / on Friday evenings, 7pm / payday. That's what / Gerry says' (Lyons 2011b, p. 222).

Though we initially assume that the poeticization of the river is per-formed by the 'poetic voice' there is, at least, some input from a friend or acquaintance in the fashioning of the central simile. Multiplicity of voice and sound effect, then, are condensed into this brief stanza by Lyons, as the whisperings of the river, caused by the moving presence of the river cruiser, are identified with the mobile populations of migrant workers one encounters in multinational supermarkets. The sibilance evident in the first half of the stanza is part of Lyons's effort to highlight the inter-actions of human and non-human ecology during the Celtic Tiger property 'boom'. Yet the choice of the word 'wake', to describe the process and the departure of the human presence along the river – an intrusive presence in this scene – is not suggestive of an easy and enduring accommodation between the human and non-human in this location and on these terms. In a similar way to this opening stanza, the subsequent two stanzas foreground the aural presences of the human construction of property along this riverside location. Likewise, there is an attempt on Lyons's part to ease the potential friction between an invasive human presence and the natural environment.

This is evident in the opening lines of stanza two: 'The river surface offers / space to the song'; yet what kind of lyricism fills out this space? Nothing but the 'hammer taps of Latvians / and Poles nailing planks of a deck. The place / between water and sky / holding sound' (Lyons 2011b, p. 222). Rather than carrying the sound effects of non-human ecology, the river side resonates with the timbres of construction. While the sibilance of the opening half of the first stanza edges towards some form of conciliation between surroundings and human presence, the sibilance apparent in the opening two lines of the second stanza is abruptly drowned out by the notes of the 'hammer taps' and the nailing of planks to decks. In this technical manner we see how the tone of the poetic voice changes over the body of the poem, becoming more and more cynical about the human incursions into this resonant 'amphitheater' (Lyons 2011b, p. 222). The insistent hammering continues into the third stanza as we progress further away from the early sibilant identification of the river with the cadences of language. Significantly, in the third stanza the poetic voice alters tense, and the products of the 'tapping' labours of Poles, Latvians and Lithuanians '*will* be [...] nice features / of that riverside property [my emphasis]' (Lyons 2011b, p. 222). The migrant labourers are employed to realize, in physical constructed forms, the aspirations of the Irish nouveau riche. Equally, the landscape, which reverberates with the mechanical processes of construction, must be 'nailed' and 'decked', fixed in place and pruned. And, again, this is brought out by the replacement of the softer sonics of the earlier parts of the poem with the emphatic and harsher consonantal sounds of the building process.

In the concluding stanza that we return to a scene of aftermath, and, just as we witnessed in 'Developers', it is an aftermath of lives that were never actually lived at this location. Rather than presenting another 'aural' voice in this stanza, Lyons inserts a visual/verbal 'sign' in a register familiar across most of the Irish landscape in recent times. Presented in a typography that distinguishes it from the body of the poem, we read '42 LUXURY BUNGALOWS ONLY TWO / REMAINING' (Lyons 2011b,

p. 223). As the poem progresses from past to present, this bold 'sign' of the times is rendered redundant in the contemporary. At the same time as the houses it advertises stand incomplete and/or unoccupied, 'Winter gales have made swift work / of the billboard' (Lyons 2011b, p. 223). There may have been a similed convergence of human and non-human in the opening stanza, but by the close the relationship is no longer so benign. In a concluding spectacle that combines pathos and bathos, Lyons describes the legacies of Ireland's construction 'boom' in terms of waste and failure: 'Crumpled up / on the roadside now / two-by-four legs akimbo – / a circus-horse curtsy / or steeplechase mishap' (Lyons 2011b, p. 223). This abject symbol of Ireland's economic decline and fall reprises the sibilance of the poem's outset, as Lyons formally conjoins beginning and ending, without suggesting such an accommodation in Ireland's ecological relationships. Lyons's poems, then, confront localized but resonant examples of property frenzy in Ireland, focusing on one facet, perhaps the most debilitating, of the financial excesses of the Celtic Tiger years in Ireland.

Conclusion

In the 'Introduction' to their 2009 volume *Transforming Ireland: Challenges, Critiques and Resources*, Debbie Ging, Michael Cronin and Peadar Kirby highlight the linguistic contortions that were, and are, characteristic of public political debate in Ireland during, and since, the Celtic Tiger. They identify 'the restricted vocabulary of the business studies vulgate [which] is applied indiscriminately to health, education, the arts, policing' (Ging, Cronin and Kirby 2009, p. 4), as inimical to the cultivation of radical and progressive critical debate in Ireland. Yet, in the same piece, they retain a utopian faith in the transience of such hollowed-out idioms, arguing that 'it is important to bear in mind that languages have a past and future as well as a present. In other words, the present infestation of public language with the default rhetoric of the market is, in historical terms, relatively recent' (Ging, Cronin and Kirby 2009, p. 5). The poets under consideration here have each, differentially, but often in parallel ways, attended to these transient languages of consumption and moral corruption. Both critics and artists are keenly attuned to the semiotics of excess that structured public and private discourse in Ireland during the country's economic boom times. But what is just as true is that, as Higgins displays, much of this phoney discourse of acquisition and plenty was utterly alien to scores of lives and communities across Ireland. If public language has been 'infested', as Ging, Cronin and Kirby attest, then these poetic artists avail of the creative contingency of language to expose and to critique further the legacies and the ruins of this recent, passing, infestation. In another way, and if we return to Dewey's comments in our epigraph, these poets are representative of a critical mindset that can, potentially, speak out for those who have been victims of the Celtic Tiger's 'indirect consequences'.

Works cited

Dewey, John (1991) [1927] *The Public and Its Problems*, Athens: Ohio University Press.

Durcan, Paul (2004) *The Art of Life*, London: Harvill.

Franke, Astrid (2010) *Pursue the Illusion: Problems of Public Poetry in America*, Heidelberg: Universitätsverlag Winter.

Ging, Debbie, Cronin, Michael, and Kirby, Peadar, (2009) 'Transforming Ireland: Challenges', in Ging, Debbie, Cronin, Michael, and Kirby, Peadar (eds), *Transforming Ireland: Challenges, Critiques and Resources*, Manchester: Manchester University Press, pp. 1–17.

Higgins, Rita Ann (2011) *Ireland Is Changing Mother*, Tarset: Bloodaxe.

Lippman, Walter (1925) *The Phantom Public*, New York: Macmillan.

Lyons, Alice (2011a) 'Developers', *Poetry*, 129:3, p. 218.

Lyons, Alice (2011b) 'The Boom and After the Boom', *Poetry*, 129:3, pp. 222–223

Lyons, Alice (2011c) 'Interview with Alice Lyons', *Poetry*, 129:3, p. 224.

O'Driscoll, Dennis (1999) *Weather Permitting*, London: Anvil.

O'Toole, Fintan (2009) *Ship of Fools: How Stupidity and Corruption Sank the Celtic Tiger*, London: Faber.

O'Toole, Fintan (2010) *Enough Is Enough: How to Build a New Republic*, London: Faber and Faber.

O'Toole, Fintan (2011) 'Now the Bubble Has Burst, We're Left with Our Real Treasures', *The Irish Times*, 24 September.

Updike, John (2009) *Endpoint and Other Poems*, New York: Alfred A. Knopf.

15

Between modernity and marginality: Celtic Tiger cinema

Ruth Barton

By the late 1990s, it was obvious that Irish film production had changed sufficiently for the phrase 'Celtic Tiger cinema' to signal something new. Although the term is used consensually, its exact definition is elusive. In keeping with the debate around what we knew and what we said during the boom, I will be considering later in this chapter the various political and social interpretations the films offer. In particular, I will be discussing how themes of social and geographical marginality came to dominate the films of the era. Cinema, however, is not just a medium of expression or reflection of ideas, it is also a business shaped both by movements of capital and by advances in technology. In that sense, it provides an interesting insight into how a small, local industry, which was itself internationally marginalized, developed in the years of the boom. I will start, then with a discussion of the economic background to the Celtic Tiger cinema, and the role that technological change played in shaping the content of the films. I am also concerned to nuance the overall debate with a reminder that not all of the changes that occurred during the late 1990s and through to the 2000s were due to the new economic order; some were as a result of an interweaving of circumstances, not least of which was the end of the Troubles. For reasons of concision, I am excluding discussions of television and other new media; I am also bearing in mind that films often have a long production time; therefore many of the releases that fall within the early years of the Celtic Tiger have their origins in the pre-Celtic Tiger era, while others that have been released since the crash have their origins in the boom years.

The economics of film production (1994–2007)

The years 1994–2007 saw an increase in film production in Ireland. In 1994, eight feature films were produced, of which four were local, and the remainder overseas productions (including *Braveheart* (Mel Gibson

1995)) (IBEC 1995). Production peaked in 2003 with the making of fourteen feature films, including the major Hollywood productions *King Arthur* (Antoine Fuqua 2003) and *Tristan & Isolde* (Kevin Reynolds 2006); the remaining twelve were Irish, in theme or at least partially in setting. In that year, feature films and major TV dramas combined to create a spend of €244.3 million, compared to €127.7 million in 2002 and €196.6 million in 2001 (IBEC 2004, p. 7).[1] In 2007, twelve feature films were produced in Ireland (this figure includes feature length documentaries such as *Waveriders* (Joel Conroy 2008)); the combined production value of feature films and major TV dramas in this year was €154 million, a decrease of 77 per cent from 2006 (Moriarty 2008, p. 7). What is significant about the listing of films in 2007 is that they were all either Irish productions, or Irish/European co-productions with an Irish theme or location. During that year, Ireland failed to attract any foreign feature film productions, although the country hosted a substantial number of foreign television productions, notably *The Tudors*. The reason for this disparity was that in Ireland the tax break system (Section 481) applied to television productions, whereas in competing territories it was available only for feature filmmaking. Also in 2007, eleven animated films were released, of which most were short films; some were international co-productions (*The Flight Before Christmas* (Michael Hegner, Karl Juusonen, 2008)) and others were television series (*Ballybraddan* (broadcast RTÉ 2, 2009)), making animation the largest provider of full-time and permanent employment in the independent audiovisual sector (Moriarty 2008, p. 7). Animation also became an increasingly prestigious medium, picking up multiple awards and nominations.

The overseas productions provided major knock-on benefits, both to the economy (in terms of accommodation and ancillary services) and to tourism (visitors coming to the country as a result of seeing it on film) and also as a way of training technical and other staff, actors and extras, who secured employment on set. The audiovisual sector has consistently argued that, for the tax forgone on Section 481, the benefits in terms of employment, training and secondary services more than compensate. However, as these figures indicate, foreign productions dwindled in number long before the end of the boom. This occurred in part because of more attractive competing tax breaks

[1] 'The IBEC (Irish Business and Employers Confederation) report, as it is commonly called, does not distinguish between feature films and major TV dramas when computing the value of the audiovisual sector to the economy. Dates given in brackets following film titles are the year of release not the year of production.

systems in other territories (most of them based on the Irish model) but also because, during the boom, Ireland priced itself out of the market. As the national economy was transformed, the price of accommodation and services in Ireland grew exponentially. At the same time, the euro increased in value against the US dollar, further inflating the cost of working here.

In this period, therefore, the film sector increasingly became reliant on indigenous productions, most of the funding for which came from a combination of Section 481 tax breaks and Irish Film Board subsidies, and from co-production funding. Section 481, however, was based on a system of claiming investment in production against tax; as tax rates fell, so the system in turn lost attractiveness. Ultimately it fell to the State-subsidised Irish Film Board to provide the majority of the funding for Irish cinema in the latter years of the Celtic Tiger, a responsibility it was able to take on as a result of the well-stocked State coffers.

The Board's budget increased significantly through the years of the Celtic Tiger; in 1994 it received IR£2 million (€2,539,476) in state funding; by 2007 this had reached €17 million (Woodworth 1993; Madden 2007). During the same period, the cost of filmmaking dropped as new digital production methods enabled filmmakers to work on much lower budgets. Increasingly, Irish films have followed the low-budget formula, particularly since, under European Commission rules, the State (through the Film Board) can finance only up to 50 per cent of any project, unless it is considered 'Low Budget' or 'Difficult' (in which case it can fund up to 65 per cent with a cap of €750,000) or if it costs less than €100,000 ('Micro Budget'), in which case the Board can fully fund the project (Irish Film Board 2012). Thus, to summarize, most local Irish films are low-budget or micro-budget productions, and most are reliant on a combination of Irish Film Board and Section 481 funding. Had there not been an economic boom, it is impossible to envisage how Irish production would have survived; the only benefit would have been that Ireland would have remained a low-cost economy. The question arises, then, as to whether Irish filmmakers felt themselves in a position to critique government policy (or the lack of it) when that same government was its chief, if indirect, source of funding.

Technology, ideology, the Troubles

Although digital technology has developed to such an extent that most filmgoers would be hard-pressed to distinguish between a high-end project made on digital or one on 35mm, in the early days of digital filmmaking the technology largely dictated the aesthetics. The first digital films looked grainy, often with poor lighting, particularly for night-time sequences, and many camera operators were influenced by the Danish Dogme movement, which started in 1995 with a Manifesto that dictated a naturalistic look for digital filmmaking (Hjort and Bondebjerg 2003). With its frequent use of hand-held cameras, often employed to mimic eye-movement, and the corresponding favouring of rapid editing techniques, films made on digital cameras and edited using digital technology became quickly identified with contemporary urban narratives, often featuring edgy, dispossessed central characters.

This too was the direction Celtic Tiger cinema took, though not only for reasons of technology. Filmmaking in Ireland had been, until the 1970s, a patchy affair, dominated by outside filmmakers with their own perspectives – both ideological and visual. For the consummate example of how the work of outside filmmakers dictated the identity of Irish film, we have only to think of John Ford's *The Quiet Man* (1952) with its mix of sentimentality and humour, its play on stereotypes and its Technicolor landscapes. Another such film, although made from quite a different perspective, was David Lean's *Ryan's Daughter* (1970). It was only in the 1970s that indigenous Irish filmmakers began consistently to make their own films, often with the intention of deconstructing the imagery they had inherited from their overseas predecessors. Now films began to be set in the contemporary city; works such as *Down the Corner* (Joe Comerford 1977) and *Pigs* (Cathal Black 1984) were shot in Dublin's new suburbs and its decaying tenements. In 1989, Jim Sheridan made his breakthrough into film with *My Left Foot*, again set in Dublin's inner city (Rockett, Gibbons, Hill 1988; McLoone, 2000; Pettitt 2000; Barton 2004). However, it was the Irish countryside that remained the most common backdrop to Irish film narratives of the pre-Celtic Tiger years.

Key films of this era – *The Ballroom of Romance* (Pat O'Connor 1982), *The Field* (Jim Sheridan 1990), *December Bride* (Thaddeus O'Sullivan 1991), *Korea* (Cathal Black 1995) – all have rural settings, and all associate the Irish countryside with traumatic narratives of loneliness, sexual repression and an oppressive patriarchal culture. Their central characters not only function as vehicles for the dramatic action but also bear the symbolic weight of history. To take just one example, Cathal Black's *Korea*, a film released during the Celtic Tiger period but ideologically located in the preceding era (and adapted from the John McGahern short story of the same name, published in 1970), deals with a father–son relationship, with Donal Donnelly playing the father, John Doyle, and Andrew Scott the son, Eamon. Set against a background of rural electrification, and the Korean War, Eamon believes that his father wishes him to emigrate to the United States so that if he is conscripted and killed, as was their neighbour's son, Luke Moran, he will benefit financially. The story is sparse and elegiac in keeping with the McGahern original (and much of McGahern's work), with a shot of freshwater eels tangled in a trap punctuating the encounters between the various characters.

Informing many of these narratives, whether explicitly or otherwise, are the Troubles, so that the characters occupy a symbolic function as the bearers of a traumatic history. The films must also negotiate unanswered questions about the legacy of violence and revolution in the present. In *Korea*, for instance, the rift between the Doyles and the Morans dates back to the Irish Civil War (1922–1923), its ramifications continuing to affect the next generation, particularly when Eamon starts seeing Luke Moran's sister, Una (Fiona Molony).

With the ending of the Troubles, such issues receded in urgency. Celtic Tiger cinema has its own Troubles films, the most notable being *Hunger* (Steve McQueen 2008) and *Five Minutes of Heaven* (Oliver Hirschbiegel 2009), but these are reflective works that look back on events that are signalled as over, and in the past, rather than part of the everyday structures of Irish society. Instead, therefore, of being informed by political events deriving from the conflict in Northern Ireland, and from the violent establishment of the State, the films of the Celtic Tiger era have shown themselves to be largely unconcerned with history, locating their narratives firmly in the present, and most often in present-day Dublin.

Animation and global Irishness

Before looking more closely at the city-set films, we need to acknowledge that other significant development in terms of production – the rise of Irish animation. It is impossible to provide a general overview of an eclectic industry that produces work for multinationals such as Disney and for television (the Cartoon Network, BBC, RTÉ), and circulates as arthouse cinema. Animation increased its profile in Ireland following Academy Award nominations for *Give Up Yer Aul Sins* (Cathal Gaffney 2000) and *Fifty Percent Grey* (Ruairí Robinson 2001). The former is based on a 1960 recording made by schoolteacher Peig Cunningham of inner-city Dublin children telling Bible stories. A young schoolchild recounts the tale of John the Baptist with some gusto, and with particular emphasis on the more violent aspects of the Saint's misfortunes. The cartoon is tinted sepia, and has a deliberately artisanal quality, using hand-drawn 24fps cell animation. Its global success had a David versus

Goliath ring to it (the Academy Awards pitted it against Hollywood multinational Pixar, who eventually carried away the prize), while its capturing of bygone Dublin attitudes propelled it into the nostalgia category. Thus, its origins and model of production combined to erase the sophistication that in fact marks contemporary animation practice to produce an image of pastness and innocence.

A similar discourse accompanied the 2010 Academy Award-nominated feature-length *The Secret of Kells* (Tomm Moore 2009) which was heralded by the *New York Times* as 'a hand-drawn labor of love made for 6 million euros (about $8 million), the equivalent of what, in headier days, some studios would spend on a film's Oscar campaign alone' (Ryzik 2010). It too is positioned outside of the mainstream in terms of both production and aesthetic; it is also noteworthy for its refusal to contribute to a faith-based religious discourse, in other words to the tenets of Catholicism (Walsh 2011). This is not to suggest that all Irish animation positions itself as an antidote to corporate, computer-driven cartoon work (many Irish animation companies are working in highly sophisticated production environments), but it does indicate that the global appeal of Irish animation depends on it consciously disassociating itself from technology and promoting itself via its marginality.

The city and the Tiger

Discussing the first Dublin-set films of the Celtic Tiger cinema, specifically *About Adam* (Gerard Stembridge 2000) and *Goldfish Memory* (Elizabeth Gill 2003), Martin McLoone wrote: 'These films celebrate and even glorify a certain kind of urban lifestyle, dressed in the signifiers of contemporary global youth culture, and populated by the beautiful people of Celtic Tiger Ireland' (McLoone 2007, p. 212) Such films, he went on to argue, epitomize a kind of 'transglobal "cool"', are lighter in tone than earlier Irish films, are marked by an irreverent humour and are visually identifiable by their settings in the new landscape of Celtic Tiger Dublin with its coffee shops, wine bars and trendy restaurants (McLoone 2007, p. 212).

Both films certainly did delight in the new freedoms afforded the city's youth, most particularly to imitate the kind of lifestyles already familiar from imported American television programmes. In the same manner, Irish filmmakers moved much closer to a global model of production, in particular that of genre cinema. Concurrently, then, with the rise of the new Dublin film, came an outbreak of genre productions. Horror films included *Dead Meat* (2004), *Boy Eats Girl* (Stephen Bradley 2005) and *Shrooms* (Paddy Breathnach 2007). Romcoms numbered *About Adam*, *When Brendan Met Trudy* (Kieron J. Walsh 2000) and *Goldfish Memory*, with bigger-budget, US–Irish co-productions such as *The Matchmaker* (Mark Joffe 1997), *P.S. I Love You* (Richard LaGravenese 2007) and *Leap Year* (Anand Tucker) tapping into the international popularity of Irish chick lit. The decision of so many of these filmmakers to cast Hollywood stars in their leads (Janeane Garofaolo in *The Matchmaker*; Kate Hudson in *About Adam*; Hilary Swank and Gerard Butler in *P.S. I Love You*; Amy Adams and Matthew Goode in *Leap Year*) further highlights their global identity. Several of the films – *The Matchmaker*, *P.S. I Love You* and *Leap Year* – involve a journey from America to Ireland and a series of comic and/or romantic encounters with the Irish that point to a new conception of Ireland as a playground for entertainment and romance, rather than as a country wrapped in a traumatic postcolonial history. These films specifically, unlike other of the genre films, locate the romance of Ireland in its countryside, transporting their metropolitan Americans to the Wicklow hills and to Atlantic villages apparently untouched by Celtic Tiger housing developments.

It is this complex relationship between modernity and marginality that fuels much of the output of the Celtic Tiger cinema. In an article on one of the period's most internationally successful films, *Once*, Neasa Hardiman has argued that the film's amateur acting and unsophisticated camerawork locate it artistically outside the filmmaking mainstream, while its location as an Irish film emphasises its geographic peripherality. At the same time sequences such as the drunken post-production party play up regressive stereotypes of Irishness. Further, *Once*'s positioning within global filmmaking practices (as the rank outsider, virtually a home movie, that won an Academy Award) echoed its own rags-to-riches narrative (Hardiman 2011).

Such tensions – between participation in global filmmaking practices and global capital, and acknowledgement, even celebration, of the specificities of Irish culture – also inform the most popular genre to emerge during the Celtic Tiger era – the crime/caper movie. The gangster film has long provided a lens through which to examine issues of class and social mobility in the contemporary city – as Robert Warshow writes in his classic 1948 examination of the genre:

> At bottom, the gangster is doomed because he is under the obligation to succeed, not because the means he employs are unlawful. In the deeper layers of the modern consciousness, *all* means are unlawful, every attempt to succeed is an act of aggression, leaving one alone and guilty and defense-

less among enemies: one is *punished* for success. This is our intolerable dilemma: that failure is a kind of death and success is evil and dangerous, is – ultimately – impossible. The effect of the gangster film is to embody this dilemma in the person of the gangster and resolve it by his death. (Warshow 1962, p. 102; italics in original)

Of course, the genre has altered since 1948; the success of comedy gangster films such as *Lock Stock and Two Smoking Barrels* (Guy Ritchie 1998) has sanctioned an irreverent approach that celebrates violent, antisocial masculinity. This (globally recognizable) model has informed numerous recent Irish and Irish-themed films, including *Ordinary Decent Criminal* (Thaddeus O'Sullivan 2000), *Intermission* (John Crowley 2003), *In Bruges* (Martin McDonagh 2008), *Perrier's Bounty* (Ian Fitzgibbon 2009), *Between the Canals* (Mark O'Connor 2007) and *The Guard* (John Michael McDonagh 2011). These films have tended to favour working-class Dublin characters or settings (*The Guard* is an exception) and to foreground tensions between a volatile central male character with a proclivity to violence who is associated with the city and working-class suburbs, and the occupiers of domestic and professional spaces, such as homes, work, cafés, hotels, supermarkets and other locations where public and private converge. Only the pub provides an intermediary space where this lone, socially disadvantaged character may circulate with ease, providing he complies with its unspoken rules of homosociality.

The opening of *Intermission* illustrates this tension and its treatment concisely. Lehiff (Colin Farrell) saunters into a café and engages the counter server (Kerry Condon) in light banter:

'Time comes you have to leave behind the old hellraiser man, take some responsibility for your life, prepare the groundwork.'
    'How do you do that?' she enquires.
    'Well to begin with, I'd say by nestbuilding,' comes the response. 'You have to find an abode you feel secure in. You have to furnish that abode; procure the necessaries – furniture etc., kitchen utensils, your wok, your juicers.'
    'What about love?'
    'Well, that's not something you can plan for, is it?' (Crowley, *Intermission*)

The banter continues as the camera moves from a close-up to a wider-angled shot, better revealing the space in which the encounter is taking place. As greater intimacy seems on the cards, so the camera moves in tighter again. Finally, the pay-off comes:

'A fellow like meself could just be a stranger, a bit of fun in the sack,' Lehiff
confides. 'No more than that, or ... or, it's not that crazy, your soulmate.'
'Yeah,' she replies, 'you've got a point.'
'Other hand,' he comes back, 'I could just be a thief or something.'
(Crowley, *Intermission*)

By the end of the next sentence he has pulled back, smashed her in the
face, and robbed the till. As the sequence is coming to an end, a wider
shot cuts to two guards (police) coming through a revolving door to the
shopping centre where the café is located, another cut takes us to a child
licking an ice-cream, and, to the beat of an exhilarating soundtrack,
the guards pursue Lehiff out through the shoppers on to the street,
where he grabs a shovel, jumps on to the bonnet of a car and threatens
the driver. A freeze frame leads the viewer into the main credits.

The film continues to play off the encounter between a freewheel-
ing masculinity and domesticity, working through these antinomies in
a series of locations from a bourgeois home to the local pub and the
wide, abandoned public spaces of this down-at-heel suburb (the film
was shot in Tallaght, where in the 1970s many inner-city working families were resettled as part of an urban development programme). Colin
Farrell was a little-known actor when he was cast, though by the time
Intermission was released he was a rising name in Hollywood, where he
played out a 'bad boy' version of Irish masculinity that was dependent
on him being identified as working-class Irish (in fact, Farrell was born
in the middle-class suburb of Castleknock) (Barton 2006, pp. 203–222).
Farrell resumed this persona in *In Bruges* and also in a cameo in
Veronica Guerin (Joel Schumacher 2003). Still, the dilemma facing the
gangster outlined by Warshow (above) remains recognizable, in particular his positioning *vis-à-vis* mainstream capitalism. Their central, usually
criminal, characters know that there is in Ireland a world of easy access
to comfort and consumer goods; they may despise this world but that
does not prevent them from feeling entitled to its possessions. That these
films reject the new Dublin of the Celtic Tiger is emphasized by their out-
of-town settings, their hostility to bourgeois or new money lifestyles and
their often breathless celebration of transgressive masculine identities.

As a number of non-genre films of the period went on to illustrate,
the assumption that the cinema of the Celtic Tiger was reflective of the
values of the new society it spawned came to be unrealized. Instead of
abandoning social issues, the emergent cinema of the 2000s addressed
them in numerous ways, some more successfully than others. Ironically,
the film that most directly critiqued Celtic Tiger corruption and loss of
values, John Boorman's *The Tiger's Tale* (2006), was the least effective

of the cycle. The most exciting work of the decade, instead, has come from the creative partnership of director Lenny Abrahamson and writer Mark O'Halloran. They were responsible for two feature films, *Adam and Paul* (2004) and *Garage* (2007) and the four-part RTÉ television series *Prosperity* (broadcast September 2007). Favouring a shooting style that consists of long takes, a slow pacing, elliptical, heavily accented dialogue and the placing of their characters mid-frame, often facing the camera, and often against an immobile backdrop, their work has a distinctive look that is more reminiscent of European art cinema than the Hollywood or even American indie model. Their work has focused on issues of exclusion from the new Ireland; in *Adam and Paul*, two junkies (played by O'Halloran and the late Tom Murphy) wander from the outskirts of Dublin to the inner city in search of a fix. Recalling both the seminal 'day in the life of the city' novel, James Joyce's *Ulysses*, and the plays of Samuel Beckett, notably *Waiting for Godot*, the film features a series of encounters that serve to highlight the utter degradation of the two men. Unlike the gangster films, *Adam and Paul* does not solicit the audience's sympathy for its eponymous leads; on the contrary, in one of the film's most chilling and alienating sequences, the pair mug a Down's Syndrome boy, ransacking his backpack for change or a mobile phone. In common with the gangster films, *Adam and Paul* distinguishes between the public spaces of the street and urban waste grounds that the junkies inhabit, and the domestic and professional spaces of apartments and supermarkets from which they are excluded. In both *Adam and Paul* and *Prosperity*, Dublin is configured as an excremental city, the pavements fouled, and the public spaces littered with the abandoned consumer goods now deemed redundant by the new moneyed classes.

The central character of *Garage*, Josie (played in a surprisingly effective piece of casting by the Irish comedian Pat Shortt), is a lonely, moderately intellectually challenged petrol station attendant, who is again excluded, both physically and psychologically, from the mainstream, in this case, a small Irish midlands town. A series of misunderstandings sees him come under suspicion of paedophilia, leading to an ending as bleak as that of *Adam and Paul*, which concludes with the death of one of the junkies. Although Abrahamson and O'Halloran's work is highly distinctive, it shares with other films of the Celtic Tiger era a focus on marginalized masculinity. Through that marginalized male figure, the audience is invited to read a wider critique of the new society with its solipsistic concerns and focus on material gain.

In summary, then, the Celtic Tiger years coincided with a conglomeration of events – alterations in the financial structure of Irish filmmaking, the advent of digital technology, the adoption of global models of genre filmmaking, the end of the Troubles and of course the new economy – to produce a range of films that, if they have one theme in common, are marked by a discourse of marginality. For some, the romcoms and certain of the animated films, this sense of being outside of the mainstream of global culture became a calling card, one that could be guaranteed only by erasing completely all the visual signifiers of contemporary Ireland. For others, the gangster/caper films in particular, their focus was on rediscovering in the marginalized working-class male an energy and iconoclasm that, it was implied, had been lost in the overall gentrification of the nation. Yet others saw in this figure only tragedy, a recognition that in Celtic Tiger Ireland access to wealth was not universal. In certain ways, the films tell us as much about themselves and their trajectories when we consider the topics they exclude – few concern themselves greatly with the experiences of the country's new immigrants; there is a surprising silence regarding clerical child abuse; women remain of interest only in so far as they illuminate aspects of masculinity. Any critique of the new society of the Celtic Tiger tends to be inferred rather than explicated.

Before the Celtic Tiger, and while the Troubles still dominated Irish politics, it was common to discuss Irish cinema in terms of how it reflected, and reflected on, issues of national politics and civil society. The significant change that this new body of film has effected is to reorient that focus. Viewed as a whole, these films suggest a culture that, to a much greater extent than previously, is interested in questions of personal rather than political identities. Their critique of Irish society is thus modest, though none displays any affection for the dominant political order to whom they owe their funding Liberated from the requirement that it reflect on the national, the new cinema focused instead on the individual – for in this new solipsistic society, it is the individual, defined most often by their marginality, who reigns supreme.

Works cited

Barton, Ruth (2004) *Irish National Cinema*, New York and London: Routledge.
Barton, Ruth (2006) *Acting Irish in Hollywood: From Fitzgerald to Farrell*, Dublin: Irish Academic Press.
Hardiman, Neasa (2011) '*Once* Won't Happen Twice', in Huber, Werner and Crosson, Sean (eds), *Contemporary Irish Film*, Vienna: Braumüller, pp. 81–90.
Hjort, Mette, and Bondebjerg, Ib (2003) *The Danish Directors: Dialogues on a Contemporary National Cinema*, Bristol: Intellect.

IBEC (1995) *The Economic Impact of Film Production in Ireland 1994*, Dublin: Irish Business and Employers Confederation.

IBEC (2004) *Film Production in Ireland*, available: www.ibec.ie/Sectors/avf/avfDoclib4.nsf/wvICCS/1A216215FDA1393C80256FE8004E126F?OpenDocument [accessed 9 July 2012].

Irish Film Board (2012) 'Regulations and Limits', available: www.irishfilmboard.ie/funding_programme/Regulations_amp_Limits/40 [accessed 9 July 2012].

Madden, Caroline (2007) 'Film Adaptation', *The Irish Times*, 4 May, p. 14.

McLoone, Martin (2000) *Irish Film: The Emergence of a Contemporary Cinema*, London: British Film Institute.

McLoone, Martin (2007) 'Cinema, City and Imaginative Space: "Hip Hedonism" and Recent Irish Cinema', in: McIlroy, B. (ed), *Genre and Cinema: Ireland and Transnationalism*, New York and London: Routledge, pp. 205–216.

Moriarty, Kevin (2008) 'Foreword', in IBEC, *Film and Television Production in Ireland*, 7, available: www.ibec.ie/Sectors/avf/avfDoclib4.nsf/wvICCS/96A5875699133994802575280035991 5?OpenDocument [accessed 9 July 2012].

Pettitt, Lance (2000) *Screening Ireland: Film and Television Representation*, Manchester: Manchester University Press.

Rockett, Kevin, Gibbons, Luke, and Hill, John (1988) *Cinema and Ireland*, London: Routledge.

Ryzik, Melena (2010) 'An Indie Takes on Animation's Big Boys', *New York Times*, 2 March, available: www.nytimes.com/2010/03/03/movies/awardsseason/03kells.html?pagewanted=1&_r=1&sq=The%20Secret%20of%20Kells&st=cse&scp=2 [accessed 11 July 2012].

Walsh, Thomas (2011) '*The Secret of Kells*: Ireland's European Identity in Feature Animation', in Huber, Werner and Crosson, Sean (eds), *Contemporary Irish Film*, Vienna: Braumüller, pp. 91–104.

Warshow, Robert (1962) *The Immediate Experience: Movies, Comics, Theatre & Other Aspects of Popular Culture*, Cambridge, MA: Harvard University Press.

Woodworth, Patrick (1993) 'Mixed Reaction as Cash for Culture Falls Short of High Expectations', *The Irish Times*, 10 December, p. A3.

Conclusion

Eamon Maher and Eugene O'Brien

This book has not attempted to provide a final, definitive account of the strange period of history that has come to be called the Celtic Tiger, or of the transformation that ensued in its aftermath. Equally, it has not tried to compete with the many economic and political treatises currently available on this period. It does not offer a comprehensive or forensic analysis of why the economy developed, and then collapsed, at such alarmingly high speeds. Instead, the writers in the preceding chapters have focused on the aspects of the body politic that Karl Marx would call the 'superstructure', the realm of language, culture and the aesthetic. The book has examined how Ireland and the changes in its economy were signified and symbolized in poems, plays, novels, films, as well as in religious and sociological terms.

Of necessity, such cultural productions and analyses will be specific as opposed to general, and will focus on an individual, real or imagined, and his/her own particular interaction with the forces of politics and economics that led to the boom and the subsequent bust: we feel that this is a vital and somewhat neglected aspect in the analysis of the whole period. The Celtic Tiger, in terms of both prosperity and austerity, affected us all as individuals, and it is through the stories of individuals, and an analysis of these stories, that any real sense of empathy and understanding of the truth of the situation will be ultimately gleaned.

There is an apocryphal story told of this period with which we will close our analysis. This story encapsulates much of what we have termed the 'real' of the Celtic Tiger and yet it may not be factually true. The story goes that a teacher, having prepared her primary children for their First Communion, waited anxiously on a breezy Saturday morning for one child who had not appeared at the church. The ceremony was delayed and some mobile phone calls were made, but to no avail. Reluctantly the teacher agreed to the delayed beginning of the ceremony, but kept casting anxious glances to the back of the church, in the hope that the missing child would arrive. However, this did not happen, and the ceremony went ahead in her absence.

The following Monday morning, as is the general custom, the children gathered in the school, wearing their communion dresses, for a school photograph, and there, in the middle of the crowd of milling mothers and daughters, was the missing child, and her mother, dressed in a snow-white and quite ornate communion dress. The teacher asked the child's mother what had happened, and was given the following reply:

> Well, the whole morning was fraught – there was the hair and nails to be done, the dress to be slightly altered, the false tan to be applied, the photographs and videos to be taken, there was so much activity that the morning got away from us. We had lunch booked in the hotel for two o'clock, and then we had organized appointments with friends and a party, followed by dinner. Something had to give, so we skipped the ceremony and went straight to the hotel!

As already said, this story may not be factually true, but it has a truth at a deeper level. It captures the heady excitement of a time when there was significant money to spend in Ireland, and when the old authority of Church, State and a vague social and cultural memory of poverty and deprivation, if not quite stretching back to famine, was gradually fading into the background. It conveys a sense of the commodification that became rife at the time, and captures how individual self-actualization came with the money, the property, the decking and electric gates that were to be seen throughout the length and breadth of the country. While over-arching analyses are valuable, the feeling and sensations of this period are best accessed through the individual, and in our opinion, this is best achieved through aesthetic and cultural critique.

From Prosperity to Austerity offers a different lens or interpretation of the motivations, causes and effects of this period. It is hoped that the value which the contributors to this book attach to cultural analysis and critique will be shared by its readers.

Index